A Grammar
for
New Testament
Greek

A.K.M. Adam

Abingdon Press

Contents

XI

XII

XIII

XIV

XV

XVI

XVII

XVIII

XIX

XX

XXI

XXII

XXIII

XXIV

XXV

XXVI

XXVII

XXVIII

XXIX

Preface

This book is dedicated to my many Greek students at Eckerd College, Columbia Seminary's Center for Theological Education in Florida, and Princeton Theological Seminary. I learned from them what I was looking for in a textbook, and it is for them that I agreed to revise this volume for Abingdon Press. The 1996 and 1998 Summer Greek classes at Princeton Seminary endured photocopied drafts of the book, spotted mistakes, and challenged my exposition of grammatical points. To all those students — especially those who have helpfully pointed out specific frustrations they experienced with other textbooks — I dedicate my labors.

This textbook rests on the premise that vocabulary and morphology are easy to forget and easy to refresh, but that a thorough engagement with the principles of syntax is the most helpful basis for study of the Greek New Testament. The text is arranged to be used either at an intensive pace for a summer or a one-semester course, or at a more leisurely pace for a one-year course. If it is used in a short-term course, students should concentrate on recognizing the morphology and syntactical structures rather than cramming vocabulary. Students will, after all, have a lifetime to acquire vocabulary, and it is easier to memorize vocabulary on one's own than it is to come to understand Greek syntax on one's own. If the text is used in a one-year course, the pace ought probably be set to enable students to learn the syntactical and morphological lessons and to acquire the vocabulary. In either case, the student should be encouraged to make free use of reference tools. Familiarity with a good lexicon, concordance, and grammar is probably the surest foundation for a long-term relationship with the Greek New Testament.

I could not have revised this text had not my wife and children graciously — temporarily — exempted me from my minimal duties as a civilized, responsible husband and father. Margaret, Nate, Si, and Pippa have contributed vast amounts of patience and indulgence toward the timely completion of this project.

I herewith acknowledge the great contributions that Charles Low, Lidija Novakovic, and Frank Yamada have made to this text. Charles read the lessons as they came through, corrected errors, clarified ambiguities, added exercises, and reminded me that the readers of this book probably would not already know Greek as well as I supposed. Lidija composed numerous exercises for the book and dug out exercise sentences from Scripture. Marie Adam, Jen Bird, Caroline Gupton, James Miller, Virginia Mischen, Scott Rasnic, Juliet Richardson, Graham Robinson, and especially Jung Sook Kim and Kirianne Weaver were of great help in catching typographical errors in an earlier draft of the text. Clayton Croy sent suggestions for improving the material. Robert Ratcliff, Jeff Tucker, and Kelby and Teresa Bowers — the editorial and design team for Abingdon Press — transformed a rough manuscript into this polished work. And generations of students have made helpful comments about how I could do a better job as a Greek teacher. I thank them all very much.

I

The Alphabet

		Name	Erasmian Pronunciation	Modern Greek Pronunciation
A	α	alpha	*f*ather	
B	β	beta	*b*at	*v*at
Γ	γ	gamma	*g*o[1]	*g*as, *y*es[2]
Δ	δ	delta	*d*og	*th*is
E	ε	epsilon	m*e*t	
Z	ζ	zeta	a*dz*e[3]	*z*oo
H	η	eta	h*a*te	*ee*rie
Θ	θ	theta	*th*in[4]	
I	ι	iota	s*i*t/p*i*que[5]	
K	κ	kappa	*k*eep	
Λ	λ	lambda	*l*imp	
M	μ	mu	*m*at	
N	ν	nu	*n*ot	
Ξ	ξ	xi	e*x*it[6]	
O	o	omicron	n*o*t	
Π	π	pi	*p*at	
P	ρ	rho	*r*at	
Σ	σ, ς	sigma	*s*at[7]	σσ = *sh*
T	τ	tau	*t*aught	
Y	υ	upsilon	r*u*de	French t*u*/*ee*rie[5]
Φ	φ	phi	*ph*one	
X	χ	chi	*ch*orus[8]	
Ψ	ψ	psi	ri*ps*[9]	
Ω	ω	omega	h*o*pe	h*o*rn

1. Gamma preceding another gamma, a kappa, a xi, or a chi makes an *ng* sound.
2. Gamma preceding an alpha, omicron, upsilon, or omega makes a *g* sound; preceding a iota, epsilon, or eta, a *y* sound.
3. A combined *dz* sound.
4. A soft *th* sound.
5. Short/long.
6. A *ks* sound, even at the start of a word.
7. When sigma occurs as the last letter of a word, it takes the form ς.
8. Or aspirated, as the German *ich* or Scottish *loch*.
9. The *ps* sound persists when psi occurs at the beginning of a word.

1

Some students will already know many of these twenty-four letters from physics, mathematics, and college fraternities or sororities. Be sure to learn both upper and lower case letters. There are two approaches to pronouncing New Testament Greek. Many teachers find the Erasmian pronunciation system to be helpful for learning spelling and for distinguishing certain words from one another. The conventional Modern Greek pronunciation is used less often, but is probably closer to what New Testament Greek actually sounded like. Learn the system your teacher uses, but do not confuse yourself by trying to learn both. Where no pronunciation is listed for Modern Greek, it is the same as the Erasmian pronunciation.

The sooner students learn the order of the letters in the Greek alphabet, the easier it will be for them to consult a glossary or lexicon. At the outset, students may want to devise mnemonic devices to remember Greek alphabetical order; for instance, "All Barthians Get Dogmatically Educated," for the first five letters.

Vowels and Diphthongs

There are seven vowels in the Greek language: α, ε, η, ι, ο, υ, ω. Two of these (η and ω) are always long; two (ε and ο) are always short. The remaining three (α, ι, and υ) may be short or long, depending on the word in which they occur.

A diphthong combines two vowel sounds into one. Whereas English permits a wide variety of diphthongs, Greek permits only eight.

	Erasmian	*Modern*		*Erasmian*	*Modern*
αι	*ai*sle	m*e*t	αυ	h*ou*se	*a*vid
ει	fr*ei*ght	*ee*rie	ευ	f*eu*d	*e*ver
οι	*oi*l	*ee*rie	ου	gr*ou*p	gr*ou*p
υι	q*uee*n	q*uee*n	ηυ	f*eu*d	*e*ver

When a long α, an η, or an ω is combined with a iota, the iota appears *under* the other vowels: ᾳ, ῃ, ῳ. This is called a *iota subscript*. When the previous vowel is capitalized, the iota appears *after* the vowel — a iota *adscript*. The diphthongs with a iota subscript are pronounced just as the long vowel would be without a subscript. All these diphthongs count as long vowels, with one exception: when αι or οι occur as the last letters of a word, the diphthong is short. In the word λόγοις, the οι is long; in λόγοι, the οι is short.

Breathing Marks

When a Greek word begins with a vowel sound or a ρ, a diacritical mark called a "breathing mark" is used. The breathing mark indicates whether the word begins with an "h" sound. If the word begins with a *rough breathing mark* (ʽ), the word begins with a voiced "h" sound. If the word begins with a *smooth breathing mark* (ʼ), the word does not begin with a voiced "h" sound. For instance, the word ἐξ is pronounced "ex" and means "out [of]," but the word ἕξ — the same spelling, but with a rough breathing mark instead of a smooth one — is pronounced "hex" and means "six."

When a Greek word begins with ρ, the initial rho will *always* have a rough breathing mark. This is why English words derived from Greek, such as "rhythm" or "rhinoceros," have an "h" embedded in them. This odd combination is pronounced in Greek as though the "h" came before the "r" sound: *hr*. When a breathing mark appears over a diphthong, it should be placed over the *second* letter of the diphthong.

$$οὐ = oo \qquad\qquad οὑ = hoo$$

When an accented syllable takes a breathing mark, the breathing mark falls before or underneath the accent.

Consonants

Greek consonants fall into five categories. You will not need to know these categories immediately. They will play a significant role in morphology (word formation) starting in lesson IV, however, so start learning the categories right away.

β, π, φ	labial
γ, κ, χ	guttural
δ, θ, τ	dental
λ, μ, ν, ρ	liquid
ζ, ξ, ψ	compound

Syllables

Greek words divide into syllables so as to distribute one vowel or diphthong for each syllable. The last three syllables of Greek words have technical names. The last syllable is called the *ultima*; the second-to-last syllable is called the *penult*; and the third-to-last syllable is called the *antepenult*.

Accent

Most modern editions of ancient Greek texts are printed with three sorts of accent marks: the *acute* ('), the *circumflex* (ˆ), and the *grave* (`). Accent marks originally indicated the tone with which the word was to be spoken. The acute indicated a higher tone, the grave a lower tone, and the circumflex a rising and falling combination. The practice of marking accents on written manuscripts did not become standard until a relatively late date. If a diphthong is accented, the accent mark appears over the second letter of the diphthong (τοῦ). If an initial vowel or diphthong is accented, the breathing mark appears before an initial acute or grave accent (οἴκος, ὄν) and under an initial circumflex (ἦν).

An *acute* accent can appear on any of the last three syllables. It is the only accent mark that can appear on an antepenult. If the antepenult is accented, it must take an acute accent.

A *circumflex* accent can appear on either of the last two syllables, the penult or ultima. The circumflex will only appear on a syllable with a long vowel, however. A long penult followed by a short ultima *must* take a circumflex.

A *grave* accent can appear only on the last syllable, the ultima. If a word that would ordinarily receive a grave accent ends a sentence or clause, it takes an acute accent.

The following matrix provides a short guide for applying accents.

Accent	Short Ultima	Long Ultima
ultima	acute (θεός)	acute or circumflex (ψυχή, ἡμῶν)
short penult	acute (νόμος)	acute (λόγους)
long penult	circumflex (γλῶσσα)	acute (μήτηρ)
antepenult	acute (ἄνθρωπος)	—

When a word that would take an acute on the ultima is followed by an accented word (not an unaccented word or a punctuation mark), the acute changes to a grave: ὁ θεὸς πιστός. Observe that the acute on the ultima of θεός changes to a grave since it is followed by an accented word. The acute on the ultima of πιστός remains since it is followed by a punctuation mark.

Some teachers expect students to master the rules of accentuation, others do not. This textbook does not takes sides. The best way to learn the patterns of accentuation is to pay attention to the ways that the rules take effect in actual use. Read the exercises aloud and explain to yourself the reasons why an accent falls where it does.

Punctuation

Though there are few punctuation marks in the ancient manuscripts of the Greek New Testament, modern editions use several punctuation marks to help readers. Declarative sentences end with a mark equivalent to an English period (.). Questions are marked with the symbol used in English as a semicolon (;). Major breaks in a sentence, punctuated in English with a colon or semicolon, are marked in Greek with a dot or period raised above the line (·). Commas serve the same purpose in Greek texts as in English.

Exercises

The best exercise at this point is to practice forming the letters of the alphabet and to practice pronunciation by reading aloud from the Greek New Testament. If you do not already have a copy of the Greek New Testament, you may want to obtain one. In the meantime, try copying and reading aloud the following passage.

Καὶ ταῦτα γράφομεν ἡμεῖς ἵνα ἡ χαρὰ ἡμῶν ᾖ πεπληρωμένη. Καὶ ἔστιν αὕτη ἡ ἀγγελία ἣν ἀκηκόαμεν ἀπ᾽ αὐτοῦ καὶ ἀναγγέλλομεν ὑμῖν, ὅτι ὁ θεὸς φῶς ἐστιν καὶ σκοτία ἐν αὐτῷ οὐκ ἔστιν οὐδεμία. Ἐὰν εἴπωμεν ὅτι κοινωνίαν ἔχομεν μετ᾽ αὐτοῦ καὶ ἐν τῷ σκότει περιπατῶμεν, ψευδόμεθα καὶ οὐ ποιοῦμεν τὴν ἀλήθειαν· ἐὰν δὲ ἐν τῷ φωτὶ περιπατῶμεν ὡς αὐτός ἐστιν ἐν τῷ φωτί, κοινωνίαν ἔχομεν μετ᾽ ἀλλήλων καὶ τὸ αἷμα Ἰησοῦ τοῦ υἱοῦ αὐτοῦ καθαρίζει ἡμᾶς ἀπὸ πάσης ἁμαρτίας. (1 John 1:4–7)

II

Verbs

The Greek verbal system can be relatively simple or relatively complex, depending on how a student goes about learning it. A student who devotes hard work to studying the Greek verbal system from the beginning will later recognize patterns and regularities that make the whole phenomenon easier to learn and retain. Students who devote only minimal attention to the Greek verb at the early stages will have to memorize each new lesson afresh, and will see only irregularities and surprises where the more thorough student sees a discernable pattern.

Every form of a Greek verb has *tense, voice,* and *mood.*

Tense in Greek verbs expresses a combination of dimensions of verbal meaning. Greek tenses can express verbal aspect (the verbal action as a process, the verbal action as an undifferentiated whole, or the the verbal action as a particular state in a complex situation) and time of action (past, present, or future) in distinct combinations.

Voice expresses the relation of the verb's action to the verb's subject. In an active verb, the subject is the agent of the verb's action, "I hit the ball"; in a passive verb, the subject receives the verb's action, "I was hit by the ball."

Mood expresses a relation to reality: the indicative mood states that, or asks whether, a claim is true; the subjunctive mood marks a claim as more or less possible; the imperative mood instructs that an action be made real, "Make it so!"

Infinitives ("to run," "to fry") will have only the three aforementioned elements. Finite (conjugated) verbs will have a *person* and *number* as well as tense, voice, and mood. Person and number function in Greek just as in English: the first person is "I" (sg) and "we" (pl), the second person is "you" (both singular and plural in English), and the third person is "he," "she," or "it" (sg) and "they" (pl). Participles will have tense, voice, and mood, but will have gender, case, and number instead of person and number.

Look up verbs in glossaries and lexicons by searching for the first person singular, present active indicative. This form is called the verb's *lexical form*. Some verbs will appear in other forms, a phenomenon that will be explained later in the text.

When beginning students encounter a verb, they will do well to *parse* the form in question — that is, to analyze the elements that determine the given form. It is helpful to follow the same order of elements when one is parsing verbs. This book will suggest the order *person, number, tense, voice, mood*. Always conclude your parsing by giving the *lexical form* of the verb.

Present Tense

The present tense form of a Greek verb expresses what linguists call *imperfective aspect*. That means that in a present tense Greek verb the action is viewed as progressive, or as an action in process. This process may be taking place in past, present, or future time, depending on the context. The principal use of the present tense in the indicative mood, however, is to express progressive action in the present. Therefore our provisional translation for the present active indicative will adopt the progressive form of the English present tense:

ἄγω   I am leading, I am bringing

The simple present, "I lead," is not *incorrect*, but it is usually not as specifically appropriate for expressing the imperfective aspect of the present tense. Some English verbs convey imperfective aspect adequately in the simple present; one can say, "I see the apostle," since English-speakers would hardly say, "I am seeing the apostle." We will use the simple present in definitions, for simplicity's sake, but students translating the homework exercises should consider the progressive form of the present tense especially appropriate for most verbs.

Active Voice

The active voice indicates that the subject of the verb is the one performing the action of the verb. In the sentence, "I speak," it is I who am doing the speaking.

Indicative Mood

The indicative mood is used for discussing matters presumed to be fact. This does not imply that the indicative assertion is actually grounded in reality, but simply that the topic is treated as if it were factual. One can raise questions in the indicative mood, provided that the question concerns a topic that may be regarded as a matter of fact. "Is it raining outside?" belongs in the indicative. "May we go to the dance?" opens a topic whose relation to reality is not yet determined, and which therefore does not belong in the indicative.

Present Active Indicative

The present active indicative of a Greek verb is formed by ascertaining the verb stem, then adding the present tense endings to it. This usually entails finding the lexical form of the verb, then (since the lexical form is usually the first person singular, present active indicative) removing the first person singular ending from it and adding the appropriate endings for the other persons and numbers. Using the verb λύω as an example, the present stem is λυ- and the endings are:

	Singular	*Plural*
1st	λύ-ω	λύ-ομεν
2nd	λύ-εις	λύ-ετε
3rd	λύ-ει	λύ-ουσι (or λύ-ουσιν)

$$λύ\text{-}ω$$

Stem ⌐   ⌐ Present Ending

These two elements constitute the present stem — the first principal part.

Memorize the present active indicative form of the verb, and memorize the endings as well. They will not only make it possible for you to recognize the present active indicative, but also to recognize many other forms of the verb. The present active indicative constitutes the *first principal part* of the verb, from which a variety of tenses, voices, and moods are formed. The endings also recur in other tenses and moods.

Note that the third person plural form of the present active indicative can end either with a ι or with an added ν. This ν, the "movable nu," is commonly added to forms that end with a short ι or ε. The movable nu frequently occurs before a word that begins with a vowel or a diphthong, but it may also occur before the punctuation mark at the end of a clause or before a word that begins with a consonant. No rule can predict reliably when a movable nu will occur. The text will indicate forms that take the movable nu by showing a (ν). Do not add the movable nu to any form other than those whose paradigm indicates a movable nu.

Implied Subject

The Greek verb does not require that its subject be explicitly expressed in the sentence. The form of the verb implies its subject. When there is no explicit subject supplied in the sentence, use the appropriate pronoun to express the subject in English.

λύομεν   we are loosing

λαμβάνει   he (she, or it) is receiving

Negation

In Greek, an indicative mood verb is negated with the particle οὐ. Use the alternate form οὐκ before words that begin with a vowel and smooth breathing, and οὐχ before words that begin with a vowel and rough breathing. Remember that οὐ is used to negate words other than verbs, too.

λύομεν	we are loosing	οὐ λύομεν	we are *not* loosing
ἄγω	I am leading	οὐκ ἄγω	I am *not* leading
εὑρίσκει	she is finding	οὐχ εὑρίσκει	she is *not* finding

Principal Parts

Earlier in the chapter, the present active indicative was called the *first principal part*. The term "principal part" refers to the several forms of the verb that provide the basis for constructing various other forms. The present active indicative provides the basis for forming the present middle and passive indicative, the present subjunctive, the present imperative, the present participle, the present infinitive, the present optative, and the imperfect indicative.

There are six principal parts for the Greek verb. They are the present active indicative, the future active indicative, the aorist active indicative, the perfect active indicative, the perfect passive indicative, and the aorist passive indicative. These principal parts will be given in the vocabulary when a verb is first introduced even though students do not yet know the tenses of the various parts. As students learn new verbs, they will do well to go back and ascertain all the forms of the principal parts with which they are already acquainted. As students learn new principal parts, they should go back and find that principal part's forms for the verbs they know.

Accent

Greek verbs have a *recessive* accent; that is, the accent belongs as far toward the beginning of the word as it can go while still respecting the general rules of accentuation. Verbs whose last syllable (ultima) is long will have their accent on the penult, and it must be an acute accent. Verbs whose ultima is short will take their accent on the antepenult, and this, too, will be an acute accent. There will be refinements to these rules, but these two principles provide the basic pattern that verbs will follow.

Study Checklist

The aspect of the present tense
Present active indicative endings
The implied subject
The particle of negation

Vocabulary

Verbs

ἄγω ἄγω, ἄξω, ἤγαγον, ἦχα, ἦγμαι, ἤχθην   I lead, I bring

ἀκούω ἀκούω, ἀκούσω, ἤκουσα, ἀκήκοα, ἤκουσμαι, ἠκούσθην   I hear

βλέπω βλέπω, βλέψω, ἔβλεψα, βέβλεφα, βέβλεμμαι, ἐβλέφθην   I see

γινώσκω γίνώσκω, γνώσομαι, ἔγνων, ἔγνωκα, ἔγνωσμαι, ἐγνώσθην
I know

γράφω γράφω, γράψω, ἔγραψα, γέγραφα, γέγραμμαι, ἐγράφην   I write

διδάσκω διδάσκω, διδάξω, ἐδίδαξα, δεδίδαχα, δεδίδαγμαι, ἐδιδάχθην
I teach

εὑρίσκω εὑρίσκω, εὑρήσω, εὗρον, εὕρηκα, εὕρημαι, εὑρέθην I find

ἔχω ἔχω, ἕξω, ἔσχον, ἔσχηκα, ἔσχημαι, — I have

λαμβάνω λαμβάνω, λήμψομαι, ἔλαβον, εἴληφα, εἴλημμαι, ἐλήφθην / ἐλήμφθην I take, I receive

λέγω λέγω, ἐρῶ, εἶπον, εἴρηκα, εἴρημαι, ἐρρέθην I say, I speak

λύω λύω, λύσω, ἔλυσα, λέλυκα, λέλυμαι, ἐλύθην I loose, I release

πιστεύω πιστεύω, πιστεύσω, ἐπίστευσα, πεπίστευκα, πεπίστευμαι, ἐπιστεύθην I believe

Conjunctions

καί and (or "also," or "even"); καί ... καί ..., both ... and ...

ἀλλά but

Particle

οὐ, οὐκ, οὐχ not

Exercises

Read aloud, translate, and parse the following Greek expressions.

1. ἄγω	7. πιστεύουσιν	13. λέγει	19. εὑρίσκει
2. λέγουσιν	8. βλέπει	14. λαμβάνουσι	20. ἄγομεν
3. διδάσκω	9. πιστεύομεν	15. ἀκούετε	21. ἔχεις
4. γράφετε	10. ἔχει	16. ἔχομεν	22. γράφω
5. γινώσκουσι	11. βλέπομεν	17. λαμβάνετε	23. λύω
6. εὑρίσκεις	12. λύεις	18. ἀκούεις	24. διδάσκετε

25. διδάσκω καὶ γράφω, ἀλλὰ οὐ πιστεύω.

26. βλέπεις καὶ ἀκούετε, ἀλλὰ γινώσκουσιν.

27. ἄγει καὶ εὑρίσκει;

28. λαμβάνουσι καὶ οὐ λύουσιν.

Translate the following expressions into Greek.

1. I see

2. He is loosing

3. We know

4. They are teaching

5. You (sg) believe

6. She is hearing

7. They are writing

8. He is leading

9. I am finding

10. We have

11. You (sg) are saying

12. You (pl) are receiving

13. We are leading

14. You (pl) are teaching

15. I have

16. We teach and write.

17. You (sg) speak but do not lead.

18. They see and hear, but they do not believe.

III

Second Declension Nouns

The Greek noun comes in three *declensions*. The term "declension" means that these words follow similar patterns as they are inflected, or declined, for the cases and numbers. This lesson will introduce nouns of the *second declension*, a relatively simple declension that includes many common, useful nouns.

The grammatical categories that determine the form and use of a Greek noun are its *case, gender,* and *number*. Those are the characteristics to list when parsing a noun. Number is a simple matter since Greek operates with the same singular and plural distinction familiar to English-speakers. The *lexical form* of the noun is the nominative singular.

Gender

Grammatical gender is a category independent of biology, though it is not unrelated. Every Greek noun is categorized as masculine, feminine, or neuter. As an illustration of grammatical gender's independence of biology, note that the word "child" (τέκνον) is of neuter gender in Greek. There are no absolute guidelines for grammatical gender, but most second declension nouns are either masculine or neuter.

Cases

The role of a Greek noun is indicated by its *case*. English nouns have two inflected forms: an all-purpose form ("ball"), and a possessive form ("ball's"). The English pronoun has three forms: the nominative ("we," used for the subject), the possessive ("our"), and the accusative ("us," used for direct, indirect, and prepositional objects). The Greek noun has five cases: the *nominative,* the *genitive,* the *dative,* the *accusative,* and the *vocative*. Each case delimits several possible roles for the noun.

The nominative case is used almost exclusively for the *subject of a verb*. The nominative may also be used as the object of a verb of being; this is called the *predicate nominative*.

The genitive case is a very flexible means of indicating particular sorts

13

of relationships between nouns. Most genitive nouns can be provisionally translated by adding "of" to the noun: "of the message," "of love," "of the children." This simple device, however, covers various more or less distinct uses.

The most common sort of genitive in New Testament Greek is the *possessive genitive*. The provisional translation — for instance, "the meaning *of the message*" — could be translated into English more idiomatically, and just as correctly, by setting the English noun in the possessive case ("*the message's* meaning"). The possessive genitive answers the question, "Whose is it?"

The genitive is also commonly used to indicate source or origin. "Jesus *of Nazareth*" comes from Nazareth, "eye *of newt*" comes from newts, and so on. The *genitive of origin* answers the question, "Where is it from?"

The genitive can be used with certain nouns that imply activity, hence "action nouns," to indicate the agent who is responsible for the implied action. If one were to transmute the action noun into a verb, the genitive noun related to it would then become the subject of that verb. For example, in the phrase "the lust of the flesh," the flesh lusts after something; on that basis, one might categorize this as a *subjective genitive*. (One might also construe this as a possessive genitive — "the flesh's lust" — though that does not clarify the force of the construction as precisely as does construing it as a subjective genitive.)

The *objective genitive* is just the opposite of the subjective genitive. If the genitive is used with an action noun such that the noun in the genitive would receive the action of the action noun, we call the genitive construction an "objective genitive." Thus, "the word of the cross" is not a word that the cross speaks (subjective genitive), nor is it the cross's own word (possessive), but it is the word *about* the cross. What is discussed is the cross; thus, the cross constitutes the *object* of the action noun "word," and is appropriately construed as an objective genitive.

A noun in the genitive may be used to describe another noun, and this is called the *qualitative genitive*. In the phrase "a house of cards," the genitive expression "of cards" functions as if it were an adjective ("a card house"). The qualitative genitive answers the question, "What kind is it?"

Finally, some verbs (especially verbs of perception) take their direct object in the genitive case. Among the words already introduced, ἀκούω sometimes takes its object in the genitive, usually when its direct object is a person; impersonal objects usually take the accusative case.

The dative case is almost as flexible as the genitive. While the provisional translation of datives will usually rely on translating the dative with "to," "by," or "for," the student will use other ways of marking the dative case in certain contexts.

When the dative is used for the *indirect object* of the verb, it is customarily translated with "to." In the sentence "I spoke a word to the apostle," the phrase "to the apostle" (the indirect object) would be expressed in the dative case (τῷ ἀποστόλῳ).

The dative can be used to indicate the instrument or agent by which an action is effected. This usage, the *dative of means,* is most commonly translated with "by." In the sentence "I was hit by the rock," the phrase "by the rock" could be cast in the dative case in Greek as an instance of the dative of means, also known as the *instrumental dative.* In some cases, the best translation of a dative of means requires that we use "with," as in "I defended myself with a sword."

The dative can also be used to express *for whom* or *for what* an action occurred. This usage is usually translated with "for," and we refer to it as the *dative of advantage*; if the action is unwelcome, the *dative of disadvantage.* When we say, "I bought some carnations *for you,*" the phrase "for you" expresses a dative of advantage.

The dative is also translated with "to" when it is used to express destination in time or space. This is called the *local dative.* Though New Testament Greek usually uses a preposition to express motion toward a place, sometimes the dative identifies the terminus of a verb of movement. In "My children are coming to me," for instance, the local dative expresses the destination of the trip.

Certain verbs can take their direct objects in the dative case. For instance, πιστεύω takes its object in the dative case when it is a person (πιστεύω τῷ διδασκάλῳ); it can take either the dative or accusative when its object is a thing. Such a construction may be translated either as any comparable verb plus accusative construction.

The accusative case has a much more limited range. Its principal purpose, and the only one introduced here, is to indicate the direct object of a sentence.

The vocative case expresses direct address, and it is relatively rare in the New Testament. Its purpose is to indicate the addressee of a call for attention. "Lord!" "Teacher!" "Mama!" — all these would be expressed in the vocative case. The familiar liturgical formulation "Kyrie eleison" (κύριε, ἐλέησον — "Lord, have mercy!") features a noun ("Lord") in the vocative case.

All cases may be used in *appositional* structures. When an author wishes to define further or to clarify the characteristics of a noun that occurs earlier in the sentence, he or she may set another noun *in the same case* in close proximity to it. The noun in apposition usually occurs immediately adjacent to the noun it is modifying. The classic example is where Paul begins his letters, Παῦλος, ἀπόστολος Χριστοῦ Ἰησοῦ ("Paul, an apostle of Christ Jesus"). The Greek phrase ἀπόστολος Χριστοῦ Ἰησοῦ has no direct syntactical connection to Παῦλος, rather it simply amplifies what we know about Paul.

Second Declension Noun Forms

A second declension noun is declined by applying the following endings to the noun stem. The noun stem is found by removing the nominative singular ending from the lexical form. Using the masculine noun λόγος as an example, the noun stem is λογ- and the endings are:

	Singular	*Plural*
N	λόγ-ος	λόγ-οι
G	λόγ-ου	λόγ-ων
D	λόγ-ῳ	λόγ-οις
A	λόγ-ον	λόγ-ους
V	λόγ-ε	λόγ-οι

λόγ-ος

Stem ⤴   ⤴ Case/Number Ending

Neuter second declension nouns, like τέκνον, follow a similar pattern:

	Singular	*Plural*
N	τέκν-ον	τέκν-α
G	τέκν-ου	τέκν-ων
D	τέκν-ῳ	τέκν-οις
A	τέκν-ον	τέκν-α
V	τέκν-ον	τέκν-α

Neuter Plural Subjects

Watch out for a common Greek peculiarity: Koiné Greek customarily associates a neuter plural subject with a *singular* form of the verb. In other words, the neuter plural subject τέκνα takes the verb λύει where we would expect to find λύουσιν. This phenomenon trips up almost all students at one time or another, so learn now to be alert for this usage.

Masculine and Neuter Articles

Although English uses the indefinite article "a" or "an," Greek has no such article. *Anarthrous* ("without a definite article") Greek nouns may be translated with or without an indefinite article. Usually, though not always, it is best not to supply a definite article for an anarthrous Greek noun.

The definite article, "the," is extremely common in Greek. It is even used in some cases where English usually omits the definite article. While English does not use a definite article with abstract nouns like "love" or "truth," Greek will use a definite article for such nouns. We need not feel constrained to carry the definite article into our English translation, however; thus not "The love will abide," but "Love will abide." Likewise, Greek often uses the definite article with proper nouns like (ὁ) Ἰησοῦς. Here, we do not translate the article into English, either.

In certain cases, we supply a definite article in the English translation where the Greek text does not have the article. Greek permits speakers to use one-of-a-kind nouns without the definite article, presumably because a unique entity does not need specification with "the." John's Gospel, for instance, begins ἐν ἀρχή, without an article, but we translate this as "In *the* beginning." John risks no ambiguity because he imagines only one primal beginning. In such cases, the translator must be guided by context. There is no hard and fast rule to simplify the task of translation.

The article is declined in a pattern similar to that of the noun, and the article will agree in gender, case, and number with the noun it is modifying. *Attention to the definite article can be of tremendous help when construing unfamiliar words and clauses.* Observe that the endings for the articles resemble, though they do not duplicate, the endings for the corresponding noun forms. The masculine and neuter definite articles are:

	Singular		*Plural*	
	M	*N*	*M*	*N*
N	ὁ	τό	οἱ	τά
G	τοῦ	τοῦ	τῶν	τῶν
D	τῷ	τῷ	τοῖς	τοῖς
A	τόν	τό	τούς	τά

Word Order

Greek syntax permits great variation in word order. Therefore, students should concentrate on permitting the case endings to clarify the sentence structure, not simply using English sentence structure to figure out Greek texts. The most ordinary, though not necessarily the most frequent, word order in a Greek sentence is verb, then subject, then object. An author will often mark a particular word or phrase for emphasis by moving it to the beginning or end of the sentence; for example, the prologue of Luke's Gospel (1:1–4) emphasizes the word for "certainty," ἀσφάλεια, by placing it last in the sentence.

Word order is particularly important, however, in handling the genitive case. Nouns in the genitive typically, though not at all invariably, follow closely upon the noun they modify. A student who is doubtful about what a genitive construction might mean should check to see whether it might be modifying a preceding noun or noun phrase.

Accent

Although a verb's accent is recessive, a noun's accent is *persistent*; that is, it tends to stay on the same syllable unless the rules of accentuation require that the accent change. There is no general rule to determine where the accent will fall on a noun. The position of the accent must be learned with the lexical form of the word. When a long vowel in the ultima could take either an acute accent or a circumflex, use a circumflex in the genitive and dative cases, and an acute accent in the accusative plural. The vowel in the nominative case and in the accusative singular is usually short.

Study Checklist

Parsing the noun: Case, gender, number, and lexical form

Uses of the five cases
Nominative: Subject, predicate nominative
Genitive ("of"): Possessive, source or origin, qualitative, subjective
   genitive, objective genitive, direct object of certain verbs
Dative ("to," "by," "for"): Indirect object, local dative, dative of means,
   dative of advantage, direct object of certain verbs
Accusative: Direct object
Vocative: Direct address

Form of second declension nouns
The neuter plural trap
The use of the article
Syntax: Attend to the article

Vocabulary

Nouns

ἄνθρωπος, ὁ   person

ἀπόστολος, ὁ   apostle (secular Greek: "ambassador," "envoy")

ἄρτος, ὁ   bread (sg), loaf (pl)

διδάσκαλος, ὁ   teacher

δοῦλος, ὁ   slave

ἔργον, τό   work

θάνατος, ὁ   death

θεός, ὁ   God

ἱερόν, τό   temple
κύριος, ὁ   master, lord
λόγος, ὁ   word
νόμος, ὁ   law
οἶκος, ὁ   house
τέκνον, τό   child

Exercises

Read aloud and translate the following sentences from Greek to English.
Parse the verbs and nouns, and identify the ways the various cases are used.

1. ὁ κύριος ἄγει τὰ τέκνα τῷ ἱερῷ.

2. ὁ διδάσκαλος οὐ γινώσκει τὸν λόγον τοῦ νόμου.

3. τοὺς δούλους τοῦ θανάτου λύομεν τῷ κυρίῳ.

4. βλέπετε τὸν οἶκον ἀλλὰ οὐκ ἀκούετε τῶν ἀνθρώπων.

5. ἔχομεν νόμον, καὶ γινώσκομεν τὰ ἔργα τοῦ νόμου.

6. λαμβάνεις τὸν ἄρτον τοῦ δούλου.

7. γράφει ὁ ἀπόστολος τὸν λόγον τοῖς διδασκάλοις.

8. τὰ τέκνα πιστεύει τῷ ἀποστόλῳ.

9. διδάσκω τοὺς ἀνθρώπους τοῦ θεοῦ.

10. ἄγεις τοὺς ἄρτους τῷ οἴκῳ.

11. ὁ θεὸς γινώσκει τὸ τέκνον, ἀλλὰ τὸ τέκνον οὐ γινώσκει τὸν θεόν.

12. οὐχ εὑρίσκομεν τὸν οἶκον τοῦ διδάσκαλου.

13. ἔχετε τὸν ἄρτον τοῦ ἱεροῦ.

14. διδάσκει καὶ γράφει τοὺς λόγους.

15. λαμβάνουσιν οἱ δοῦλοι τὰ τέκνα.

16. οὐ πιστεύομεν τῷ κυρίῳ τοῦ θανάτου.

17. ὁ διδάσκαλος λύει τὰ τέκνα.

18. οἱ ἄνθρωποι οὐ λαμβάνουσι τὸν ἀπόστολον τοῦ κυρίου.

19. οὐ λέγω λόγους τῶν ἱερῶν, ἀλλὰ τοῦ νόμου.

20. βλέπετε τὸν νόμον· βλέπετε καὶ τὸ ἔργον τοῦ θανάτου.

Translate the following English sentences into Greek.

1. You (sg) have a master.

2. God is loosing the slave.

3. I am teaching the word of the law.

4. The teacher is leading the apostle to the house of God.

5. A person does not know God, but God knows the person.

6. We are writing the word for the children of God, but not for the slaves of death.

7. You (pl) are leading the people to the temple, and they are seeing the house of God.

8. The slaves of the law are not receiving the Lord.

9. I do not believe the words of the teacher; I believe the words of the Lord.

10. I see the work of the apostle, but not the work of God.

11. You (pl) are not finding the slave, but the child of the teacher.

12. The master of the house does not have children.

13. I am not speaking to the apostle, but to the Lord.

14. The slave brings bread for the master and the teacher of the law.

15. The people hear, but they do not receive the word of God.

16. You (pl) have the temple, but you do not know the law.

17. We find the servants of God, and we believe the Lord.

18. The apostle says, "The works of the law bring death."

19. I know the teacher, the child of the Lord. ("The child of the Lord" is in apposition to "the teacher.")

20. We are releasing the slaves of the law.

IV

First Aorist Verbs

Lesson II introduced the present tense, the first principal part of the Greek verb. This lesson examines the *aorist* tense, the *third principal part*. The present tense indicates imperfective aspect; that is, the present tense depicts the action as an action in progress. The aorist tense indicates *perfective* or *aoristic aspect,* which means that it depicts the action as a unified whole or a complete event rather than as an extended process. This distinction is not immediately obvious to English-speakers, but students will gradually get accustomed to it.

Although the aorist is not a "past tense," the aorist indicative most commonly narrates past actions. The provisional translations given in this text will adopt the English "simple past" as their reference point. This usage can be called the *historical* aorist, the *narrative* aorist, or *constative* aorist. Sometimes the aorist is used for timeless or eternal activity ("it never rains but it pours"), which is commonly called the *gnomic* aorist.

The aorist tense takes two forms: the "first" or "weak" aorist, and the "second" or "strong" aorist. The two forms of the aorist do not differ in meaning (both express perfective aspect), they differ only in form. The first aorist uses a stem that closely resembles the present stem, with endings characterized by a -σα combination, whereas the second aorist uses a markedly different stem with a different set of endings. The first aorist stem is formed on the present stem (for λύω, that means λυ-). The present and first aorist stems are usually identical. Prefix an augment ε- to this stem and add a -σ suffix. The result (ἔλυσ-) takes the following aorist endings.

	Singular		Plural	
1ST	-α	ἔλυσα	-αμεν	ἐλύσαμεν
2ND	-ας	ἔλυσας	-ατε	ἐλύσατε
3RD	-ε(ν)	ἔλυσεν	-αν	ἔλυσαν

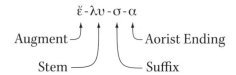

ἔ-λυ-σ-α

Augment ⌐ Aorist Ending
Stem ⌐ Suffix

Verbs that begin with a prepositional prefix will take the augment *on the stem*, not on the prepositional prefix. For example, the verb ἀπολύω (ἀπο = prepositional prefix, λύω = stem) forms its aorist as ἀπέλυσα. The augment modifies the λυ- stem, not the ἀπο- prefix.

Verb stems that begin with a vowel or diphthong will require special treatment when adding the ε- augment. Greek will not simply tack another vowel onto the front of the verb stem, but will combine the ε- augment with the stem vowel. This changes the stem vowel or diphthong (see the chart below). Since very few verbs in the Greek New Testament begin with vowels other than α or ε and their related dipthongs, for the time being you need not learn any combinations other than these:

ε + α = η   ε + ε = η

ε + αι = η   ε + ει = η (sometimes remains ει)

ε + αυ = ηυ   ε + ευ = ηυ (sometimes remains ευ)

For instance, the present form ἀκούω becomes the aorist ἤκουσα; ἐλπίζω becomes ἤλπισα; and so on.

Likewise, certain Greek consonants will not readily accept a -σ suffix. When one of those consonants occurs at the end of the verb stem, the -σ suffix will either combine with the stem consonant to produce a compound consonant, or it will quiesce into the -σ itself. For instance, διώκω becomes ἐδίωξα; βλέπω becomes ἔβλεψα; and σώζω becomes ἔσωσα.

Stems ending in	*Conclude with*
γ, κ, χ, or σσ (gutturals)	ξ
β, π, or φ (labials)	ψ
δ, ζ, θ, or τ (dentals)	σ

To repeat, there is no difference in meaning between the first aorist and the second aorist. The difference is purely morphological. The verbs we have learned that take a second aorist form include ἄγω, γινώσκω, ἔχω, λαμβάνω, and λέγω (see lesson VI). One verb, διδάσκω, forms its first aorist principal part somewhat unpredictably: ἐδίδαξα. Another verb, εὑρίσκω, occasionally forms an unusual first aorist, εὗρα, and more often a second aorist.

Prepositions

Greek prepositions dictate the cases in which their objects appear. Some prepositions are associated with one case only; others take two or more cases, often with different meanings depending on the case in which the object of the preposition appears. In this lesson, we will study the single case prepositions.

Prepositions can usually be glossed fairly simply with a basic English equivalent. Do not permit yourself to be locked into that gloss, however, because sometimes the context will require a different English translation. The principal alternate translations will be given in parentheses.

ἐν requires the *dative* case; it is usually translated "in."
 ἐν τῷ οἴκῳ means "in the house."
εἰς requires the *accusative* case; it is usually translated "into."
 εἰς τὸν οἶκον means "into the house."
ἀπό requires the *genitive* case; it is usually translated "from."
 ἀπό τοῦ νόμου means "from (or "away from") the law."
ἐκ (ἐξ before vowels) requires the *genitive*; it is usually translated "out of."
 ἐκ τοῦ θανάτου means "out of death."
σύν requires the *dative* case; it is usually translated "with."
 σὺν τῷ διδασκάλῳ means "along with the teacher."

Accent

Some forms of the aorist verb take their accent on the *augment*. That is because the recessive pattern of verb accentuation pushes the accent as far toward the beginning of the verb as the rules of accentuation permit. If the ultima is short, the accent may fall on the antepenult, which in some instances is the augment.

Study Checklist

First aorist principal part

First aorist endings

Usage of the first aorist

Historical, narrative, or constative aorist

Gnomic aorist

Single case prepositions

Vocabulary

Verbs

ἀπολύω *ἀπολύω, ἀπολύσω, ἀπέλυσα, –, ἀπολέλυμαι, ἀπελύθην*   I release,
I divorce

βαπτίζω *βαπτίζω, βαπτίσω, ἐβάπτισα, –, βεβάπτισμαι, ἐβαπτίσθην*
I baptize (secular Greek: "I dip, I plunge")

δοξάζω *δοξάζω, δοξάσω, ἐδόξασα, –, δεδόξασμαι, ἐδοξάσθην*   I glorify

θεραπεύω *θεραπεύω, θεραπεύσω, ἐθεράπευσα, –, τεθεράπευμαι,*
ἐθεραπεύθην   I heal, I cure

καταλύω *καταλύω, καταλύσω, κατέλυσα, –, –, κατέλυθην*   I destroy,
I bring down

κηρύσσω *κηρύσσω, κηρύξω, ἐκήρυξα, κεκήρυχα, κεκήρυγμαι, ἐκηρύχθην*
I proclaim, I announce, I preach

πείθω *πείθω, πείσω, ἔπεισα, πέποιθα, πέπεισμαι, ἐπείσθην*   I persuade

πειράζω *πειράζω, πειράσω, ἐπείρασα, πεπείρακα, πεπείραμαι,*
ἐπειράθην   I test, I tempt

πέμπω *πέμπω, πέμψω, ἔπεμψα, πέπομφα, πέπεμμαι, ἐπέμφθην*   I send

σώζω *σώζω/σῴζω, σώσω, ἔσωσα, σέσωκα, σέσωμαι, ἐσώθην*   I save, I heal

Prepositions

ἀπό   from [away] (takes its object in the genitive)

ἐκ, ἐξ   out of [from] (takes its object in the genitive)

εἰς   into [toward, for] (takes its object in the accusative)

ἐν   in [among, by means of] (takes its object in the dative)

σύν   with, along with (takes its object in the dative)

Exercises

Read aloud and translate the following sentences into English. Parse the verbs, and be prepared to construe the syntactical structures.

1. ἀπέλυσεν ὁ κύριος τὸν δοῦλον, ἀλλὰ ὁ δοῦλος οὐκ ἀπέλυσε τὸ τέκνον.

2. ἐπιστεύσαμεν τῷ κυρίῳ καὶ σώζει τὰ τέκνα τοῦ θεοῦ.

3. ἔπεμψεν ὁ ἀπόστολος τὸν δοῦλον εἰς τὸ ἱερόν.

4. οὐκ ἠκούσαμεν τοῦ διδασκάλου· ἐκήρυξε τὸν θάνατον τῶν ἀνθρώπων.

5. ἄγουσιν οἱ δοῦλοι τοὺς ἄρτους ἐκ τοῦ οἴκου.

6. ἔσωσεν ὁ θεὸς τὸν ἄνθρωπον ἐκ τοῦ θανάτου.

7. ἐθεράπευσεν ὁ κύριος τὸ τέκνον καὶ οἱ ἄνθρωποι ἐδόξασαν τὸν θεόν.

8. ἐπίστευσαν οἱ δοῦλοι σὺν τοῖς τέκνοις τὸν λόγον τοῦ ἀποστόλου.

9. λόγους τοῦ θανάτου λέγεις καὶ οὐκ ἐδόξασας τὸν κύριον.

10. ἐν τῷ ἱερῷ ἐδόξασε τὰ τέκνα τὸν θεόν.

11. ἄγει ὁ ἀπόστολος τὸν ἄνθρωπον ἐκ τοῦ οἴκου τοῦ θανάτου εἰς τὸν οἶκον τοῦ θεοῦ.

12. οἱ λόγοι τοῦ διδασκάλου ἔπεισαν τοὺς δούλους.

13. ἠκούσαμεν τοῦ κυρίου καὶ ἄγομεν τοὺς ἀνθρώπους ἀπὸ τῶν ἔργων τοῦ νόμου.

14. ἐπείρασεν ὁ διδάσκαλος τὰ τέκνα καὶ τὰ τέκνα ἤκουσε τὸν λόγον τοῦ κυρίου.

15. ἐκηρύξατε τὰ ἔργα τοῦ νόμου, ἀλλὰ ἐκηρύξαμεν τὰ ἔργα τοῦ κυρίου.

16. τὸν ἄρτον τοῦ ἱεροῦ εἰς τὸν οἶκον τοῦ θεοῦ ἔπεμψας.

17. ὁ διδάσκαλος τὸν νόμου ἐν τῷ ἱερῷ ἐδίδαξεν.

18. ἠκούσαμεν τοὺς λογοὺς τοῦ ἀποστόλου καὶ ἐθεράπευσε τὰ τέκνα.

19. ἔπεισαν τὸ τέκνον τοῦ θεοῦ ἀλλὰ πειράζει ὁ θάνατος τοὺς ἀνθρώπους.

20. ἐβλέψατε τὰ ἔργα τοῦ κυρίου ἀλλὰ οὐκ ἐπιστεύσατε τὸν λόγον τοῦ θεοῦ.

Translate the following sentences from English into Greek.

1. The Lord saved the child from death.

2. I heard the apostle in the temple, and I believed.

3. We did not preach the words of death, but we proclaim the Lord.

4. I proclaimed the word of God, but you (pl) are not hearing the Lord.

5. The Lord tempted the child, but did not test the apostle.

6. You (pl) are leading the people out of death.

7. You (sg) heard the law in the temple, and you saw the works of the teacher of the law.

8. The apostle tested the slaves along with the children.

9. The apostle baptized the people, and they are glorifying God.

10. She leads the people away from the temple into the house of the Lord.

11. God sent the apostle into the house of death and cured the slaves.

12. The word of God destroyed the work of death, and the people glorified God.

13. The Lord saved the slave from the law of death.

14. You (sg) heard and you saw, but you do not know God.

15. The apostle wrote to the teacher and sent the slave away from the house.

16. You (pl) have the word of God in the law, but the law did not persuade the people.

17. I baptized the servant in the house of the apostle.

18. The law tested the people, but the Lord saved and healed the children of God.

19. I preached, you (pl) believed, but they destroyed God's work.

20. The apostle announced the death of the slave to the master of the house.

V

First Declension Nouns

First declension nouns are usually feminine, and they typically end in α or η. The second declension is somewhat more uniform than the first declension. First declension nouns have a common form in the plural, but their singular forms depend on the ending of the noun. Nouns that end with η will have η-based forms throughout the singular. If the α that ends a first declension noun is preceded by ι, ε, or ρ, that noun will fluctuate between α and η in the singular. Other α-based first declension nouns will use α throughout the singular.

Form of the First Declension Noun

Using the feminine nouns ἀρχή, σοφία, and δόξα as examples, the first declension noun is formed this way:

	Singular	*Plural*
N	ἀρχ-ή	ἀρχ-αί
G	ἀρχ-ῆς	ἀρχ-ῶν
D	ἀρχ-ῇ	ἀρχ-αῖς
A	ἀρχ-ήν	ἀρχ-άς
V	ἀρχ-ή	ἀρχ-αί

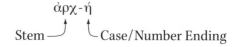

ἀρχ-ή
Stem ⌐ ⌐ Case/Number Ending

	Singular	Plural
N	σοφί-α	σοφί-αι
G	σοφί-ας	σοφι-ῶν
D	σοφί-ᾳ	σοφί-αις
A	σοφί-αν	σοφί-ας
V	σοφί-α	σοφί-αι
N	δόξ-α	δόξ-αι
G	δόξ-ης	δοξ-ῶν
D	δόξ-ῃ	δόξ-αις
A	δόξ-αν	δόξ-ας
V	δόξ-α	δόξ-αι

Feminine Article

Observe that the endings for the feminine article resemble the endings for the ἀρχή type of the first declension noun, though they do not duplicate them.

	Singular	Plural
N	ἡ	αἱ
G	τῆς	τῶν
D	τῇ	ταῖς
A	τήν	τάς

Reference Works

One of the most important skills students develop is the capacity to use reference works — a lexicon and a reference grammar. The lexicon is the most important tool at this stage. The first step in using these reference works is to learn how to find the information you need. The key to finding information in a lexicon is ascertaining the lexical form of the word you are seeking. If the lexical form is not obvious at first, strip away letters that look like augments and endings. Remember that verbs with prepositional prefixes take the augment between the prefix and the stem. You will be left with a stem from which you can guess the lexical form of the original word. The lexical entry may well begin with a list of the various forms the word takes, and that can help you recognize the form with which you are dealing.

The second step in using a reference tool is learning to use it critically. A lexicon or reference grammar is not an infallible oracle. If they were infallible, we would need only one of each, but scholars still produce competing and different versions. If you are not convinced by the first lexicon you consult, think out the basis for your doubt, and then consult another lexicon (or several more). This critical attitude is an essential component in developing exegetical judgment.

Beginning with this lesson, the exercises may include words you do not yet know. At first, the lexical form will be supplied in parentheses beside unfamiliar words. From lesson X forward, the unfamiliar words will be marked, but you will have to determine the lexical form yourself.

Understanding Sentence Structure

Greek sentences can seem extremely complicated. One way to reduce confusion is to work outward from the main verb of a sentence clause. Find the main verb first; determine the person and number of the verb, and look to see whether it has an explicit subject (a noun or pronoun in the nominative case); look for a direct object (usually in the accusative case); then account for the remaining words based on your previous work. Approaching the sentence from the verb outward, rather than simply beginning from the start of a clause, will help clarify your interpretation of Greek sentences.

Accent

First declension nouns have a special characteristic. The genitive plural of a first declension noun always takes a circumflex on the ultima — no matter where the accent falls in the lexical form.

Study Checklist

The form of the first declension noun (three types)
The feminine article
Using reference works
Understanding sentence structure

Vocabulary

Nouns

ἀγάπη, ἡ   love

ἀλήθεια, ἡ   truth

ἁμαρτία, ἡ   sin

ἀρχή, ἡ   beginning

βασιλεία, ἡ   kingdom

δόξα, ἡ   glory

εἰρήνη, ἡ   peace

ἐκκλησία, ἡ   assembly, congregation; church

ἐξουσία, ἡ   authority

ζωή, ἡ   life

ἡμέρα, ἡ   day

καρδία, ἡ   heart

κεφαλή, ἡ   head

σοφία, ἡ   wisdom

φωνή, ἡ   voice, sound

ὥρα, ἡ   hour

Exercises

Read aloud and translate the following sentences into English.
Parse all verbs, and be prepared to construe the syntactical structures.

1. ἤκουσας τὴν φωνὴν τοῦ διδασκάλου ἐκ τοῦ οἴκου.

2. ἐκηρύξαμεν τὴν ἄρχην τῆς εἰρήνης τοῖς δούλοις.

3. τὰ τέκνα λαμβάνει τὴν εἰρήνην τοῦ κυρίου.

4. ἔγραψε τῇ ἐκκλησίᾳ λόγον ζωῆς.

5. ἡ ἀγάπη τοῦ θεοῦ κατέλυσεν τὴν ἐξουσίαν τοῦ θανάτου.

6. γράφεις τὰς ἐντολὰς [*ἡ ἐντολή] ἐν ταῖς καρδίαις τῶν τέκνων.

7. ἡ φωνὴ τῶν ἀποστόλων ἔλυσε τὰς ἁμαρτίας τῶν δούλων.

8. ἤκουσαν οἱ ἄνθρωποι τὴν φωνὴν τῆς ἀληθείας.

9. τὴν ἐκκλησίαν ἐδίδαξεν ὁ ἀπόστολος καὶ τὴν βασιλείαν διδάσκει
   ὁ δοῦλος.

10. ἡ βασιλεία τῆς εἰρήνης ἐθεράπευσεν τὰς ψυχάς [*ἡ ψυχή] τῶν διδασκάλων.

11. ἐθεράπευσεν ὁ κύριος τὴν κεφαλὴν τοῦ οἴκου σὺν τοῖς δούλοις καὶ ἐδόξασε τὰ τέκνα τὴν ἀγάπην τοῦ θεοῦ.

12. ἐκηρύξαμεν τὴν ἀγάπην τοῖς ἀδελφοῖς [*ὁ ἀδελφός].

13. ἐν τῇ ζωῇ τοῦ ἀποστόλου βλέπομεν τὴν ἀλήθειαν.

14. οὐ λαμβάνουσιν οἱ ἄνθρωποι τὴν διδαχὴν [*ἡ διδαχή] τῆς σοφίας.

15. ἐκηρύξατε τὴν ὥραν τοῦ θανάτου, ἀλλὰ κηρύσσομεν τὴν βασιλείαν τοῦ θεοῦ.

16. οὐχ εὑρίσκομεν τὴν δόξαν ἐν τῇ ζωῇ τοῦ δούλου.

17. σώζει ὁ ἄγγελος [*ὁ ἄγγελος] τοὺς ἀνθρώπους ἐκ τῆς ἁμαρτίας, ἀλλὰ ἡ ὥρα τοῦ θανάτου καταλύει τὰς βασιλείας.

18. ἐν τῷ κόσμῳ [*ὁ κόσμος] ἔχει ὁ κύριος τὴν ἐξουσίαν.

19. ἐδόξασα τὸν θεὸν ἐν ἀρχῇ τῆς ἡμέρας, καὶ ἔβλεψα τὴν ἀγάπην τοῦ κυρίου.

20. ὁ διδάσκαλος ἐκήρυξεν τοῖς ἀποστόλοις ἐν τῇ ἐξουσίᾳ τῆς σοφίας.

Translate from English to Greek.

1. By the authority of the Lord we are proclaiming the beginning of the kingdom of God.

2. You (sg) heard the voice of the teacher, but you did not believe the words of wisdom.

3. The apostle has the authority in the assembly, and he is releasing the slaves of sin.

4. I did not find the wisdom of life in the authority of the law.

5. A person knows God by the head, but believes by the heart.

6. The works of the law did not save the people from sin.

7. They heard the words of the wisdom of the apostles, but they are not receiving peace in the hearts.

8. You (pl) proclaimed the love of God and the glory of God's kingdom.

9. I did not destroy the authority of the law.

10. The servant believed by the heart and has peace in life.

11. The Lord is speaking in glory, but you (pl) are not hearing God's voice.

12. The wisdom of the apostles persuaded the assembly, and the authority of the children of God released the slaves of sin.

13. The love of God saved the people from sins and destroyed the kingdom of death.

14. The Lord healed the man in the temple, and the children saw the glory of God.

15. The sin of the head of the house destroyed the kingdom of the assembly, but the slave did not glorify sin.

16. At the beginning of life the children do not have wisdom in the hearts.

17. Sin destroys the life of the person and leads to death.

18. You (sg) did not write the laws, but taught love for life with the people.

19. We saw the beginning of the wisdom of God in the assembly.

20. The voice of sin persuades the slaves of death and leads away from peace with God.

VI

Second Aorist Active Indicative

In lesson IV, the aorist principal part of verbs was introduced with a study of the first aorist forms. This lesson will focus on the second aorist form of the verb. There is no difference between first and second aorist in meaning or translation, and both aorists represent the third principal part of the verb. The aorist active verb is simply formed in two different ways.

The second aorist, like the first, takes an augment to the verb stem. While the first aorist adds a σ between the stem and the endings, the second aorist is marked by a significant change in the stem itself.

First aorist	λύω	ἔλυσα
Second aorist	λαμβάνω	ἔλαβον

Although the endings look somewhat different for the second aorist forms, the apparent dissimilarity derives mostly from different connecting vowels (α for the first aorist, o/ε for the second aorist). Note that the third person singular form may take a movable nu.

	Singular	*Plural*
1ST	ἔλαβ-ον	ἐλάβ-ομεν
2ND	ἔλαβ-ες	ἐλάβ-ετε
3RD	ἔλαβ-ε(ν)	ἔλαβ-ον

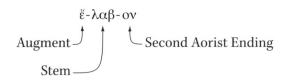

ἔ-λαβ-ον

Augment ⌐ ⌐ Second Aorist Ending

Stem

The same principles for augmenting the verb stem hold for the second aorist. For instance, the aorist modified stem of φέρω, a verb meaning "I carry," is

34

ἐνεγκ-. When the augment is applied, the stem becomes ἠνεγκ-. Several verbs that form a strong aorist principal part have already been encountered:

Principal Part

1st (present)	3rd (aorist)
ἄγω	ἤγαγον
γινώσκω	ἔγνων
εὑρίσκω	εὗρον
ἔχω	ἔσχον
λαμβάνω	ἔλαβον
λέγω	εἶπον
(ὁράω)	εἶδον

The aorist form of γινώσκω is conjugated somewhat irregularly:

	Singular	*Plural*
1ST	ἔγνων	ἔγνωμεν
2ND	ἔγνως	ἔγνωτε
3RD	ἔγνω	ἔγνωσαν

This pattern recurs in several other verbs, such as the μι verbs. Hereafter, it will be the student's responsibility to observe when a new verb takes a strong or weak aorist form.

Nouns with Unexpected Genders

We observed that second declension nouns are mostly masculine and neuter; likewise, first declension nouns are usually feminine. There are a few exceptions to this pattern, however.

There are several masculine nouns of the first declension. These can be recognized by noting that the definite article is masculine (ὁ) and that the nominative ending on the noun will be -ης or -ας (-ας only if the noun stem ends in ε, ι, or ρ). Remember that the article must agree with the noun in gender, number, and case, but not necessarily in ending. Note that the nominative and genitive singular differ from the usual first declension noun forms; otherwise the endings are the same.

	Singular		*Plural*	
N	ὁ	προφήτης	οἱ	προφῆται
G	τοῦ	προφήτου	τῶν	προφητῶν
D	τῷ	προφήτῃ	τοῖς	προφήταις
A	τὸν	προφήτην	τοὺς	προφήτας
V		προφῆτα		προφῆται

There are a few feminine nouns of the second declension. These nouns are declined with the usual second declension endings, but they take the feminine article.

	Singular		*Plural*	
N	ἡ	ὁδός	αἱ	ὁδοί
G	τῆς	ὁδοῦ	τῶν	ὁδῶν
D	τῇ	ὁδῷ	ταῖς	ὁδοῖς
A	τὴν	ὁδόν	τὰς	ὁδούς

Study Checklist

The form of the second aorist active indicative
Nouns with unexpected genders
Singular forms of the masculine first declension noun

Vocabulary

Nouns

ἀδελφός, ὁ   brother (used of Christian"brethren," hence presumably intended to be gender-inclusive in many contexts, especially in the plural)

ἀδελφή, ἡ   sister

ἔρημος, ἡ   wilderness, desert

ὁδός, ἡ   path, way

μαθητής, ὁ   disciple

προφήτης, ὁ   prophet

Verbs

βάλλω   *βάλλω, βαλῶ, ἔβαλον, βέβληκα, βέβλημαι, ἐβλήθην*   I throw

ἐκβάλλω   *ἐκβάλλω, ἐκβαλῶ, ἐξέβαλον, ἐκβέβληκα, ἐκβέβλημαι, ἐξεβλήθην*
I throw out

ἐσθίω   *ἐσθίω, φάγομαι, ἔφαγον, —, —, —*   I eat

πίνω   *πίνω, πίομαι, ἔπιον, πέπωκα, —, ἐπόθην*   I drink

πίπτω   *πίπτω, πεσοῦμαι, ἔπεσον/ἔπεσα, πέπτωκα, —, —*   I fall

φέρω   *φέρω, οἴσω, ἤνεγκα, ἐνήνοχα, ἐνήνεγμαι, ἠνέχθην*   I bear, I carry
(observe that φέρω has a second aorist stem, but takes *first* aorist endings)

ὁράω/εἶδον   *ὁράω, ὄψομαι, εἶδον, ἑώρακα, —, ὤφθην*   I see/I saw (Εἶδον
is the third principal part of the verb ὁράω. You will not be held responsible
for *present* forms of ὁράω for the time being, but you should keep up with
its other principal parts as they are introduced.)

Exercises

Read aloud and translate the following sentences into English. Parse all
verbs, and be prepared to construe the syntactical structures.

1. εὕρομεν τὸν προφήτην καὶ ἠκούσαμεν τοὺς λόγους τῆς ἀληθείας.

2. ἤγαγον οἱ μαθηταὶ τοὺς ἀδελφοὺς εἰς τὸ ἱερὸν καὶ ἔλαβον τὸν ἄρτον
τῆς ζωῆς.

3. ὁ προφήτης τῇ ἀδελφῇ τοῦ μαθητοῦ εἶπεν· ἐδίδαξεν τὰ τέκνα τοὺς
λόγους τῆς σοφίας.

4. οἱ νεανίσκοι (*νεανίσκος) σὺν τοῖς δούλοις τοῦ προφήτου ἐξέβαλον τοὺς προφήτας ἐκ τοῦ οἴκου.

5. ἔγνων τὴν ὁδὸν τῆς ζωῆς, ἀλλὰ οὐκ ἐπίστευσας *ὅτι ἐθεράπευσεν ὁ κύριος τὴν κεφαλὴν τοῦ ἀποστόλου.

6. ἐν τῇ ἡμέρᾳ τῆς δόξης ἠγάγομεν τοὺς ἀδελφούς ἀπὸ τῆς ὁδοῦ τοῦ θανάτου.

7. ἤνεγκαν οἱ μαθηταὶ τοὺς ἄρτους ἐκ τῆς ἐρήμου εἰς τὸν οἶκον τοῦ προφητοῦ.

8. ἠγάγετε ἡμᾶς ("us") ἐν τῇ ὁδῷ τοῦ διδάσκαλου, ἀλλὰ οὐκ ἔγνωτε τὴν φωνὴν τῆς σοφίας.

9. ἔσχες τὴν ἀγάπην ἐν τῇ καρδίᾳ, εἶπεν ὁ ἀπόστολος τῇ ἀδελφῇ.

10. οὐκ ἤνεγκεν ὁ *Ἰησοῦς εἰρήνην εἰς τὸν κοσμὸν (*κόσμος) ἀλλὰ μάχαιραν (*μάχαιρα).

11. ὦ ("O!") μαθηταὶ, ἐλάβετε ἐξουσίαν ἐν τῇ βασιλείᾳ, ἀλλὰ οὐκ ἔχετε ἐξουσίαν ἐν τῷ ἱερῷ.

12. ἐπέσετε εἰς τὴν ἁμάρτιαν, καὶ ἡ ἁμαρτία κατέλυσε τὰ ἔργα τῆς ἐκκλησίας.

13. ἤνεγκεν τὰ τέκνα τοὺς νόμους τῷ διδασκάλῳ ἐκ τῶν ἐκκλησιῶν.

14. καὶ εἴδομεν τὸν κύριον καὶ ἐδοξάσαμεν τὴν βασιλείαν τῆς ζωῆς.

15. ἔπεσεν ἐκ τοῦ οὐρανοῦ (*οὐρανός) τὰ τέκνα τῆς ἁμαρτίας.

16. οὐκ ἔφαγε τὸν ἄρτον ὁ προφήτης καὶ οὐκ ἔπιε τὸν οἶνον (*ὁ οἶνος) ἐν τῇ ἐρήμῳ.

17. εἶπεν ὁ *Ἰησοῦς τοῖς ἀδελφοῖς· οὐκ ἦλθεν ("it came") ἡ βασιλεία τοῦ θεοῦ ἐκ τοῦ κοσμοῦ (*κόσμος) ἀλλὰ ἐκ τοῦ οὐρανοῦ (*οὐρανός).

18. εἶδον οἱ ἄνθρωποι τὸν υἱὸν τοῦ θεοῦ, ἀλλὰ οὐχ εὗρον τὴν ὁδὸν εἰς τὴν βασιλείαν.

19. ἀδελφὴ ἀδελφῇ εἶπεν· εἶδον τὸν προφήτην ἐν τῷ ἱερῷ.

20. ἔσχετε τὸν διδάσκαλον τῆς δικαιοσύνης (*δικαιοσύνη) ἀλλ᾽ ἔχομεν τὸν κύριον.

Translate from English to Greek.

1. The prophets had the authority of the law, but we have the authority of the Lord.

2. The master threw the servant of the apostle out of the house.

3. We received but did not eat the bread of life.

4. The slave fell from the house, but the Lord saved the life of the slave.

5. You (pl) ate and drank with the disciples in the temple.

6. The sister brought the child into the house.

7. The apostle did not have the authority in the assembly.

8. The voice of the disciple led the brethren into the house of the Lord.

9. The children led the master into the desert, but the prophet found the children.

10. They found the path of wisdom and saw the glory of God.

11. Lord, you knew the sins in the hearts of human beings.

12. The child received the bread from the sister of the master.

13. You (sg) found the wisdom, but you do not have peace in the heart.

14. The brother fell from the path of life into sins.

15. The prophet proclaimed the word of the Lord in the wilderness.

16. The teacher said to the children: "I wrote a word to the master, and the master sent the servant with bread."

17. I did not have wisdom, but God's ways led the people of authority into the assembly.

18. He saw and heard the teacher, but he did not believe.

19. The love of God and the peace of the Lord led the assemblies into glory.

20. I brought the bread for the prophet in the wilderness.

VII

Adjectives

Greek adjectives and English adjectives have similar functions, but Greek syntax differs from familiar English syntax in important ways. An adjective in Greek must agree in gender, case, and number with the noun that it modifies. This frequently means that the endings of the adjective and noun will be the same, but there are so many variations in endings that a student is ill advised to count on recognizing an adjective's antecedent — that is, the noun it modifies — by the ending. For example, an adjective may follow the ἀρχή pattern from the first declension, while the noun follows the σοφία pattern; or the antecedent may be a noun of unexpected gender.

Form of the Adjective

The adjective is declined like the noun and article. Adjectives also follow different patterns. The adjectives in this lesson are declined according to second declension patterns for the masculine and neuter forms, and according to first declension patterns for the feminine.

	Singular			Plural		
	M	F	N	M	F	N
N	δίκαι-ος	δικαί-α	δίκαι-ον	δίκαι-οι	δίκαι-αι	δίκαι-α
G	δικαί-ου	δικαί-ας	δικαί-ου	δικαί-ων	δικαί-ων	δικαί-ων
D	δικαί-ῳ	δικαί-ᾳ	δικαί-ῳ	δικαί-οις	δικαί-αις	δικαί-οις
A	δίκαι-ον	δικαί-αν	δίκαι-ον	δικαί-ους	δικαί-ας	δίκαι-α
N	ἀγαθ-ός	ἀγαθ-ή	ἀγαθ-όν	ἀγαθ-οί	ἀγαθ-αί	ἀγαθ-ά
G	ἀγαθ-οῦ	ἀγαθ-ῆς	ἀγαθ-οῦ	ἀγαθ-ῶν	ἀγαθ-ῶν	ἀγαθ-ῶν
D	ἀγαθ-ῷ	ἀγαθ-ῇ	ἀγαθ-ῷ	ἀγαθ-οῖς	ἀγαθ-αῖς	ἀγαθ-οῖς
A	ἀγαθ-όν	ἀγαθ-ήν	ἀγαθ-όν	ἀγαθ-ούς	ἀγαθ-άς	ἀγαθ-ά

Just as some first declension nouns are declined with α instead of η in the singular, note that some adjectives take their feminine singular form with α instead of η.

Uses of Adjectives

An adjective may have one of three syntactical functions: it may have an attributive relation to a noun; it may have a predicative relation to a noun; or it may function substantively, as though it were itself a noun.

Attributive function. An adjective functions attributively when it serves to modify or describe a noun. In the phrase "the terrible teacher," the adjective "terrible" functions attributively.

The Greek adjective functions attributively when it is situated in one of two positions with respect to the article and noun. The attributive adjective may appear between an article and the noun it governs.

ὁ μικρὸς διδάσκαλος   the small teacher

The attributive adjective may also occur outside the article-noun sandwich so long as it also is governed by an article. The most familiar sequence is article, noun, article, adjective (of course, the article and adjective must agree with the noun they modify).

ὁ διδάσκαλος ὁ μικρός   the teacher, the small one
or the small teacher

There is no difference in meaning between attributive adjectives in the sandwich position and attributive adjectives in the outside position.

ἡ ἀγαθὴ ἀδελφή   the good sister
ἡ ἀδελφὴ ἡ ἀγαθή   the good sister

Predicative function. An adjective functions predicatively when it is not governed by an article — that is, when it is anarthrous — and the noun it modifies is governed by an article. English typically requires a verb of being for predicative constructions, such as "the homework is difficult." When translating predicative constructions into English, supply the verb of being omitted in the Greek construction. Once again, there is no difference in meaning between the two predicative positions.

κακὸς ὁ διδάσκαλος   The teacher [is] bad.
ὁ διδάσκαλος κακός   The teacher [is] bad.

Substantive function. An adjective functions substantively when it is governed by an article but has no explicit noun to modify. In such constructions the noun is implied, but the adjective functions as if it were itself a noun. The same construction occurs in English expressions like "the diligent will prosper." The noun ("people" or "students") is implicit, and the adjective "diligent" functions as if it were a noun.

ἐγείρει τοὺς νεκρούς   He (or she) is raising the
dead [people].

In summary, the three uses of the adjective include the attributive adjective governed by an article, modifying a noun:

ὁ διδάσκαλος ὁ μικρός   the small teacher

The predicative adjective not governed by an article, modifying a noun:

ὁ διδάσκαλος μικρός   the teacher [is] small

The substantive adjective governed by an article with no explicit noun:

ὁ μικρός   the small [person]

Another point: Just as adjectives may appear in an attributive construction, so also entire phrases may function attributively. A prepositional phrase may be used this way:

ἡ ἐκ τῆς καρδίας σοφία   the wisdom from the heart
(the from-the-heart wisdom)

Noun phrases (ὁ τῆς ζωῆς ἄρτος) can also be used this way, as can a variety of constructions yet to be introduced.

Demonstrative Pronouns

Like English, Greek has two demonstrative pronouns: οὗτος ("this") for the near demonstrative, and ἐκεῖνος ("that") for the far demonstrative. The demonstrative pronoun, like the adjective, must agree in gender, case, and number with the noun that it modifies. Unlike the adjective, the demonstratative pronoun *always* stands in the predicate position. Do not be misled by this construction.

The near demonstrative, οὗτος, is declined as follows:

	Singular			Plural		
	M	*F*	*N*	*M*	*F*	*N*
N	οὗτος	αὕτη	τοῦτο	οὗτοι	αὗται	ταῦτα
G	τούτου	ταύτης	τούτου	τούτων	τούτων	τούτων
D	τούτῳ	ταύτῃ	τούτῳ	τούτοις	ταύταις	τούτοις
A	τοῦτον	ταύτην	τοῦτο	τούτους	ταύτας	ταῦτα

The far demonstrative, ἐκεῖνος, is declined as follows:

	Singular			Plural		
	M	*F*	*N*	*M*	*F*	*N*
N	ἐκεῖνος	ἐκείνη	ἐκεῖνο	ἐκεῖνοι	ἐκεῖναι	ἐκεῖνα
G	ἐκείνου	ἐκείνης	ἐκείνου	ἐκείνων	ἐκείνων	ἐκείνων
D	ἐκείνῳ	ἐκείνῃ	ἐκείνῳ	ἐκείνοις	ἐκείναις	ἐκείνοις
A	ἐκεῖνον	ἐκείνην	ἐκεῖνο	ἐκείνους	ἐκείνας	ἐκεῖνα

The demonstrative pronoun can modify a noun, in which case the noun must have the article and the demonstrative pronoun stands in the predicative position: οὗτος ὁ λόγος means "this word"; ἐκείνη ἡ καρδία means "that heart." The use of the predicative position for demonstrative pronouns defies most students' expectations. Be careful to remember this peculiarity.

The demonstrative pronoun can also function substantively, as though it were an adjective. Thus, οὗτος, when used substantively, would mean "this person"; τοῦτο, "this thing," and so on.

Study Checklist

Form of the adjective

Uses of adjectives
Attributive
Predicative
Substantive

Demonstrative pronouns; they assume predicative position when modifying a noun

Vocabulary

Adjectives

ἀγαθός, -ή, -όν   good

ἀγαπητός, -ή, -όν   beloved

δίκαιος, -αία, -ον   righteous, just

ἔσχατος, -η, -ον   last, final

κακός, -ή, -όν   bad, evil

καλός, -ή, -όν   good, beautiful

μικρός, -ά, -όν   small, little

μόνος, -η, -ον   only, alone

πιστός, -ή, -όν   faithful

πονηρός, -ά, -όν   wicked, evil

πρῶτος, -η, -ον   first

Demonstrative Pronouns

οὗτος   this (near demonstrative)   ἐκεῖνος   that (far demonstrative)

Exercises

Translate from Greek to English.

1. ὁ δοῦλος τοῦ ἀποστολοῦ εὗρεν τὰ ἀγαπητὰ τέκνα ἐν τῷ οἴκῳ ἐκείνῳ.

2. ἀπὸ ἐκείνης τῆς ἡμέρας οὐκ ἦλθον (translate, "[they] came") οἱ μαθηταὶ τοῦ διδασκάλου εἰς ταύτην τὴν ἐκκλησίαν.

3. ἐν τῇ ὥρᾳ τῇ πρώτῃ τούτους τοὺς λόγους εἶπεν.

4. ἐκεῖνοι οἱ ἄνθρωποι πονηροὶ ἐν ταῖς ἐσχάταις ἡμέραις.

5. ἠνέγκαμεν τὸν ἄρτον τὸν μικρὸν τῷ ἀγαπητῷ μαθητῇ.

6. ἡ ἀγάπη ταύτης τῆς δικαίας ἀδελφῆς πιστή.

7. ἠγάγομεν τὰ τέκνα σὺν τοῖς πιστοῖς ἀπὸ τῆς θαλάσσης (*θάλασσα) εἰς τὸν οἶκον τὸν μικρόν.

8. ὁ μόνος λόγος τοῦ δικαίου προφήτου ἔσωσεν τὴν ζωὴν τοῦ ἀγαθοῦ δούλου ἐκ τοῦ θανάτου.

9. ἐν ταῖς ἡμέραις ἐκείναις ἐδίδαξεν τοὺς μικροὺς καὶ τοὺς παλαιούς (*παλαιός).

10. ἔβαλεν ταῦτα τὰ τέκνα τὰ πονηρὰ τὰς γραφὰς (*γραφή) ἐκ τοῦ οἴκου τῆς καλῆς ἀδελφῆς.

11. αὕτη ἡ ὁδὸς εἰς τὸν καινὸν (*καινός) οἶκον ἄγει.

12. δίκαιος καὶ πιστὸς ὁ ἔσχατος τῶν προφητῶν.

13. ἀγαθὴ ἡ ἐκκλησία καὶ ἡ βασιλεία κακή.

14. ταῖς πισταῖς καὶ τοῖς πιστοῖς ὁ κύριος τὴν καλὴν παραβολὴν (*παραβολή) εἶπεν.

15. ὁ προφήτης τοῖς δικαίοις εἶπεν· πρῶτοι οἱ δοῦλοι, ἔσχατοι οἱ κύριοι.

16. τῇ ἐκκλησίᾳ τῇ μόνῃ ἔγραψεν ὁ κύριος τοῦτον τὸν λόγον τὸν ἀγαθόν.

17. ὁ ἀγαθὸς ἐδίδαξεν τὰ ἀγαθά, ὁ κακὸς τὰ κακά.

18. ἀγαθὸς καὶ πιστὸς ὁ δοῦλος ἐκεῖνος καὶ εἶδεν τὰ καλά.

19. τοὺς οἴκους τοὺς μικροὺς καὶ τὰς παλαιὰς (*παλαιός) ὁδοὺς οὗτοι οἱ σοφοὶ (*σοφός) ἀπόστολοι εὗρον.

20. ἔσχατος ὁ πρῶτος, καὶ πρῶτος ὁ ἔσχατος ἐν τῇ βασιλείᾳ τῇ δικαίᾳ τοῦ οὐρανοῦ (*οὐρανός).

Translate from English to Greek.

1. This faithful apostle wrote the last word to the first assembly in the wilderness.

2. The beloved sister saw a small path in the desert, but she did not know that way.

3. This woman did not say these evil things.

4. In the lives of the faithful man and the faithful woman, the good things are first and the bad things last.

5. We said good words to this assembly, but we wrote bad words to those brethren.

6. The works of the evil people destroyed the beautiful temples and the small houses.

7. The last prophet sent the just laws to the wicked men and the wicked women.

8. The beloved teacher taught the only way into the beautiful kingdom of God.

9. The wicked child destroyed the peace of that house.

10. I heard that beautiful voice, and I received the last law from the Lord.

11. The righteous laws led the wicked assembly into death, but the love of God saved the small ones.

12. The first sound from the house persuaded the brethren, and they released those wicked slaves of the evil master.

13. The works of a good man are good, and the works of an evil man are evil.

14. I received this authority from the beloved apostle of the Lord.

15. The evil works brought the bad things to this house, but the good works of the just servant brought peace.

16. You (sg) did not have that wisdom, the only authority in this church.

17. The faithful servant does not destroy the works of the beloved teacher.

18. These children found the way from the wilderness to the small house of the teacher.

19. I glorified the righteous ways of God, the only master of this kingdom.

20. Death is bad, and life is good; bad works lead a person into death, and good works into life.

VIII

Passive Voice

So far, only the active voice of the verb has been explored. Active voice verbs express verbal action when the subject of the verb is the *agent* of the verb. In the sentence, "The student broke the pencil," the verb "broke" is in the active voice; "the student" is the agent, the one who made the "breaking" happen. Passive voice verbs express verbal action when the subject *receives* the action of the verb. In the sentence "The pencil was broken by the student," the verb "was broken" is in the passive voice; "the pencil," which is the subject of the sentence, receives the action of "breaking." English expresses the passive voice by using a helping verb (a form of the verb "to be"), but Greek expresses the passive voice by using a different form of the verb.

Present Passive Indicative

The present passive is formed from the first principal part. The present passive indicative form begins with the present stem, then adds a different set of endings.

	Singular	*Plural*
1ST	λύ-ομαι	λυ-όμεθα
2ND	λύ-η	λύ-εσθε
3RD	λύ-εται	λύ-ονται

λύ-ομαι

Stem ⌡ ⌐ Present Passive Ending

Aorist Passive Indicative

The aorist passive form constitutes the *sixth principal part*. The aorist passive indicative form begins with the augment, then the verb stem, then a -θη suffix, then the connecting vowel η, and then adds the aorist passive endings.

47

	Singular	*Plural*
1ST	ἐλύθη-ν	ἐλύθη-μεν
2ND	ἐλύθη-ς	ἐλύθη-τε
3RD	ἐλύθη	ἐλύθη-σαν

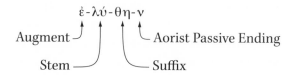

ἐ-λύ-θη-ν

Augment ⌐ Stem ⌐   Aorist Passive Ending   Suffix

There are some complications relative to the aorist passive stem. Just as consonantal stems combined with the first aorist active's -σ suffix, so also certain consonants react peculiarly with the aorist passive's -θη suffix.

Stems ending in	*Conclude with*
γ or κ (gutturals)	χ
β or π (labials)	φ
δ, ζ, or θ (dentals)	σ

For instance: διώκω becomes ἐδιώχθην; βλέπω becomes ἐβλέφθην; βαπτίζω becomes ἐβαπτίσθην.

The aorist passive form of some verbs is unpredictable. When you encounter a new verb, check its sixth principal part to make sure that you will recognize it.

Agency

Recall that the subject of a passive construction receives the action of the verb. Passive constructions themselves do not specify the agent of the action they describe, and authors may deliberately adopt the passive voice for that reason. The New Testament and the Septuagint may employ the "divine passive," which couches God's actions in the passive voice (from a reverent caution about naming God). At other times, however, authors indicate agency in passive constructions. In English, agency is expressed with the preposition "by": "The professor was mocked by the student."

Greek, however, distinguishes two types of agency, and each is expressed differently. Impersonal agents, such as inanimate objects, are expressed with a simple dative phrase: ὁ ἀπόστολος κατελύθη τοῖς λίθοις ("the apostle was destroyed by the stones"). This construction is called the *dative of means* or *instrumental dative*. Personal agency — which may be construed loosely to include people, supernatural beings, abstract entities, and so on — is expressed by the preposition ὑπό with a genitive construction: ὁ ἀπόστολος κατελύθη ὑπὸ τοῦ προφήτου ("the apostle was destroyed by the prophet"). Be alert, however, because the preposition ὑπό also takes constructions in the accusative case, in which instance it means "under."

Adverbs

Many Greek adverbs can be formed by making a simple change to the form of an adjective. Take an adjective (such as δίκαιος), construct its genitive plural form (δικαίων), and substitute a final ς for the final ν of the genitive plural (δικαίως). The adverbial form, thus, typically ends in -ως, just as English adverbs typically end in -ly. Some adverbs, however, are formed irregularly. The neuter accusative singular adjective (as, for instance, μόνον) can be used adverbially.

κακός	bad, evil	κακῶς	badly
καλός	good, beautiful	καλῶς	well
δίκαιος	righteous, just	δικαίως	righteously, justly

Postpositive Particles

Greek has a number of words which cannot stand first in a clause. For instance, the words δέ, γάρ, and οὖν cannot appear as the first word in a clause. This becomes problematic for students inasmuch as these words correspond to English words that typically *do* occur as the first word in a clause. The postpositive particle γάρ means "for" (in the sense of "for this reason"); δέ means "but" or "and." Translations should reflect English word order, not Greek, so place "but" or "for" at the beginning of the clause, where it would naturally occur in English. Note that a postpositive particle does not affect such structures as attributive phrases because the particle is syntactically blank.

Study Checklist

The meaning of passive constructions
The form of the present passive indicative
The form of the aorist passive indicative

Expressing agency in passive constructions
Dative of means for impersonal agency
Ὑπό with the genitive for personal agency

The form of adverbs
The adverbial accusative

Vocabulary

Verbs

ἀποθνῄσκω *ἀποθνῄσκω, ἀποθανοῦμαι, ἀπέθανον, —, —, —*   I die

ἀποκτείνω *ἀποκτείνω, ἀποκτενῶ, ἀπέκτεινα, ἀπέκτονα, —, ἀπεκτάνθην*
I kill

ἐγείρω *ἐγείρω, ἐγερῶ, ἤγειρα, ἐγήγερκα, ἐγήγερμαι, ἠγέρθην*   I raise (up)

Nouns

γῆ, ἡ   earth   ὄχλος, ὁ   crowd

λαός, ὁ   people   υἱός, ὁ   son

οὐρανός, ὁ   sky, heaven   ψυχή, ἡ   soul, life

Adjectives

ἅγιος, -α, -ον   holy   νεκρός, -α, -ον   dead

Conjunctions

γάρ   for (postpositive)

γέ   indeed (postpositive)

δέ   but, and (postpositive; the "mild" adversative, not as strong an opposi-
tion as that of ἀλλά; can mean either "but" or "and" depending on context)

ἤ   or

ὅτι   because, that

οὖν   therefore, then (postpositive)

ὡς   as

Prepositions

πρός   to, toward (takes the accusative)

ὑπό   by (takes the genitive; expresses personal agency); under (takes the accusative)

Adverbs

δικαίως   justly, righteously   καλῶς   well

καθώς   just as, even as   οὕτως   thus, so

κακῶς   badly

Exercises

Translate from Greek to English.

1. τῷ λόγῳ τοῦ κυρίου ἀγόμεθα εἰς τὴν ἅγιαν ἐκκλησίαν.

2. ἐγνώσθης ὑπὸ τοῦ θεοῦ καὶ πέμπῃ *νῦν ὑπὸ τοῦ υἱοῦ πρὸς τὸν κοσμόν (*κόσμος).

3. ὁ *Ἰησοῦς ἀπέθανεν ἀπεκτάνθη γὰρ ὑπὸ τῶν πονηρῶν, ἠγέρθη δὲ ἐκ τῶν νεκρῶν ὑπὸ τοῦ θεοῦ.

4. εἰρήνην ἔχει ὁ λαὸς σῴζεται γὰρ ὑπὸ τοῦ υἱοῦ τοῦ ἀνθρώπου.

5. ἐκεῖνοι οἱ ἀγαθοὶ διδάσκαλοι οὐκ ὤφθησαν ἐν τῷ οἴκῳ τῆς ἁμαρτίας.

6. ἐλήμφθησαν οἱ πιστοὶ εἰς τὸν οὐρανόν, ἀλλὰ ἐξεβλήθησαν οἱ πονηροὶ ἐκ τοῦ οὐρανοῦ.

7. ἐπέμφθησαν *τότε οἱ προφῆται, ἀλλὰ πέμπονται *νῦν οἱ μαθηταί.

8. οὐ βαπτίζεται τὰ τέκνα τὰ μικρὰ ὑπὸ τούτου τοῦ προφήτου, ἀλλὰ ὑπὸ τοῦ ἁγίου διδασκάλου.

9. εἴπετε ἐκείνοις τοῖς ἀνθρώποις ὅτι ἐσώθησαν ὑπὸ τοῦ θεοῦ ἐκ τῶν ἁμαρτιῶν.

10. αἱ ψυχαὶ τῶν ἀδελφῶν ἐθεραπεύθησαν ὑπὸ τοῦ ἐσχάτου ἁγίου.

11. ὁ νόμος ἐκηρύχθη τῷ δικαίῳ ὄχλῳ ἐν ταῖς ἡμέραις ἐκείναις, *νῦν δὲ κηρύσσεται τὸ εὐαγγέλιον (*εὐαγγέλιον) καὶ τοῖς ἀγαθοῖς καὶ τοῖς πονηροῖς.

12. *τότε ἐδιδάχθημεν ὑπὸ τοῦ προφήτου καὶ ἐδιδάξαμεν τοὺς ἀνθρώπους, ἀλλὰ *νῦν οὐ διδασκόμεθα καὶ οὐ διδάσκομεν.

13. ἐπιστεύσαμεν εἰς τὸν υἱὸν τοῦ θεοῦ ὅτι ἤχθημεν πρὸς τὸν κύριον ὑπὸ τῶν ἀδελφῶν.

14. οἱ λόγοι τοῦ υἱοῦ τοῦ ἀνθρώπου ἐγράφησαν ἐν ταῖς ψυχαῖς τῶν ἁγίων.

15. οὐχ ὑπὸ τῶν μαθητῶν σῴζῃ ἀπὸ τοῦ θανάτου, ἀλλὰ ὑπὸ τοῦ δικαίου θεοῦ.

16. ταῦτα εὑρέθη ἐν ταῖς ἁγίαις γραφαῖς (*γραφή).

17. *νῦν ἄγεται πρὸς τὸν θεὸν τῇ φωνῇ τῶν ἀποστόλων.

18. ὁ προφήτης *πάλιν εἶπεν ὅτι οἱ νεκροὶ ἠγέρθησαν ἐν ταῖς πρώταις ἡμέραις.

19. ὁ λαὸς εἰς τὸν Μωϋσῆν (*Μωϋσῆς) ἐβαπτίσθη ἐν τῇ νεφέλῃ (*νεφελή) καὶ ἐν τῇ θαλάσσῃ (*θάλασσα).

20. ἐν ἐκείναις ταῖς ἡμέραις ἦλθεν ("came") Ἰησοῦς ἀπὸ Ναζαρὲτ ("Nazareth") τῆς Γαλιλαίας ("Galilee") καὶ ἐβαπτίσθη εἰς τὸν Ἰορδάνην ("Jordan") ὑπὸ Ἰωάννου ("John"). (Mark 1:9)

Translate from English to Greek.

1. The people were persuaded that Jesus was sent by God.

2. The sons of evil people did not have the wisdom of God, but they are now seen and received by the Lord.

3. The Son of Man was raised from the dead and was glorified.

4. Those churches are saved by God from death.

5. He is now teaching the crowd because he was taught by this apostle.

6. These things are said by the sister of the disciple because they were written in the hearts of the faithful ones.

7. In these last days the holy ones are being risen from the dead by the voice of the Lord.

8. You (pl) were known by the Lord and are now led by the authority of the only Son of God.

9. The child of the righteous woman died, but he was raised by the word of the prophet.

10. That small path in the wilderness is found by the beloved children.

11. You (sg) wrote these words because you were healed by Lord's love and baptized by the head of the assembly.

12. The good things are glorified by God, but the bad things are destroyed by the word of the Lord.

13. That woman again received the bread because she was thrown out from the house of the wicked master.

14. When we were baptized by the first disciple, we received the wisdom and the authority from God.

15. Those words were heard by the crowd in the desert, but now they are heard again in the assembly.

16. This assembly is holy because the sins of the people were released by God.

17. The works of the evil ones were seen by that crowd because the wicked people killed the prophet from the wilderness.

18. That bread was not thrown from the house, but is being eaten again.

19. The disciples brought the small ones to the Lord, but we were not led by the apostles.

20. The authority of the teacher was destroyed by the works of the wicked ones.

IX

Middle Voice

In addition to active and passive voices, Greek has a third voice, the *middle voice*, which has no parallel in English. The middle voice is impossible to categorize adequately. The conventional definition suggests that the middle voice expresses *action with respect to the agent*, yet there are instances in which middle voice verbs have developed meanings where the action bears no obvious relation to the agent. The middle voice is *not* simply equivalent to a construction with a reflexive pronoun. Greek has a reflexive pronoun which will be introduced later. It is best to reckon that the meaning of the middle voice may vary from verb to verb, and careful students will observe the middle meaning of any new verbs they learn. None of the verbs encountered thus far appears in the middle voice, indicative mood. Among those already studied, only ἐγείρω and ἔχω appear in the middle voice in the New Testament: ἐγείρομαι, "I get up," and ἔχομαι, "I hold onto, I am near to."

First Aorist Middle Indicative

The present middle indicative form is identical to the present passive form. This occasionally generates ambiguity, but the context almost always makes either the passive or middle more likely. If the syntax specifies agency with one of the constructions described in lesson VIII, it can be safely surmised that the verb is passive. When beginning students encounter a verb and they are unsure whether it has a specific middle usage, and the context does not provide sufficient clues, they would do well to assume that the verb in question is passive.

The aorist middle indicative is formed from the *aorist active indicative* principal part. Thus, the aorist middle pattern varies depending on whether the verb forms a first or a second aorist principal part.

	Singular	*Plural*
1ST	ἐλυσ-άμην	ἐλυσ-άμεθα
2ND	ἐλύσ-ω	ἐλύσ-ασθε
3RD	ἐλύσ-ατο	ἐλύσ-αντο

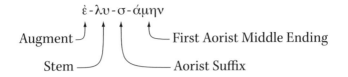

Second Aorist Middle Indicative

	Singular	*Plural*
1ST	ἐλαβ-όμην	ἐλαβ-όμεθα
2ND	ἐλάβ-ου	ἐλάβ-εσθε
3RD	ἐλάβ-ετο	ἐλάβ-οντο

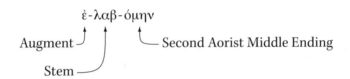

Note that the first and second aorist middle endings differ principally in their connecting vowel; the basic endings are the same.

Personal Pronouns

The Greek personal pronoun takes the place of a noun. The noun a pronoun replaces is called its *antecedent*. The personal pronoun always agrees with its antecedent in number. The first and second person pronouns have no gender and are declined by case and number. The third person pronoun agrees with its antecedent in gender, and is declined by gender, case, and number. The first and second person pronouns are declined as follows:

	First		*Second*	
	singular	*plural*	*singular*	*plural*
N	ἐγω	ἡμεῖς	συ	ὑμεῖς
G	ἐμοῦ, μου	ἡμῶν	σοῦ	ὑμῶν
D	ἐμοί, μοι	ἡμῖν	σοί	ὑμῖν
A	ἐμέ, με	ἡμᾶς	σέ	ὑμᾶς

The first and second person singular pronouns sometimes appear in monosyllabic forms without an accent. These forms are called *enclitic*. Enclitics draw their accent from the preceding word, as though they were the ultima of the preceding word. The accented form and the enclitic form have no difference in meaning. The third person pronoun is declined as follows:

		Singular			*Plural*	
	M	F	N	M	F	N
N	αὐτός	αὐτή	αὐτό	αὐτοί	αὐταί	αὐτά
G	αὐτοῦ	αὐτῆς	αὐτοῦ	αὐτῶν	αὐτῶν	αὐτῶν
D	αὐτῷ	αὐτῇ	αὐτῷ	αὐτοῖς	αὐταῖς	αὐτοῖς
A	αὐτόν	αὐτήν	αὐτό	αὐτούς	αὐτάς	αὐτά

Uses of Personal Pronouns

A personal pronoun substitutes for a noun in contexts where the noun itself would seem awkward or repetitive. In this common use, the pronoun agrees with its antecedent in number, or gender and number, and derives its case from its function in the clause.

Personal pronouns also have several special uses. The nominative case of the pronoun would frequently be redundant, since the verb implies its own subject. When the nominative personal pronoun appears, it emphasizes the subject. This *emphatic use* of the personal pronoun may be hard to translate. The student should underline — or italicize, or mark in some other way — the pronoun.

> ἐγὼ δὲ λέγω ὑμῖν...   But *I* am telling you
> (saying to you)... (Matthew 5:22)

The third person pronoun can be used as though it were an adjective meaning "the same." In this usage, called the *identical use* of the pronoun, the form of αὐτός always appears in the attributive position and agrees with the noun it is modifying.

> διαιρέσεις διακονιῶν εἰσιν,   There are varieties of ministries,
> καὶ *ὁ αὐτὸς κύριος.*   and *the same Lord.* (1 Corinthians 12:5)

The third person pronoun can also be used to intensify a noun or pronoun. The *intensive use* of the pronoun employs a pronoun in the predicate position which agrees with the noun it modifies in gender, case, and number.

It is translated as an intensive pronoun ("myself," "yourselves," and so on) whose person depends on the noun it intensifies.

αὐτὰ τὰ ἔργα ... *The works themselves ...*
μαρτυρεῖ περὶ ἐμοῦ   testify about me. (John 5:36)

Accent

Certain words in Greek have no accent of their own. Some are called "enclitic" because they "lean back" on the preceding word in the sentence, and others are called "proclitic" because they "lean forward" to the following word in the sentence. Enclitics are treated as though they were the last syllable of the preceding word, proclitics as though they were the first syllable of the following word.

If the word preceding an enclitic has an accent on the antepenult, that word receives an additional accent on the ultima. This acute accent will not change to a grave, since the enclitic now counts as the last syllable of the preceding word.

If the word preceding an enclitic has an accent on the penult, the accent depends on whether the penult takes a circumflex or an acute. If the penult takes a circumflex, the word receives an additional acute accent on the ultima. If the penult takes an acute accent *and* the enclitic is a single syllable, then the preceding word takes no additional accent. If the penult takes an acute accent and the enclitic has two syllables, the enclitic takes an acute accent on the ultima.

If the word preceding an enclitic has an accent on the ultima, there is usually no change, regardless of whether the enclitic has one or two syllables. This point, however, is not a clear matter, and students may well find counterexamples. When a proclitic precedes an enclitic, the first of the two words gets an accent on the ultima.

Study Checklist

The meaning of the middle voice
The forms of the present and aorist middle indicative
Personal pronouns

The uses of the personal pronoun
Standard pronominal usage
Emphatic use of the pronoun
Identical use of αὐτός
Intensive use of αὐτός

Vocabulary

Pronouns

αὐτός, -ή, -ό   he, she, it; same (attributive position); -self (predicative position)

ἐγώ   I

σύ   you (sg)

Adverbs

νῦν   now   πάλιν   again

ὅτε   when   τότε   then

Verbs (middle voice glosses for verbs that have already been introduced)

ἀπολύομαι (ἀπολύω)   I depart

βαπτίζομαι (βαπτίζω)   I wash up; I get baptized

ἐγείρομαι (ἐγείρω)   I get up

ἔχομαι (ἔχω)   I cling to; I am next to

Exercises

Translate from Greek to English.

1. αὐτὸς γὰρ ἔσωσεν τὸν λαὸν αὐτοῦ ἀπὸ τῶν ἁμαρτιῶν τοῦ κόσμου (*κόσμος).

2. ταῦτα εἶπεν, καὶ νῦν τοῦτο λέγει αὐτοῖς· ὁ *φίλος ἡμῶν ἀπέθανεν.

3. τότε ἐπιστεύσαμεν τὸν νόμον ὑμῶν καὶ ἀπελύοντο ὁ πονηρὸς ἐκεῖνος καὶ οἱ αὐτοὶ δοῦλοι πρὸς τὸν Ῥωμαῖον (*Ῥωμαῖος).

4. γινώσκομεν τὴν μόνην ὁδόν, καὶ αὐτὴ ἄγει σε εἰς τὸν οἶκον ἡμῶν.

5. αὐτὸς δὲ ὁ κύριος τῆς εἰρήνης πέμπει ὑμῖν τὴν εἰρήνην. (as in 2 Thessalonians 3:16)

6. εἰς τὴν αὐτὴν γῆν ἤχθημεν ὑπὸ τῶν διδασκάλων ἡμῶν τῶν ἀγαθῶν.

7. ἡμεῖς αὐτοὶ οὐκ ἐσώσαμεν ὑμᾶς, ἀλλ᾽ ἐσώθητε ὑπὸ Χριστοῦ (*Χριστός).

8. ἡ δόξα σου γράφεται ἐν τῷ νόμῳ, ἀλλὰ ἡ ἁμαρτία τῶν ἀνθρώπων κηρύσσεται ὑπὸ τοῦ ἀποστόλου ἐν τῷ ἱερῷ.

9. ὁ διδάσκαλος ὁ ἀγαπητὸς λαμβάνεται ὡς ἀδελφός, τὸν γὰρ ἄρτον αὐτοῦ οὐκ ἔφαγεν σὺν τοῖς πονηροῖς.

10. ἡμεῖς ἀπεθάνομεν σὺν Χριστῷ (*Χριστός), καὶ πιστεύομεν ὅτι καὶ σωζόμεθα ὑπ᾽ αὐτοῦ.

11. πάλιν λέγω ὑμῖν ὅτι εἴδετε τοὺς προφήτας καὶ ἠκούσατε τοὺς λόγους αὐτῶν, ἀποκτείνετε δὲ τὰ τέκνα αὐτῶν.

12. ἐπίστευσεν δὲ Ἀβραὰμ (*Ἀβραάμ) τῷ θεῷ καὶ ἐλογίσθη (*λογίζομαι) αὐτῷ εἰς δικαιοσύνην (*δικαιοσύνη). (Romans 4:3)

13. *Χριστὸς (Χριστός) ἀπέθανεν *ὑπὲρ τῶν ἁμαρτιῶν ἡμῶν κατὰ τὰς γραφὰς καὶ ἐτάφη (*θάπτω). (as in 1 Corinthians 15:3–4)

14. ἠγείρατο ὁ κύριος, ἐπίστευσαν δὲ εἰς αὐτὸν οἱ ἄνθρωποι τῆς ἐκκλησίας ἐκείνης.

15. καὶ αὐτοὶ τὸ αὐτὸ βρῶμα (*βρῶμα) ἔφαγον καὶ τὸ αὐτὸ πόμα (*πόμα) ἔπιον. (as in 1 Corinthians 10:3–4a)

16. ἐν τούτῳ γινώσκομεν ὅτι ἐν αὐτῷ μένομεν (*μένω) καὶ αὐτὸς ἐν ἡμῖν. (1 John 4:13)

17. Οὐκ ἔστιν (translate as "is") μαθητὴς *ὑπὲρ τὸν διδάσκαλον· οὐ δοῦλος ὑπὲρ τὸν κύριον αὐτοῦ. (cp. Matthew 10:24)

18. ἐπέμφθη οὖν οὗτος ὁ λόγος εἰς τοὺς ἀδελφοὺς ὅτι ὁ μαθητὴς ἐκεῖνος οὐκ ἀπέθανεν. (cp. John 21:23)

19. ἐπείσθησαν δὲ αὐτῷ, καὶ ἀπελύσαν τοὺς ἀποστόλους. (as in Acts 5:39–40)

20. οὐκ ἔχομεν ταύτην τὴν ἐξουσίαν, ὡς καὶ οἱ λοιποὶ (*λοιπός) ἀπόστολοι καὶ οἱ ἀδελφοὶ τοῦ κυρίου; (as in 1 Corinthians 9:5)

Translate from English to Greek.

1. They justly persuaded us, and we were led to the same path.

2. You yourself proclaimed this word in this assembly.

3. Just as you (pl), we believe in the same God.

4. Her teacher was sent into the house and again brought the same prophet with him.

5. Our love for you (pl) and your love for us are known by them.

6. I myself wrote these words, but you (sg) were not taught by them.

7. We ourselves have these sins in our hearts.

8. You (sg) are sent into the same house, just as Christ was sent into it.

9. He fell into the same sin again, for he did not hear the words of the Lord.

10. You (sg) ate bread with them; therefore they are now receiving your slave well.

11. The same words were spoken again by the teacher, but they were badly received by the children.

12. This disciple had the same authority as his master.

13. She spoke well among her brothers and sisters.

14. I preached to you (pl) in those days, but now you yourselves are preaching my words to them.

15. When this house was destroyed by you (pl), my heart had no peace.

16. Thus says the Lord, "I see your (pl) works."

17. My brother and I found the same way out of the wilderness as you (sg) found.

18. With his final word he did not glorify God, but his teacher.

19. We heard the same things, for they were spoken by the same person.

20. They saw his son, but they were not persuaded by him.

X

Imperfect Tense

The imperfect tense is part of the present tense system, and it shares the imperfective aspect of the present tense. The imperfect tense is formed from the present active principal part (the first principal part). The imperfect differs from the present in that the imperfect locates the imperfective or progressive aspect of the present tense *in past time*. Where the present expresses imperfective or progressive aspect ("I am running") without regard to time and the aorist expresses perfective aspect ("I ran," "I run") without regard to time, the imperfect tense expresses past progressive action ("I was running").

Imperfect Active Indicative

The imperfect active indicative applies the endings introduced for the second aorist (the *secondary endings*) to the present stem, preceded by the ε-augment.

	Singular	*Plural*
1ST	ἔλυ-ον	ἐλύ-ομεν
2ND	ἔλυ-ες	ἐλύ-ετε
3RD	ἔλυ-ε(ν)	ἔλυ-ον

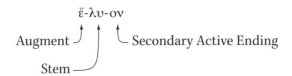

ἔ-λυ-ον

Augment ⌐ | ⌐ Secondary Active Ending

Stem ⌐

The augment affects the imperfect in the same way as it does the aorist. Stems that begin with a vowel will show contraction, and stems with prepositional prefixes will take the augment on the stem proper, not on the prefix. Some verbs have slightly irregular imperfect forms; for instance, ἔχω becomes εἶχον in the imperfect. This is the only verb we have studied so far that takes an irregular form in the imperfect.

Imperfect Middle / Passive Indicative

The imperfect middle and imperfect passive take identical forms, as do the present middle and passive. The imperfect middle/passive indicative begins with the augment, then the present stem, then the secondary middle/passive endings. As in the aorist middle endings, the imperfect uses ε and ο as its connecting vowels.

	Singular	*Plural*
1ST	ἐλυ-όμην	ἐλυ-όμεθα
2ND	ἐλύ-ου	ἐλύ-εσθε
3RD	ἐλύ-ετο	ἐλύ-οντο

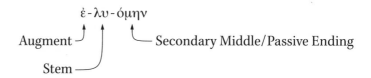

ἐ-λυ-όμην

Augment ⌐   ⌐ Secondary Middle/Passive Ending

Stem

Uses of the Imperfect

The imperfect has various uses. First, it is usually used simply to express progressive action in past time.

[Ἰωάννης] ἐκήρυσσεν ...   [John] *was preaching* ... (Mark 1:7)

Second, the imperfect can express intended action, as in "I was trying to loose" (the *conative* imperfect).

ὁ δὲ Ἰωάννης διεκώλυεν αὐτόν ...   But John *was trying to prevent* him ... (Matthew 3:14)

Third, the imperfect can express customary or habitual action, as in "I used to loose" (the *customary* imperfect).

κατὰ δὲ ἑορτὴν ἀπέλυεν   At the feast he *used to release* one
αὐτοῖς ἕνα δέσμιον ...   prisoner for them... (Mark 15:6)

Finally, the imperfect can be used to express the beginning of an action, as in "I began to loose" (the *inceptive* imperfect).

ἔστη καὶ *περιεπάτει* καὶ	He stood and *began to walk* and
εἰσῆλθεν σὺν αὐτοῖς ...	entered with them ... (Acts 3:8)

In each of these special uses of the imperfect, the conventional translation of progressive aspect in past time would be problematic. One would not say of Pontius Pilate that "he was releasing" a prisoner at the feast. When a conventional translation seems unsatisfactory, one of these special uses may better express the force of the verb. There are other nuances of the imperfect, but these four examples provide an ample beginning.

The Verb Εἰμί

The Greek verb meaning "to be" is εἰμί. Learn the present and imperfect conjugation:

	Present		*Imperfect*	
	singular	*plural*	*singular*	*plural*
1ST	εἰμί	ἐσμέν	ἤμην	ἦμεν, ἤμεθα
2ND	εἶ	ἐστέ	ἦς, ἦσθα	ἦτε
3RD	ἐστί(ν)	εἰσί(ν)	ἦν	ἦσαν

The present forms of εἰμί are enclitic, except for the second person singular. Do not try to bring out an imperfective aspect in translating εἰμί; the conventional translations ("I am," "they were," and so on) express the imperfective aspect quite well enough. Be alert to the possibility that εἰμί can be used impersonally. It may be appropriate to translate ἐστιν as "there is" or εἰσίν as "there are" (in the imperfect, "there was" or "there were").

Like other verbs of being, εἰμί takes its object in the nominative case, a phenomenon which is called the *predicate nominative*. Since the adjective (and certain other structures) can be used predicatively, it is not always necessary to include a form of εἰμί to indicate "being" in a Greek clause. To say "the word is faithful," πίστος ὁ λόγος does just as well as πιστός ἐστιν ὁ λόγος. In a clause with εἰμί, it may be hard to distinguish the subject of the verb from its object since they are both in the nominative case.

As a general rule, the more definite of the words linked by εἰμί is the subject, the less definite word is the predicate. A demonstrative pronoun or a relative pronoun is more likely to be the subject than any other nominative.

A personal pronoun or proper noun is more likely to be the subject than any of the remaining sorts of nominatives. An articular noun is more likely to be the subject than an anarthrous noun. If either nominative is distinctly more definite than the other, the linking verb may simply be equating the two, and the word that comes first is probably the subject.

Accent

All present indicative forms of the verb εἰμί are enclitic *except* for the second person singular and plural. Sometimes the word ἐστι(ν) — which usually takes an accent on the ultima — takes an acute accent on the penult. Such circumstances include: when ἐστί occurs at the beginning of the sentence; when it immediately follows οὐκ, μή, εἰ, ὡς, καί, ἀλλά, and τοῦτο; and when it means "exists" or "is possible."

Study Checklist

The form of the imperfect
Irregular imperfects

The uses of the imperfect
Continuing action, past time
Conative imperfect
Customary imperfect
Inceptive imperfect

The forms of εἰμί
Predicate nominative with verbs of being
Demonstrative or relative pronouns are the subject rather than any other noun
Proper nouns or personal pronouns are the subject rather than any other nouns
An articular noun is the subject rather than an anarthrous noun
Impersonal use of εἰμί

Vocabulary

Verbs

ἀποστέλλω ἀποστέλλω, ἀποστελῶ, ἀπέστειλα, ἀπέσταλκα, ἀπέσταλμαι, ἀπεστάλην   I send

εἰμί εἰμί, ἔσομαι, —, —, —,—   I am

Nouns

ἄγγελος, ὁ   messenger (angel)

γραφή, ἡ   writing, scripture

κόσμος, ὁ   world

ὀψία, ἡ   evening

σάββατον, τό   sabbath, week (dative plural = σάββασιν)

χριστός, ὁ   anointed one; messiah; Christ

Adjectives

ἄλλος, -η, -ο   other, another (the accent on the α helps distinguish
ἄλλος from ἀλλά)

Ἰουδαῖος, -αία, -ον   Judean (frequently used substantively as "a Judean,"
"a Jew")

Exercises

Translate from Greek to English.

1. οἱ ἀδελφοὶ τῆς ἐκκλησίας τῆς δικαίας ἐθεραπεύοντο τῇ ἐξουσίᾳ τοῦ
μόνου προφήτου.

2. ὅτε ἤγαγεν ὁ διδάσκαλος ἡμᾶς ἀπὸ τῶν ὄχλων τῶν πονηρῶν, εἶπεν
αὐτῷ ὁ ἄγγελος, Ἤνεγκας αὐτοὺς δικαίως.

3. ὁ μαθητὴς ὁ ἀγαπητὸς ἐδίδασκεν τὰ τέκνα τῆς ἐκκλησίας,
ὅτι ἦν ἅγιος.

4. ἐκεῖοι οἱ αὐτοὶ πονηροὶ ἀπεκτάνθησαν ὑπὸ τοῦ *κεντυριῶνος τοῦ
ἐσχάτου.

5. οἱ Ἰουδαῖοι φέρουσιν τὰς ἀδελφὰς εἰς τὸν οἶκον, ὀψία γὰρ ἐστίν.

6. οὐ δοξάζετε τὸν θεὸν τοῦ οὐρανοῦ ὅτε πίνετε καὶ ἐσθίετε, ὅτι οὐκ
ἐκβάλλετε τὰς ψυχὰς τὰς κακάς ἐκ τοῦ λαοῦ.

7. ἔγνως τὰς γράφας, ἀλλ᾽ οὐ ἀπέστειλας τὸν ἄλλον δοῦλον πρὸς τὴν
βασιλείαν.

8. αἱ ψυχαὶ τῶν μαθητῶν τούτων ἀπέθανον τῇ ἁμαρτίᾳ, ἀλλ᾽
ἠγέρθησαν τῇ ζωῇ.

9. οὕτως λέγει ὁ κύριος ὅτι ἔπεμψα τὸν χριστὸν ὑμῖν, ἀλλ᾽ ὑμεῖς
οὐ ἐλάβετε αὐτόν.

10. κύριος γάρ ἐστιν τοῦ σαββάτου ὁ υἱὸς τοῦ ἀνθρώπου. (Matthew 12:8)

11. ὅτε ὀψία ἦν, οἱ δοῦλοι ἐβαπτίσαντο ἐν τῷ *ποτάμῳ.

12. τότε ἐπείρασεν αὐτὸν ὁ *διάβολος, καὶ ἄγγελοι ἄρτον ἤνεγκον καὶ ἔφαγεν αὐτόν.

13. ἐν ἀρχῇ ἦν ὁ λόγος, καὶ ὁ λόγος ἦν πρὸς τὸν θεόν, καὶ θεὸς ἦν ὁ λόγος. οὗτος ἦν ἐν ἀρχῇ πρὸς τὸν θεόν. (John 1:1–2)

14. ὑμεῖς ἐστε τὸ *ἅλας τῆς γῆς· ὑμεῖς ἐστε τὸ *φῶς τοῦ κόσμου. (Matthew 5:13a, 14a)

15. *μακάριοι οἱ *πτωχοί, ὅτι αὐτῶν ἐστιν ἡ βασιλεία τῶν οὐρανῶν. (as in Matthew 5:3)

16. *Πέτρος εἶπεν, Σὺ εἶ ὁ Χριστός, ὁ υἱὸς τοῦ θεοῦ. (Matthew 16:16)

17. (*ἀνέγνωτε τὸν λόγον), Ἐγώ εἰμι ὁ θεὸς *Ἀβραὰμ καὶ ὁ θεὸς *Ἰσαὰκ καὶ ὁ θεὸς *Ἰακώβ; οὐκ ἔστιν ὁ θεὸς νεκρῶν ἀλλὰ ζωῆς. (see Matthew 22:32)

18. ἐν ταῖς *συναγωγαῖς τῶν Ἰουδαίων ἐκήρυσσεν τὸν Ἰησοῦν· ἔλεγεν, Οὗτός ἐστιν ὁ υἱὸς τοῦ θεοῦ. (see Acts 9:20)

19. ὅτε γὰρ δοῦλοι ἦτε τῆς ἁμαρτίας, *ἐλεύθεροι ἦτε ἐν ταῖς καρδίαις ὑμῶν.

20. ἔστιν δὲ αὕτη ἡ *παραβολή· Ὁ *σπόρος ἐστὶν ὁ λόγος τοῦ θεοῦ. (Luke 8:11)

Translate from English to Greek.

1. The voice was leading us into the temple, but we did not find the child of the kingdom in the house of God.

2. *I* am hearing a voice in the assembly, and it is saying that you (sg) are not a slave.

3. Then God said to the beautiful world, "I see the sky and the land and the people. You (pl) are my beloved."

4. *We* know that the Messiah was Judean because thus the scriptures say to us.

5. By the authority of the beloved prophet, the faithful assembly itself writes to the sisters of the anointed one.

6. The scriptures of the assembly are bringing a final word, just as those prophets themselves were saying and were teaching in the beginning.

7. We saw a beautiful evening, but the same hour of sin destroyed the life of the world.

8. For you (pl) took the kingdom of peace, and you are proclaiming it to the evil masters.

9. They received the holy person from the crowd when he was healed by those righteous messengers.

10. Again, the sisters are being cast out by the people because the bad messengers are persuading the crowd.

11. We said to the evil ones, "You are eating the bread of the prophet on the sabbath."

12. The same children of the house are being loosed by the work of the slaves, but these other children are being carried away from the holy law of that assembly.

13. Therefore, we are being saved by the words of peace, and we are proclaiming those words in the first hour of the day.

14. The teacher of wisdom was being released by the children of love because they were glorifying the only God of the world.

15. When they did not baptize the prophets, the other disciples did not glorify their master with love and peace.

16. The people were being healed by the disciples as those final slaves were released from the wicked sins of their hearts.

17. The teachers destroyed the wisdom of sin, and they taught the disciples a righteous path out of the desert.

18. When the land was being killed by this work of death, the people of life sent bread to the last slaves.

19. The masters themselves brought the people to the path of life, but the apostles are leading them to peace in God.

20. God is sending authority into the world, but the world continues eating and drinking.

21. The faithful love of the disciples is good for the work of God.

XI

Mι Verbs

The verbs we have studied thus far have lexical forms that end with ω. In this lesson, we encounter a family of verbs whose lexical forms end in -μι. These μι verbs are the more ancient forms, and they had generally been displaced by ω verbs in the New Testament period. However, some particularly common μι verbs survived, including the verb of being, εἰμί, and these occur throughout the New Testament.

The differences between μι verbs and ω verbs seem imposing at first glance. The differences in the two families appear mainly in the first and third principal parts, the present and aorist active indicative; in the other principal parts, both families are conjugated in the same way. The most important trick to learning μι verbs is that their present principal part does not reveal the verb stem directly, as is the case with ω verbs. Μι verbs *reduplicate* their initial consonant — that is, the initial consonant of the verb stem is repeated *before* the verb, with a ι- augment.

Δίδωμι and Ἵστημι

The verb δίδωμι has δο- as its stem. The initial δ is reduplicated before the stem, and ι provides the connecting vowel for this syllable. After the stem, the stem's ο and the ο connecting vowel combine to form an ω.

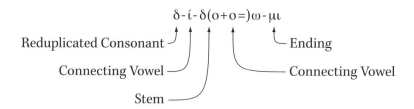

The second verb for this lesson, ἵστημι, is different inasmuch as its stem is στα-. The initial ι in ἵστημι is the connecting vowel, and the rough breathing serves as the reduplicated stem σ (to avoid an unpleasant σισ sound).

	Singular	Plural		Singular	Plural

Present Active Indicative

1ST	δίδωμι	δίδομεν		ἵστημι	ἵσταμεν
2ND	δίδως	δίδοτε		ἵστης	ἵστατε
3RD	δίδωσι(ν)	διδόασι(ν)		ἵστησι(ν)	ἱστᾶσι(ν)

Present Middle/Passive Indicative

1ST	δίδομαι	διδόμεθα		ἵσταμαι	ἱστάμεθα
2ND	δίδοσαι	δίδοσθε		ἵστασαι	ἵστασθε
3RD	δίδοται	δίδονται		ἵσταται	ἵστανται

Imperfect Active Indicative

1ST	ἐδίδουν	ἐδίδομεν		ἵστην	ἵσταμεν
2ND	ἐδίδους	ἐδίδοτε		ἵστης	ἵστατε
3RD	ἐδίδου	ἐδίδοσαν		ἵστη	ἵστασαν

Imperfect Middle/Passive Indicative

1ST	ἐδιδόμην	ἐδιδόμεθα		ἱστάμην	ἱστάμεθα
2ND	ἐδίδοσο	ἐδίδοσθε		ἵστασο	ἵστασθε
3RD	ἐδίδοτο	ἐδίδοντο		ἵστατο	ἵσταντο

First Aorist Active Indicative

1ST	ἔδωκα	ἐδώκαμεν		ἔστησα	ἐστήσαμεν
2ND	ἔδωκας	ἐδώκατε		ἔστησας	ἐστήσατε
3RD	ἔδωκε(ν)	ἔδωκαν		ἔστησεν	ἔστησαν

Second Aorist Active Indicative

1ST				ἔστην	ἔστημεν
2ND				ἔστης	ἔστητε
3RD				ἔστη	ἔστησαν

continues

	Singular	Plural		Singular	Plural

Aorist Middle Indicative

1ST	ἐδόμην	ἐδόμεθα		ἐστησάμην	ἐστησάμεθα
2ND	ἔδου	ἔδοσθε		ἐστήσω	ἐστήσασθε
3RD	ἔδοτο	ἔδοντο		ἐστήσατο	ἐστήσαντο

Aorist Passive Indicative

1ST	ἐδόθην	ἐδόθημεν		ἐστάθην	ἐστάθημεν
2ND	ἐδόθης	ἐδόθητε		ἐστάθης	ἐστάθητε
3RD	ἐδόθη	ἐδόθησαν		ἐστάθη	ἐστάθησαν

Note that δίδωμι's aorist forms are conjugated as ordinary first aorist forms, except that the consonantal suffix is κ instead of σ. The verb ἵστημι forms both a second aorist form *and* a first aorist (ἔστησα); the difference in form signifies a difference in meaning. The present and first aorist of ἵστημι are *transitive* (they take a direct object) and mean "I stand [something] up," as in "I stood a box up on its end." The second aorist and aorist passive are *intransitive* (they do not take a direct object) and mean, "I stand." A similar pattern holds for ἀνίστημι, a compound formed with the prepositional prefix for ἀνά. The verb ἀνίστημι usually means, "I raise [something]," but when ἀνίστημι appears without a direct object or in the middle voice, it means "I rise."

Conditional Sentences

A conditional sentence indicates what follows *on the condition* that certain premises are, or are not, true. The premise of a conditional clause is called the *protasis*, and the consequence of a conditional is called the *apodosis*. The protasis usually precedes the apodosis, but that is not always the case. Students may be tricked by conditionals whose protasis *follows* the apodosis. The Greek language constructs conditional sentences in four distinct ways.

The first class, the *simple conditional*, indicates that *if* a certain condition holds to be true, then certain results follow — with the assumption that, at least for the sake of the argument, the condition does in fact hold true. The second class, the *contrary to fact conditional,* indicates what would be the case if the condition were true — with the assumption that the condition is not true. The third class includes *present general* and *future more probable conditionals;* it may state what is generally the case if a certain condition holds true, or what will probably be the case if the condition turns out to be true. In both cases, the third class conditional indicates a matter that is genuinely hypothetical. The fourth class, *future less probable conditional,* introduces conditions that are genuinely hypothetical, but are less likely to be fulfilled. We will learn how to construct simple conditionals and contrary to fact conditionals in this lesson.

Simple Conditional

A simple conditional (first class) has a protasis that begins with the particle εἰ and a verb in the indicative mood, and an apodosis whose verb may appear in any mood or tense.

> Protasis εἰ + a verb in the indicative mood
> Apodosis a verb in any tense or mood

εἰ δὲ πνεύματι ἄγεσθε,　But if you are led by the Spirit,
οὐκ ἐστὲ ὑπὸ νόμον.　you are not under the law. (Galatians 5:18)

Paul presupposes that the Galatians *are* led by the Spirit. A simple conditional does not imply that the protasis is, in fact, true; the speaker or writer may be mistaken. It simply implies that the speaker or writer is presupposing the truth of the protasis.

Contrary to Fact Conditional

The contrary to fact conditional (second class) has a protasis that begins with the particle εἰ and a verb in the imperfect or aorist indicative, and an apodosis that begins with the particle ἄν and continues with a verb in the imperfect or aorist indicative. Translate a contrary to fact conditional whose verbs occur in the imperfect with a progressive or simple past construction in the protasis, and a contingent clause with "would" in the apodosis. Translate a contrary to fact conditional whose verbs occur in the aorist with a pluperfect construction ("had done," "had thought," "had brought") in the protasis, and a parallel contingent clause in the apodosis.

Protasis   εἰ + a verb in the imperfect indicative

Apodosis   ἄν + a verb in the imperfect indicative

εἰ γὰρ ἐπιστεύετε Μωϋσεῖ,   For if you believed Moses, you would believe
ἐπιστεύετε ἄν ἐμοί...   me ... (John 5:46)

Protasis   εἰ + a verb in the aorist indicative

Apodosis   ἄν + a verb in the aorist indicative

Κύριε, εἰ ἦς ὧδε οὐκ ἄν   Lord, if you had been here, my brother
ἀπέθανεν ὁ ἀδελφός μου.   would not have died. (John 11:21)

In the first example, Jesus assumes that the Judeans do not believe Moses (at least, not on his terms); in the second, Martha reproaches Jesus because he was not, in fact, in Bethany in time to prevent Lazarus from dying.

Note that the protasis of the second example includes the verb ἦς, the imperfect of εἰμί. Since there *is* no aorist form of εἰμί, one must substitute the imperfect for it in the contrary to fact conditionals. Construe a contrary to fact conditional with a form of εἰμί and an aorist as though the clause with εἰμί were also in the aorist. If the verbs in both clauses are imperfect forms of εἰμί, then you must discern from the context how best to construe the sentence.

Study Checklist

The forms of δίδωμι and ἵστημι

Simple (first class) conditionals and contrary to fact (second class) conditionals

Characteristics of simple conditionals: εἰ + indicative in protasis, any form in apodosis; protasis assumed to be true

Characteristics of contrary to fact conditionals: εἰ + imperfect/aorist in protasis, imperfect/aorist + ἄν in apodosis; protasis assumed to be untrue

Vocabulary

Verbs

ἀνίστημι *ἀνίστημι, ἀναστήσω, ἀνέστησα, ἀνέστηκα, ἀνέστημαι, ἀνεστάθην*   I raise [something] (transitive); I rise (intransitive)

ἀποδίδωμι *ἀποδίδωμι, ἀποδώσω, ἀπέδωκα/ἀπεδόμην, —, —, ἀπεδόθην*
I give back, I pay; I sell (middle voice)

δίδωμι *δίδωμι, δώσω, ἔδωκα, δέδωκα, δέδωμαι, ἐδόθην*   I give ἵστημι ἵστημι, στήσω, ἔστησα/ἔστην, ἔστηκα, ἕσταμαι, ἐστάθην I stand [something] up (transitive); I stand (intransitive)

καθίστημι καθίστημι, καταστήσω, κατέστησα, κατέστακα, κατέσταμαι, κατεστάθην I establish (transitive); I am established (intransitive)

παραδίδωμι παραδίδωμι, παραδώσω, παρέδωκα, παραδέδωκα, παραδέδομαι, παρεδόθην I hand over

παρίστημι παρίστημι, παραστήσω, παρέστησα, παρέστηκα, —, παρεστάθην I am present

Particles

ἄν   (untranslatable particle; marker of contingency)

εἰ   if

Exercises

Translate from Greek to English.

1. ἐγω γὰρ ἔλαβον ἀπὸ τοῦ κυρίου τοὺς ἅγιους λόγους τῆς σοφίας.

2. ἄλλα δὲ ἔπεσεν *ἐπὶ τὴν γῆν τὴν καλὴν καὶ ἐδίδου *καρπόν. (Matthew 13:8)

3. καὶ ἀπέδοντο οἱ ἁμαρτωλοὶ τὸν δίκαιον εἰς Αἴγυπτον· καὶ παρέστησεν ὁ θεὸς αὐτῷ καὶ ἔδωκεν αὐτῷ *χάριν καὶ σοφίαν καὶ κατέστησεν αὐτὸν.

4. ἐδίδασκεν γὰρ τοὺς μαθητὰς αὐτοῦ καὶ ἔλεγεν αὐτοῖς ὅτι ὁ υἱὸς τοῦ ἀνθρώπου παραδίδοται τοῖς κακοῖς ἀνθρώποις. (cp. Mark 9:31)

5. ἤγαγεν δὲ αὐτὸν εἰς Ἰερουσαλὴμ καὶ ἔστησεν ἐπὶ τὸ *πτερύγιον τοῦ ἱεροῦ. (Luke 4:9)

6. ταῦτα μοι παρεδόθη ὑπὸ τοῦ *πατρός μου. (cp. Matthew 11:27)

7. νῦν ἀνέστη *Ἰούδας ὁ *Γαλιλαῖος ἐν ταῖς ἡμέραις τῆς *ἀπογραφῆς καὶ ἤγαγεν τὸν λαὸν. (cp. Acts 5:37)

8. τότε παρέδωκεν αὐτοὺς ὁ θεὸς ἐν ταῖς *ἐπιθυμίαις τῶν καρδιῶν αὐτῶν εἰς *ἀκαθαρσίαν. (Romans 1:24)

9. οὐκ ἂν ἥμαρτον εἰ οὐκ ἐδώκας μοι τὸν ἄρτον τοῦ πονηροῦ.

10. ὁ δὲ κύριός μοι παρέστη καὶ εἶπεν σὺν μοι. (cp. 2 Timothy 4:17)

11. οὗτος εἰ ἦν προφήτης, ἐγίνωσκεν ἂν ὅτι αὕτη οὐκ ἔστιν ἅγια.

12. καὶ εἰ ἐγὼ ἐν *Βεελζεβοὺλ ἐκβάλλω τὰ *δαιμόνια, οἱ υἱοὶ ὑμῶν τῇ αὐτῇ ἐξουσίᾳ ἐκβάλλουσιν αὐτά; (cp. Matthew 12:27)

13. εἰ γὰρ ἐπιστεύετε *Μωϋσεῖ, ἐπιστεύετε ἂν ἐμοί· *περὶ γὰρ ἐμοῦ ἔγραψεν. (cp. John 5:46)

14. εἰ οὐκ ἐκήρυξεν αὐτοῖς καὶ ἐπείρασεν αὐτούς, ἁμαρτίαν ἂν οὐκ εἴχοσαν.

15. εἰ γὰρ *Ἀβρααμ ἐξ ἔργων ἦν δίκαιος, ἔχει *καύχημα, ἀλλ᾽ οὐ πρὸς θεόν. (cp. Romans 4:2)

16. καὶ εἰ οὐκ κατελύθησαν αἱ ἡμέραι ἐκεῖναι, οὐκ ἂν ἐσώθησαν οἱ ἄνθρωποι τῆς καλῆς γῆς. (cp. Matthew 24:22)

17. εἰ *τυφλοὶ ἦτε, οὐκ ἂν εἴχετε ἁμαρτίαν· νῦν δὲ λέγετε ὅτι βλέπομεν· ἡ ἁμαρτία ὑμῶν *μένει. (John 9:41)

18. εἰ γὰρ ἔγνωσαν, οὐκ ἂν τὸν κύριον τῆς δόξης ἀπεκτείναν.

19. εἰ κύριος *Σαβαὼθ οὐκ ἐθεράπευσεν τοὺς κακοὺς καὶ τὰς πονηρὰς, ὁ κόσμος ἂν κατέλυθη ὡς *Σόδομα καὶ ὡς *Γόμορρα.

20. εἰ ὑπὸ ὑμῶν κρίνεται ὁ κόσμος, *ἀνάξιοί ἐστε ἐν τοῖς μικροῖς τούτοις;

Translate from English to Greek.

1. If you (sg) believe in me, your life is led by my word.

2. I handed over to you (pl) that Jesus was risen from the dead.

3. If I had known that he was the Son of God, I would have received him into my house.

4. If we had drunk and eaten with you (pl), we would have destroyed the peace of your church.

5. If you (sg) had not given him that authority, you would have been the master of your life.

6. Your (sg) words are now present in my heart, for you gave me the wisdom of your law.

7. If she had known that that path was leading into death, she would not have been persuaded by the words of the evil teacher.

8. If you yourselves fell into that sin, the holy bretheren would not have received you with love into their assembly.

9. I gave back to him that writing, but he did not send a messenger with a word for me.

10. If this is the word of God, now we are hearing from God.

11. If the people do not see that Jesus has the authority in this world, they are not receiving him as the Messiah.

12. My faithful ones stand in the temple, for I knew them from the beginning of the world.

13. The anointed one was handed over to the wicked ones, but God was faithful to his holy one.

14. Had you (sg) first talked to me, I would have known that this man is a righteous one.

15. If you (pl) threw them out of the temple, they would have established another assembly.

16. If Jesus was raised from the dead, then he was the Messiah.

17. If you (sg) had known the scriptures, you would have found these words.

18. If her brother had written to me, I would not have taken that man into my house.

19. If I were you (sg), I would neither write to him, nor speak with him.

20. If Jesus had been in the house, the child of the master would not have died.

XII

Future Tense

The future tense involves learning one new principal part and using another principal part that has already been learned. The new principal part is the future active indicative, which is the *second principal part*. You now know four of the six principal parts: the present active indicative is the first principal part; the aorist active indicative is the third principal part; the aorist passive indicative is the sixth principal part. In most cases, the future active principal part is extremely easy to learn.

The future tense differs from the other tenses inasmuch as it has *only* time reference; it has no aspectual characteristics of its own. Greek does not make a formal distinction between "we will run" and "we will be running." Thus the present tense expresses imperfective, or progressive aspect without regard to time; the aorist tense expresses perfective aspect without regard to time; the imperfect tense expresses imperfective aspect in past time; and the future tense expresses future time without regard to aspect.

Tense	Aspect	Time
present	imperfective/progressive	—
aorist	perfective	—
imperfect	imperfective/progressive	past
future	—	future

Future Active Indicative

The future active principal part is usually formed simply by adding a σ between the present active stem and the endings.

	Singular	*Plural*
1ST	λύσ-ω	λύσ-ομεν
2ND	λύσ-εις	λύσ-ετε
3RD	λύσ-ει	λύσ-ουσι(ν)

λύσ - ω

Stem ⟶   ⟵ Active Ending

Future Middle Indicative

	Singular	*Plural*
1ST	λύσ-ομαι	λύσ-ομεθα
2ND	λύσ-ῃ	λύσ-εσθε
3RD	λύσ-εται	λύσ-ονται

λύσ-ομαι

Stem ⟶   ⟵ Middle Ending

Some verb stems end in consonants that combine with the σ of the future tense to form compound consonants, as in the aorist. For instance, the future principal part of διώκω, is διώξω; βλέπω becomes βλέψω; and σώζω becomes σώσω. Μι verbs take regular future active and middle forms; the final vowel of the stem lengthens, and adds the future's characteristic σ and regular endings. Some verbs have unusual future forms, so check the list of principal parts to be certain about what form the future will take. The future forms of εἰμί are:

	Singular	*Plural*
1ST	ἔσομαι	ἐσόμεθα
2ND	ἔσῃ	ἔσεσθε
3RD	ἔσται	ἔσονται

Future Passive Indicative

	Singular	Plural
1ST	λυθήσ-ομαι	λυθησ-όμεθα
2ND	λυθήσ-η	λυθήσ-εσθε
3RD	λυθήσ-εται	λυθήσ-ονται

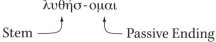

Stem ⟶ ⟵ Passive Ending

The future passive is formed from the aorist passive principal part. Take the aorist passive stem; eliminate the ε- augment; add the characteristic σ of the future tense; and add the primary middle/passive endings. The future passive of μι verbs is formed predictably from the aorist passive principal part.

Deponent Verbs

We have observed that the middle voice can express meaning in the full range from active to passive voice. When the middle voice of a verb supplants the active voice to express active meaning, it is called a *deponent* form. The verb loses its active voice form and relies on the middle (or sometimes the passive) form. For instance, the common verb meaning "I come," ἔρχομαι, is deponent: the middle form expresses the active sense of "coming." When parsing a deponent form, specify whether the form is middle or passive. (If it helps you keep aware of these distinctions, you may say "middle deponent" or "passive deponent.") Thus ἔρχεται would be parsed as third person singular present middle (deponent) indicative of ἔρχομαι. Sometimes a deponent form will obviously be passive rather than middle, since in the aorist and future the middle and passive take different forms. If a deponent form is encountered in a tense wherein the middle and passive take the same form, it is safest to reckon that the deponent is in the middle voice. Every verb has a different pattern of usage for active, present, and middle voices, so get acquainted with each verb's particular profile.

   Verbs frequently adopt deponent forms in some principal parts, but active forms in other principal parts. For instance, the future form of εἰμί is the deponent ἔσομαι. Likewise, the aorist active principal part for ἔρχομαι is ἦλθον, a simple second aorist form. A number of the verbs in the vocabulary so far have deponent future forms (γινώσκω's future principal part is γνώσομαι), while a few have deponent aorist forms.

When students learn a new verb, they should check the principal parts to make sure they will recognize all the forms of the verb.

Dual Case Prepositions

Some prepositions typically require their objects in one case only; for instance, ἐν requires its object in the dative. Prepositions can also require their objects in two or more cases, with concomitant changes in meaning. We have already learned that ὑπό with an object in the genitive, used to indicate personal agency in passive constructions, is to be translated "by," while ὑπό with its object in the accusative means "under." This lesson's vocabulary includes a number of common dual case prepositions.

Pronominal Use of the Article

Beginning with this lesson, the exercises will sometimes use an article without the noun to which it presumably refers. In such cases, the article is functioning as if it were a pronoun. Students should examine the context for clues to the article's referent.

Study Checklist

The use of the future tense (future time, unspecified aspect)
The forms of the future tense
Check the future form of every verb already introduced
Deponent verbs
Dual case prepositions
Pronominal use of the article

Vocabulary

Verbs

ἀποκρίνομαι *ἀποκρίνομαι, —, ἀπέκρινάμην, —, —, ἀπεκρίθην*   I answer

ἀσπάζομαι *ἀσπάζομαι, ἀσπάσομαι, ἠσπασάμην, —, —, —*   I greet

γίνομαι *γίνομαι, γενήσομαι, ἐγενόμην, γέγονα, γεγένημαι, ἐγενήθην*
I become, I am (verb of "being," takes predicate nominative)

δέχομαι *δέχομαι, δέξομαι, ἐδεξάμην, —, δέδεγμαι, ἐδέθην*   I receive

εἰσέρχομαι εἰσέρχομαι, εἰσελεύσομαι, εἰσῆλθον, εἰσελήλυθα, —, —
I enter (frequently takes its object with the redundant preposition εἰς)

ἐξέρχομαι ἐξέρχομαι, ἐξελεύσομαι, ἐξῆλθον, ἐξελήλυθα, —, —   I go out
(frequently takes its object with ἐκ)

ἔρχομαι ἔρχομαι, ἐλεύσομαι, ἦλθον, ἐλήλυθα, —, —   I come, I go

ἐρῶ I will say (future principal part of λέγω)

πορεύομαι πορεύομαι, πορεύσομαι, —, —, πεπόρευμαι, ἐπορεύθην   I go,
I come

Prepositions

διά   through (with genitive); on account of (with accusative)

κατά   against, down from (with genitive); according to (with accusative)

μετά   with (with genitive); after, beyond (with accusative)

περί   concerning, about (with genitive); around (with accusative)

ὑπέρ   on behalf of, for (with genitive); above (with accusative)

Exercises

Translate from Greek to English.

1. *σημεῖον οὐ δοθήσεται ὑμῖν, ἀλλὰ δέξεσθε τὸν λογὸν τοῦ Ἰωνᾶ τοῦ προφήτου μόνον. (for μόνον, see lesson VIII)

2. παρέστησαν οἱ ὄχλοι τῆς γῆς καὶ οἱ ἄνθρωποι *συνήχθησαν κατὰ τοῦ κυρίου καὶ κατὰ τοῦ Χριστοῦ αὐτοῦ. (cp. Acts 4:26)

3. ἡ δὲ ἀπεκρίθη καὶ λέγει αὐτῷ, Κύριε, καὶ ἡμεῖς μικροὶ ὑπὸ τὴν *τραπέζην ἐσθίομεν ἀπὸ τοῦ ἄρτου σου. (cp. Mark 7:28)

4. ἀπεκρίθη αὐτοῖς ὁ Ἰησοῦς, Οὐκ ἐγὼ ὑμᾶς τοὺς *δώδεκα *ἐξελεξάμην; καὶ ἐν ὑμῖν *διάβολός ἐστιν. (cp. John 6:70)

5. ἀσπάζονται ὑμᾶς αἱ ἐκκλησίαι τῆς Ἀσίας. ἀσπάζονται ὑμᾶς ἐν τῷ κυρίῳ σὺν τῇ κατ᾽οἶκον αὐτῶν ἐκκλησίᾳ. (as in 1 Corinthians 16:19)

6. καὶ αὐτὸς ἐδέξατο αὐτὸ εἰς τὸν οἶκον αὐτοῦ καὶ εἶπεν, Νῦν ἀπολύεις τὸν δοῦλόν σου κατὰ τὸν λόγόν σου ἐν εἰρήνῃ· ὅτι εἶδον τὸ *σωτήριόν σου. (cp. Luke 2:28–30)

7. ἐλεύσεται καὶ καταλύσει τοὺς *γεωργοὺς τούτους καὶ δώσει τὸν *ἀμπελῶνα ἄλλοις. (cp. Luke 20:16)

8. ἦλθεν γὰρ Ἰωάννης πρὸς ὑμᾶς ἐν τῷ ὁδῷ τῷ δικαίῳ, καὶ οὐκ ἐπιστεύσατε αὐτῷ, οἱ δὲ *τελῶναι καὶ αἱ *πόρναι ἐπίστευσαν αὐτῷ. (cp. Matthew 21:32)

9. Μαριὰμ ἐν ταῖς ἡμέραις ταύταις ἐπορεύθη εἰς τὴν ἐσχάτην *κώμην καὶ εἰσῆλθεν εἰς τὸν οἶκον Ζαχαρίου καὶ ἠσπάσατο τὴν Ἐλισάβετ. καὶ ἐγένετο ὅτι τὸ τέκνον ἤκουσεν τὸν *ἀσπασμὸν τῆς Μαρίας. (cp. Luke 1:39–41a)

10. ὅτε οὖν ἐξῆλθεν λέγει Ἰησοῦς, Νῦν ἐδοξάσθη ὁ υἱὸς τοῦ ἀνθρώπου, καὶ ὁ θεὸς ἐδοξάσθη ἐν αὐτῷ· εἰ ὁ θεὸς ἐδοξάσθη ἐν αὐτῷ καί ὁ θεὸς δοξάσει αὐτὸν ἐν αὐτῷ, καὶ *εὐθὺς δοξάσει αὐτόν. (John 13:31–32)

11. μετὰ δὲ τὴν *θλῖψιν τῶν ἡμερῶν ἐκείνων ὁ *ἥλιος καταλυθήσεται, καὶ ἡ *σελήνη οὐ δώσει τὸ *φέγγος αὐτῆς. (cp. Matthew 24:29a)

12. ἐν ἐκείνῃ τῇ ὥρᾳ ἐπορεύθη ὁ Ἰησοῦς τοῖς ἀνθρώποις διὰ τοὺς κακοὺς ὄχλους.

13. εἰ γὰρ ἐστιν ὁ *θησαυρός σου ὑπὸ τοὺς οὐρανούς, *ἐκεῖ ἔσται καὶ ἡ καρδία σου. (as in Matthew 6:21)

14. καὶ ἐπορεύθησαν *ἕκαστος εἰς τὸν οἶκον αὐτοῦ, Ἰησοῦς δὲ ἐπορεύθη εἰς τὴν ἐκκλησίαν. ὅτε δὲ πάλιν *παρεγένετο εἰς τὸ ἱερὸν ὁ λαὸς ἤρχετο πρὸς αὐτόν. (cp. John 7:53–8:2a)

15. δώσει αὐτῷ κύριος ὁ θεὸς τὸν *θρόνον Δαυίδ, καὶ *βασιλεύσει ἐπὶ τὸν οἶκον Ἰακὼβ εἰς τοὺς *αἰῶνας, καὶ τῆς βασιλείας αὐτοῦ οὐκ ἔσται *τέλος. (cp. Luke 1:32–33)

16. καὶ ἐν ταῖς ἡμέραις ἐκείναις *ζητήσουσιν οἱ ἄνθρωποι τὸν θάνατον καὶ οὐχ εὑρήσουσιν αὐτόν. (cp. Revelation 9:6a)

17. ἐγὼ δέξαμην τούς κακούς λόγους τοῦ ἀγγέλου ὅτι ὁ θεὸς κατέστησε τὴν ἐξουσίαν αὐτοῦ κατὰ αὐτοῦ.

18. ἐκεῖνος ἐμὲ δοξάσει, ὅτι ἐκ τοῦ ἐμοῦ λήμψεται τὴν εἰρήνην τῆς ζωῆς ὑμῖν. (cp. John 16:14)

19. πέμψει ὁ υἱὸς τοῦ ἀνθρώπου τοὺς ἀγγέλους αὐτοῦ, καὶ ἀπολύσει ἐκ τῆς βασιλείας αὐτοῦ τὰ *σκάνδαλα … καὶ ἐκβαλοῦσιν αὐτούς. (cp. Matthew 13:41–42)

20. καὶ ἐκηρύχθη τοῦτο τὸ εὐαγγέλιον τῆς βασιλείας ἐν ὅλῳ τῷ κόσμῳ εἰς *μαρτύριον. (cp. Matthew 24:14)

Translate from English to Greek.

1. If you (sg) give me that writing, I will go to the temple and hand it over to the prophet.

2. When Jesus entered the house, the master greeted him and his disciples.

3. I will not sell my slave because I received him from our teacher.

4. Jesus came to this world and died for it according to the scriptures.

5. We shall receive the apostles because you (sg) sent them to us.

6. We will answer your writing if you give it to the messenger.

7. This way will lead you (pl) through the desert toward our house, and at the evening you will be with us.

8. After the sabbath we will bring our children to the assembly.

9. His life is handed over to the wicked men, but they will not kill him.

10. The teacher will speak with the master about that child.

11. This authority will be given to the little ones, and they will proclaim the day of the Lord.

12. After these things I will not be your (sg) slave, but you will be under my authority.

13. You (pl) will find the prophet among the slave because they are persuaded that he is the holy one.

14. If he teaches you (pl) other things concerning the last day, you shall not believe his words.

15. These words will be written by the beloved disciple and sent to the faithful churches.

16. His messenger will be received and greeted by the apostle himself.

17. If my authority is of this world, you will not have that peace among yourselves.

18. We came to you, O Lord, because we believe that you will save us from death.

19. The love and the peace of God will be with you (pl) after this day.

20. This man is not answering the holy prophet because he does not know his words.

XIII

Subjunctive Mood

All of the verbs encountered thus far have been in the indicative mood, the mood of assertion and factuality. This lesson introduces the *subjunctive* mood, the mood of *contingency*. The subjunctive appears principally in certain specialized sorts of clauses and is negated with the particle μή, as are all non-indicative moods.

The subjunctive mood always uses the primary active and middle endings, substituting a lengthened connecting vowel for the customary short ε or ο. The subjunctive drops the ε- augment for the aorist tense, as do all other non-indicative moods. Observe that the present and aorist subjunctive often differ only in that the aorist stem has the characteristic σ suffix.

	Singular	*Plural*
	Present Active Subjunctive	
1ST	λύ-ω	λύ-ωμεν
2ND	λύ-ῃς	λύ-ητε
3RD	λύ-ῃ	λύ-ωσι(ν)
	Present Middle / Passive Subjunctive	
1ST	λύ-ωμαι	λυ-ώμεθα
2ND	λύ-ῃ	λύ-ησθε
3RD	λύ-ηται	λύ-ωνται
	Aorist Active Subjunctive	
1ST	λύσ-ω	λύσ-ωμεν
2ND	λύσ-ῃς	λύσ-ητε
3RD	λύσ-ῃ	λύσ-ωσι(ν)

	Singular	Plural
	Aorist Middle Subjunctive	
1ST	λύσ-ωμαι	λυσ-ώμεθα
2ND	λύσ-ῃ	λύσ-ησθε
3RD	λύσ-ηται	λύσ-ωνται
	Aorist Passive Subjunctive	
1ST	λυθ-ῶ	λυθ-ῶμεν
2ND	λυθ-ῆς	λυθ-ῆτε
3RD	λυθ-ῇ	λυθ-ῶσι(ν)

The pattern is the same for first and second aorists, and it is fundamentally the same for μι verbs and for ω verbs. The present middle/passive subjunctive of δίδωμι does not occur in the New Testament.

	Singular	Plural
	Present Active Subjunctive	
1ST	διδ-ῶ	διδ-ῶμεν
2ND	διδ-ῷς	διδ-ῶτε
3RD	διδ-ῷ	διδ-ῶσι(ν)
	Aorist Active Subjunctive	
1ST	δ-ῶ	δ-ῶμεν
2ND	δ-ῷς	δ-ῶτε
3RD	δ-ῷ	δ-ῶσι(ν)

The aorist middle subjunctive does not occur in the New Testament. The aorist passive follows the pattern for ω verbs (δοθῶ, δοθῇς, δοθῃ, δοθῶμεν, δοθῆτε, δοθῶσιν).

The present subjunctive of εἰμί:

	Singular	*Plural*
1ST	ὦ	ὦμεν
2ND	ᾖς	ἦτε
3RD	ᾖ	ὦσι(ν)

Uses of the Subjunctive

The subjunctive is used in a variety of situations. The subjunctive mood indicates *purpose* or *result*, specifically with the conjunctions ἵνα and ὅπως (see lesson XXIV). Note that since both ἵνα and ὅπως are subordinating conjunctions, they will not introduce a main clause. If the subjunctive appears in a main clause, it must be one of the following specialized uses.

ἦραν οὖν λίθους ἵνα   Then they took up stones in order that
βάλωσιν ἐπ᾽ αὐτόν.   *they might throw* [them] at him. (John 8:59)

The subjunctive mood can be used for first person proposals, declarative or interrogative. The declarative proposal is called the *cohortative,* or *hortatory* subjunctive, and it is translated with the phrase "Let us ..."

εἰρήνην ἔχωμεν   *Let us have* peace with God ... (Romans 5:1;
πρὸς τὸν θεὸν ...   variant reading)

The interrogative proposal is called the *deliberative* subjunctive, and it is translated with the phrase, "Shall we ...?"

δῶμεν ἢ μὴ δῶμεν;   *Shall we give,* or *shall we not give?* (Mark 12:14)

Notice that *both of these constructions are limited to the first person.* These are the principal uses that permit the subjunctive voice in the main clause.

The subjunctive is used with adverbial conjunctions of time or place when those conjunctions are used in combination with the particle ἄν. Sometimes a conjunction is compounded with ἄν; at other times, ἄν stands alone. In either case, ἄν indicates contingency and requires the subjunctive mood, except when ἄν appears in a contrary to fact conditional.

ὅταν γὰρ *ἀσθενῶ*, τότε   For whenever *I am weak,* then I am
δυνατός εἰμι.   powerful. (2 Corinthians 12:10)

The fourth use of the subjunctive arises in the (third class) conditional sentences of the *present general* or *future more probable* types. In the simple conditional, the protasis is assumed to be fulfilled; in the contrary to fact conditional, it is assumed to be *un*fulfilled. Both present general and future more probable conditionals imply no determination — they express a genuine hypothetical situation. The protasis of these conditionals contains the particle ἐάν and the subjunctive mood. The apodosis of a present general conditional usually uses the present indicative tense, while the apodosis of a future more probable conditional usually uses the future indicative.

ἐὰν μόνον *ἅψωμαι* τοῦ   If only *I touch* his robe, I will be saved.
ἱματίου αὐτου σωθήσομαι.   (Matthew 9:21; future more probable)

ἐὰν δὲ *ἀποθάνῃ*, πολὺν   If *it dies,* it bears much fruit.
καρπὸν φέρει.   (John 12:24; present general)

The fifth use of the subjunctive mood involves a verb in the *aorist* subjunctive, negated with μή, to express a prohibition, such as "Do not do it!"

μὴ *εἰσενέγκῃς* ἡμᾶς εἰς   Do not *lead* us into temptation …
πειρασμόν …   (Matthew 6:13)

The sixth use of the subjunctive likewise involves a negated aorist subjunctive, but in this case the verb is negated with οὐ *and* μή. The effect of this combination is cumulative, for the subjunctive verb is absolutely ruled out as a future possibility. There is no convenient idiomatic expression in English to express this emphatic negation, but the colloquial phrase "no way" (or, more politely, "not by any means") captures its force.

οὐ μὴ *ἴδητέ* με …   *You will* not by any means *see* me …
(or, "No way will you see me"; Luke 13:35)

Negative Questions

A negative question can be expressed in Greek in two ways. If the negative question expects a positive answer, it is negated with the particle οὐ. If the negative question expects a negative answer, it is negated by the particle μή, even if the question is in the indicative mood.

οὐχ ὁ θεὸς ἐξελέξατο   Did not God choose the poor? (Yes)
τοὺς πτωούς;

μὴ ἔχει χάριν τῷ δούλῳ;   Does he have regard for the slave? (No)

The expectation of a negative or positive answer does not guarantee that such an answer will be received. In Matthew 26:25, Judas asks Jesus, μήτι ἐγώ εἰμι; and Jesus answers, σὺ εἶπας (a *positive* response).

Triple Case Prepositions

Several prepositions can take their objects in three cases. The preposition's sense shifts depending upon the case with which it is associated.

Ἐπί has the basic sense of "upon." With the accusative case, the sense of the preposition is something like "toward." With the genitive, the sense tends simply to be "upon." With the dative, ἐπί can mean something like "at."

Παρά is flexible even by the standards of Greek prepositions. Its basic sense is "beside." The accusative with παρά retains this sense of "beside," "alongside," but it never appears with a personal object in the New Testament. The genitive with παρά *always* appears with a personal object, and it means "away from." παρά with the dative and a personal agent usually means "beside"; it can also mean "in [X's] view."

Study Checklist

The uses of the subjunctive mood
Purpose clauses governed by ἵνα (or ὅπως)
Cohortative subjunctive
Deliberative subjunctive
Conjunctions with ἄν
Present general conditional: ἐάν + subjunctive in protasis, present in apodosis; condition undetermined, genuinely hypothetical
Future more probable conditional: ἐάν + subjunctive in protasis, future in apodosis; condition undetermined, genuinely hypothetical
Prohibition: μή with aorist subjunctive
Emphatic negation: οὐ μή with aorist subjunctive

Form of the subjunctive
Negative questions with οὐ and μή
Triple case prepositions

Vocabulary

Verbs

αἴρω *αἴρω, ἀρῶ, ἦρα, ἦρκα, ἦρμαι, ἤρθην*   I take up, I take away

ἀπέρχομαι *ἀπέρχομαι, ἀπελεύσομαι, ἀπῆλθον, ἀπελήλυθα, —, —*
I go away, leave

προσέρχομαι *προσέρχομαι, προσελεύσομαι, προσῆλθον,*
προσελήλυθα, —, —   I go to, I come to

προσεύχομαι *προσεύχομαι, προσεύξομαι, προσηυξάμην, —, —, —*
I pray

Nouns

δικαιοσύνη, ἡ   righteousness

οἰκία, ἡ   house (like ὁ οἶκος)

ὀφθαλμός, ὁ   eye

τόπος, ὁ   place

Particles

ἐάν   if (takes the subjunctive)

ἵνα   in order that, so that (takes the subjunctive)

μή   not (negates non-indicative moods; introduces questions that expect
a negative answer)

ὅπου   where; ὅπου ἄν, wherever

ὅταν   whenever

Prepositions

ἐπί   upon (with genitive); at (with dative); toward (with accusative)

παρά   away from (with genitive); beside, in [X's] view (with dative);
beside, alongside (with accusative)

Exercises

Translate from Greek to English.

1. ὁ Ἰησοῦς ἦλθεν καὶ ἐθεράπευσεν ἡμᾶς ἵνα κηρύξωμεν τὸν λόγον εἰρήνης τῷ κόσμῳ.

2. τὰ οὖν τῆς εἰρήνης δοξάζωμεν καὶ διδάσκωμεν τὰ τῆς ζωῆς τοῖς ὄχλοις.

3. τότε *διεστείλατο τοῖς μαθηταῖς ἵνα μὴ εἴπωσιν ὅτι αὐτός ἐστιν ὁ Χριστός. (cp. Matthew 16:20)

4. εἰ νεκροὶ οὐκ ἐγείρονται, φάγωμεν καὶ πίωμεν, *αὔριον γὰρ ἀποθνήσκομεν. (1 Corinthians 15:32b)

5. εἰ πιστεύομεν γὰρ, τῷ κυρίῳ πιστεύομεν, εἰ δὲ ἀποθνήσκομεν, τῷ κυρίῳ ἀποθνήσκομεν. εἰ οὖν πιστεύομεν ἢ εἰ ἀποθνήσκομεν, τοῦ κυρίου ἐσμέν.

6. καὶ ἀπέστειλεν πρὸς τοὺς *γεωργοὺς τῷ *καιρῷ δοῦλον, ἵνα παρὰ τῶν *γεωργῶν λάβῃ ἀπὸ τῶν *καρπῶν τοῦ *ἀμπελῶνος. (Mark 12:2)

7. καὶ *διελογίζοντο, Ἐὰν εἴπωμεν, Ἐξ οὐρανοῦ, ἐρεῖ, Τί ("why") οὐκ οὖν ἐπιστεύσατε αὐτῷ; ἀλλὰ ἐὰν εἴπωμεν, Ἐξ ἀνθρώπων, ὁ ὄχλον καταλύσει ἡμᾶς. οἱ ἄνθρωποι γὰρ ἔγνωσαν ὅτι ὁ Ἰωάννης προφήτης ἦν. (cp. Mark 11:31–32)

8. ἐὰν οὖν προσευχώμεθα τοῖς δούλοις, ὁ θεὸς ἀκούσει ἡμᾶς καὶ ἀπολύσει αὐτοὺς ἀπὸ τῆς κεφαλῆς τῆς ἐκκλησίας.

9. ὅτε ἦλθεν οὖν τῷ οἴκῳ τῶν ἀδελφῶν μου, εἶπεν, Κύριε, μὴ πέμψῃς αὐτὸν ἀπὸ τοῦ οἶκον αὐτῶν, ἵνα μὴ αὐτοὶ ἔλθωσιν εἰς τὸν τόπον τοῦτον.

10. οὐ γὰρ ἀπέστειλεν ὁ θεὸς τὸν υἱὸν εἰς τὸν κόσμον ἵνα *κρίνῃ τὸν κόσμον, ἀλλ' ἵνα σωθῇ ὁ κόσμος δι' αὐτοῦ. (John 3:17)

11. ἐρχώμεθα πρὸς τὸν οἴκον τοῦ κυρίου, ἵνα δοξάζωμεν τὸν θεὸν τοῦ οὐρανοῦ καὶ τῆς γῆς.

12. προσευχόμεθα περὶ ὑμῶν, ἵνα δοξάσθῃ ὁ κύριος ἡμῶν Ἰησοῦς ἐν ὑμῖν, καὶ ὑμεῖς ἐν αὐτῷ, κατὰ τὴν *χάριν τοῦ θεοῦ ἡμῶν καὶ κυρίου Ἰησοῦ Χριστοῦ. (cp. 2 Thessalonians 1:11a, 12)

13. ἔλεγεν γάρ, Ἐὰν μόνον *ἅψωμαι τοῦ *ἱματίου αὐτοῦ σωθήσομαι. (cp. Matthew 9:21)

14. ἐγώ εἰμι ἡ *θύρα· δι' ἐμοῦ ἐάν ἄνθρωπος εἰσέλθῃ σωθήσεται καὶ εἰρήνην εὑρήσει ... ἐγὼ ἦλθον ἵνα ζωὴν ἔχωσιν καὶ *περισσὸν ἔχωσιν. (cp. John 10:9–10)

15. εἶπεν δὲ αὐτῷ, Ἐι Μωϋσέως καὶ τῶν προφητῶν οὐκ ἀκούουσιν, οὐ τῷ ἄλλῳ ἀγγέλῳ ἐκ νεκρῶν πεισθήσονται. (cp. Luke 16:31)

16. ἐν τούτῳ ἐδοξάσθη ὁ κύριος μου, ἵνα *καρπὸν *πολὺν ("much," accusative singular) φέρητε καὶ γένησθε ἐμοὶ μαθηταί. (cp. John 15:8)

17. ἀλλ' ἐγὼ τὴν ἀλήθειαν λέγω ὑμῖν, *συμφέρει ὑμῖν ἵνα ἐγὼ ἀπέλθω. ἐὰν γὰρ μὴ ἀπέλθω, ὁ *παράκλητος οὐκ ἐλεύσεται πρὸς ὑμᾶς· ἐὰν δὲ πορευθῶ, πέμψω αὐτὸν πρὸς ὑμᾶς. (John 16:7)

18. *κἀγὼ δέ σοι λέγω ὅτι σὺ εἶ Πέτρος, καὶ ἐπὶ ταύτῃ τῇ *πέτρᾳ καταστήσω μου τὴν ἐκκλησίαν. (cp. Matthew 16:18)

19. ἐγὼ δὲ οὐ παρὰ ἀνθρώπου τὴν *μαρτυρίαν λαμβάνω, ἀλλὰ ταῦτα λέγω ἵνα ὑμεῖς σωθῆτε. (John 5:34)

20. παρὰ ἀνθρώποις *ἀδύνατον ἀλλ' οὐ παρὰ θεῷ, *πάντα ("all things") γὰρ *δυνατὰ παρὰ τῷ θεῷ. (Mark 10:27)

Translate from English to Greek.

1. We prayed to God that you (pl) may leave the life of death and come into the holy life with him.

2. I sent a beloved brother to them that they may know the things about us.

3. The Son of Man will be taken up so that you (pl) may receive his righteousness and be his disciples.

4. These things are written that you (pl) might believe that Jesus is the Christ.

5. The prophets wrote their writings in order that we know that the Messiah will come in the last days.

6. Let us leave these evil people and come to the assembly of the righteous ones.

7. Wherever you (sg) pray, God will hear you and answer to you.

8. If you were a righteous man, you would leave this wicked place.

9. Shall we speak with them, or shall we send them our messenger?

10. If those people should say that Jesus did not rise from the dead, we will not listen to their words.

11. Let us go to the house of the Lord and pray that he heals our souls.

12. If you (sg) should go to the temple and leave your church, you will find the people of God also in that place.

13. The prophet was taken away from us in order that we ourselves might receive God's righteousness.

14. Let us have the peace with God and with one another.

15. Whenever my sins lead me away from righteousness, I lift up my eyes toward you, O Lord.

XIV

The Infinitive

The infinitive is a verb form that is technically not a mood, but a verbal noun. However, the infinitive will be treated as a mood for parsing and for simplicity. Remember that since the infinitive is a non-indicative mood, it will be negated with μή. The Greek infinitive functions in various ways, many of which are similar to those of the English infinitive.

The forms of the infinitive are simple and few. There is one form each for the present active, present middle/passive, aorist active, middle, and passive. There is no imperfect infinitive, but there is a future infinitive, which occurs only five times in the New Testament. The infinitive, like the subjunctive, has *no* ε- augment, and it is formed from the verb stem with the following endings:

Present active	λυ + ειν = λύειν
Present middle/passive	λυ + εσθαι = λύεσθαι
First aorist active	λυσ + αι = λῦσαι
Second aorist active	λαβ + ειν = λαβεῖν
First aorist middle	λυσ + ασθαι = λύσασθαι
Second aorist middle	λαβ + εσθαι = λάβεσθαι
Aorist passive	λυθ + ηναι = λυθῆναι
Present infinitive of εἰμί is εἶναι	

The provisional translation of an infinitive should be the equivalent of the English infinitive: λύειν = "to loose." The difference between an aorist infinitive and a present infinitive has nothing to do with the time of the action, but has much to do with the verbal aspect and the particular verb's characteristic usage. Some verbs simply tend to appear in the aorist, while others appear mainly in the present. It will frequently be difficult or awkward to bring out the aspectual difference (for instance, between "to loose" and "to be loosing" or "to go on loosing"). Students should be alert to aspectual difference, but they need not disrupt their idiomatic English translations to emphasize the imperfective or perfective aspect of the infinitive.

Uses of the Infinitive

Whenever the infinitive's verbal element requires a subject, the subject of the infinitive occurs in the accusative case. This is called the *accusative of general reference*. For instance, the expression πέμπειν αὐτόν in a subordinate clause is translated as though the infinitive were a finite verb: "he sends." Such constructions may generate some ambiguity, since the direct object will also occur in the accusative (πέμπειν αὐτὸν τὸν δοῦλον). The student will have to rely on context to distinguish the accusative of general reference from the accusative of the direct object.

The infinitive can function as a *verbal complement*. In this usage, the emphasis is on the verbal dimension of the infinitive; that is, the infinitive completes, or complements, the main verb of the clause. This construction occurs principally with a small group of verbs: θέλω, μέλλω, δύναμαι, κωλύω, ἄρχομαι, ὀφείλω.

Θέλεις δὲ *γνῶναι* …;   Do you want *to know* …? (James 2:20)

In a similar usage, the infinitive can be used with *impersonal* verbs: δεῖ, ἔξεστιν, and some constructions with εἰμί, especially with predicate adjectives. In such constructions, the infinitive may take the place of the subject, or an impersonal subject such as "it" or "there" may be supplied. Here, the infinitive serves as the subject of the impersonal verb.

Οὐκ ἔξεστίν σοι *ἔχειν* αὐτήν.   It is not lawful for you *to have* her.
(or, "*To have* her is not lawful for you";
Matthew 14:4)

The infinitive can be used to express a purpose or a result, and there are a variety of ways to construct purpose or result clauses. Some involve the articular infinitive (which will be explained below); others simply use the infinitive itself; and still others use the conjunction ὥστε with the infinitive.

ἤλθομεν *προσκυνῆσαι* αὐτῷ.   We have come *to worship* him.
(Matthew 2:2)

σεισμὸς ἐγένετο μέγας ὥστε σαλευθῆναι τὰ θεμέλια ...	There was a great earthquake, so that the foundations *were shaken* ... (Acts 16:26)

The preceding three uses of the infinitive draw more or less upon the *verbal* character of the infinitive; the following uses of the infinitive accent the infinitive as verbal *noun*. One characteristic of the latter is the association of the infinitive with an article, hence the term, *articular infinitive*. The articular infinitive is often used as the object of a preposition. The significance of the preposition will differ somewhat from its conventional sense, and the infinitive will often have to be translated as though it were a finite verb.

μετὰ τὸ *ἐγερθῆναί* με προάξω ὑμᾶς εἰς τὴν Γαλιλαίαν.	After I *am raised,* I will go before you into Galilee. (Mark 14:28)
ἐν τῷ *σπείρειν* αὐτὸν ὃ μὲν ἔπεσεν παρὰ τὴν ὁδόν...	While he was *sowing,* some fell along the path ... (Luke 8:5)
Πρὸ τοῦ δὲ *ἐλθεῖν* τὴν πίστιν ὑπὸ νόμον ἐφρουρούμεθα ...	Before faith *came,* we were imprisoned under the law... (Galatians 3:23)
ἐξανέτειλεν διὰ τὸ μὴ *ἔχειν* βάθος γῆς ...	[The plant] sprouted quickly, because it did not *have* deep soil ... (Matthew 13:5)
ἔπεμψα εἰς τὸ *γνῶναι* τὴν πίστιν ὑμῶν...	I sent in order *to know* your faith ... (1 Thessalonians 3:5)
Ἐξῆλθεν ὁ σπείρων τοῦ *σπεῖραι* τὸν σπόρον αὐτοῦ.	A sower went out *to sow* his seed. (Luke 8:5)

Third Declension Nouns

Though nouns of the first and second declensions have very predictable forms, *third declension* nouns are rather miscellaneous. There is certainly a pattern to the third declension, but it will not be obvious to all students, and many may opt simply to memorize the various paradigms of noun declension rather than determine how the latent pattern of the third declension works out in particular cases.

The group of third declension nouns introduced here comprises neuter nouns that end in -μα.

	Singular	Plural
N	ὄνο-μα	ὀνό-ματα
G	ὀνό-ματος	ὀνο-μάτων
A	ὀνό-ματι	ὀνό-μασι(ν)
D	ὄνο-μα	ὀνό-ματα

Hereafter, the vocabulary will list the genitive ending for all third declension nouns. Given the endings for the nominative and genitive singular, you should be able to ascertain the endings for other forms.

Study Checklist

The infinitive
The forms of the infinitive
Accusative of general reference (subject of the infinitive)

Uses of the infinitive
Verbal complement
Subject of impersonal verb
Purpose or result clause (some with ὥστε)
Articular infinitive: object of a preposition

μετὰ τὸν + *infinitive* = "*after*..."
πρὸ τοῦ + *infinitive* = "*before*..."
ἐν τῷ + *infinitive* = "*while*..."
διὰ τὸ + *infinitive* = "*because of*..."
εἰς τὸ + *infinitive* = "*in order to*..."
τοῦ + *infinitive* = "*to*..." (*purpose clause*)

Third declension nouns

Vocabulary

Verbs

ἄρχω, ἄρχομαι (ἄρχω, ἄρξω, ἦρξα, ἦρχα, ἦργμαι, ἤρχθην) (*ἄρχομαι, ἄρξομαι, ἠρξάμην, ἤργμαι, –, –*)   I rule; I begin (middle/deponent) δεῖ (imperfect ἔδει)   it is necessary (impersonal verb)

ἔξεστιν   it is lawful (impersonal verb; occurs only in this form and a participial form)

θέλω θέλω, θελήσω, ἠθέλησα, τεθέληκα, — , — (in the imperfect, ἤθελον) I wish, I want

κωλύω κωλύω, — , ἐκώλυσα, — , — , ἐκωλύθην   I hinder

μέλλω μέλλω, μελλήσω, ἐμέλλησα,— , — , —   I am about ...

ὀφείλω ὀφείλω, — , — , — , — , —   I owe; I ought ...

Nouns

αἷμα, -ατος, τό blood	πρόσωπον, τό face
εὐαγγέλιον, τό good news	σημεῖον, τό sign
ὄνομα, -ατος, τό name	στόμα, -ατος, τό mouth
πνεῦμα, -ατος, τό spirit, wind	σῶμα, -ατος, τό body

Conjunction

ὥστε   so as to, in order that

Exercises

Translate from Greek to English.

1. ἐν δὲ τῷ εἰπεῖν τὸν Ἰησοῦν ἦγεν αὐτῷ τὸν ἄρτον ὁ ὄχλος.

2. καὶ ἤρξατο διδάσκειν αὐτοὺς ὅτι δεῖ τὸν υἱὸν τοῦ ἀνθρώπου *παθεῖν καὶ ἀποκτανθῆναι καὶ μετὰ *τρεῖς ἡμέρας ἀναστῆναι. (cp. Mark 8:31)

3. οὐχ εὑρήσετέ με, ὅτι *ὅπου εἰμὶ ἐγὼ ὑμεῖς οὐ *δύνασθε ἐλθεῖν. εἶπον οὖν οἱ Ἰουδαῖοι, *ποῦ οὗτος μέλλει πορεύεσθαι ὅτι ἡμεῖς οὐχ εὑρήσομεν αὐτόν; (cp. John 7:34–35)

4. ἀπεκρίθησαν αὐτῷ οἱ Ἰουδαῖοι· ἡμεῖς ἔχομεν νόμον, καὶ κατὰ τὸν νόμον ὀφείλει ἀποθανεῖν, διὰ τὸ λέγεσθαι αὐτὸν τὸν υἱὸν τοῦ θεοῦ. (cp. John 19:7)

5. ἦλθον βαλεῖν εἰρήνην ἐπὶ τὴν γῆν· οὐκ ἦλθον βαλεῖν εἰρήνην ἀλλὰ *μάχαιραν. (cp. Matthew 10:34)

6. καὶ ἄρχονται πνεύματι ἁγίῳ οἱ ἄνθρωποι εἰπεῖν ἐν ἄλλαις *γλώσσαις καθὼς τὸ πνεῦμα ἐδίδου *ἀποφθέγγεσθαι αὐτοῖς. (cp. Acts 2:4)

7. οὐκ ἔστιν καλὸν λαβεῖν τὸν ἄρτον τῶν τέκνων καὶ αὐτὸν βαλεῖν τοῖς *κυναρίοις. (cp. Matthew 15:26)

8. καὶ λέγει αὐτοῖς, Ἔξεστιν τοῖς σάββασιν ψυχὰν σῶσαι ἢ ἀποκτεῖναι; (cp. Mark 3:4)

9. ἐν τῷ εἰσελθεῖν αὐτὴν τὸν τόπον, ὁ ἀδελφὸς αὐτῆς ἦλθεν ἀσπάζεσθαι αὐτήν.

10. καὶ *ψευδοπροφῆται ἐγερθήσονται καὶ κατελύθησαν τοὺς ὄχλους ὅτι θέλουσιν ἀρχεῖν τὸν κόσμον.

11. ἔλεγεν γὰρ ὁ Ἰωάννης αὐτῷ, Οὐκ ἔξεστίν σοι ἔχειν αὐτήν. (cp. Matthew 14:4)

12. ὁ Πέτρος εἶπεν τῷ Ἰησοῦ, κύριε, καλόν ἐστιν ἡμᾶς *ὧδε εἶναι· εἰ θέλεις, καταστήσω *ὧδε *τρεῖς *σκηνάς, σοὶ *μίαν καὶ Μωϋσεῖ *μίαν καὶ *Ἠλίᾳ *μίαν. (cp. Matthew 17:4)

13. ἤθελον πρῶτος πρὸς ὑμᾶς ἐλθεῖν, ἵνα εἰρήνην σχῆτε, καὶ δι᾽ ὑμῶν εἰσελθεῖν εἰς *Μακεδονίαν, καὶ πάλιν ἀπὸ *Μακεδονίας ἐλθεῖν πρὸς ὑμᾶς. (cp. 2 Corinthians 1:15–16)

14. καὶ οὐ θέλετε ἐλθεῖν πρός με ἵνα ζωὴν ἔχητε. (John 5:40)

15. τότε ὁ Ἰησοῦς ἤχθη εἰς τὴν ἔρημον ὑπὸ τοῦ πνεύματος, πειρασθῆναι ὑπὸ τοῦ *διαβόλου. (cp. Matthew 4:1)

16. ὁ οὖν κύριος Ἰησοῦς μετὰ τὸ εἰπεῖν αὐτοῖς ἐλήμφθη εἰς τὸν οὐρανόν. (cp. Mark 8:31)

17. ὅτι ἐὰν *ὁμολογήσῃς (ὁμολογέω) ἐν τῷ στόματί σου κύριον Ἰησοῦν, καὶ πιστεύσῃς ἐν τῇ καρδίᾳ σου ὅτι ὁ θεὸς αὐτὸν ἤγειρεν ἐκ νεκρῶν, σωθήσῃ· καρδίᾳ γὰρ πιστεύεται εἰς δικαιοσύνην, στόματι δὲ *ὁμολογεῖται εἰς σωτηρίαν. (cp. Romans 10:9–10)

18. τὸ δὲ πνεῦμα τὸ ἅγιον ἀποστελεῖ ἐν τῷ ὀνόματί μου καὶ ἐκεῖνο ὑμᾶς διδάξει λόγους μου.

19. λέγω γὰρ ὑμῖν ὅτι προφῆται καὶ δίκαιοι ἤθελον ἰδεῖν καθὼς ὑμᾶς ἀλλ᾽ οὐκ ἔβλεψαν, καὶ ἀκοῦσαι καὶ οὐκ ἤκουσαν. (cp. Luke 10:24)

20. καὶ ἂν ἄνθρωπος θέλῃ ἐν ὑμῖν εἶναι πρῶτος ἔσται ὑμῶν δοῦλος· *ὥσπερ ὁ υἱὸς τοῦ ἀνθρώπου ἦλθεν δοῦναι τὴν ψυχὴν αὐτοῦ *λύτρον. (cp. Matthew 20:27–28)

Translate from English to Greek.

1. If we wish to see Jesus, let us go into that house beside the temple.

2. It is not lawful to eat this loaf because it will be given to the teacher of righteousness.

3. If you (pl) are baptized in Jesus' name, you will receive his Spirit.

4. The disciples hindered children to come to Jesus, but he received them with love.

5. I am about to write the good news to my son, but first I will answer the writing of my sister.

6. While they were praying to God, the Spirit of God fell upon them.

7. You (sg) ought to persuade that man not to take our beloved child away from us.

8. Before he saw her face, he knew that she did not want to speak about these things.

9. After the master died and was raised, his disciples began to proclaim good news about him.

10. Jesus gave his body and his blood for us in order that we have life through him.

11. Because you (pl) were teaching these things, it is not necessary to speak again about them.

12. If the words of your (sg) mouth should not praise God, I will hinder your teaching (hinder you to teach) in our assembly.

13. I handed over to you (pl) the words of my master in order that you knew that he gave his life for us.

14. You (pl) wish to see a sign, but no sign will be given to you beside my own words and signs.

15. After I am taken away, my Spirit will be sent to you (pl) in order that you know that I am present among you.

XV

More Third Declension Nouns

There is an underlying pattern to the endings added to nouns of the third declension.

	Singular	Plural
N	-ς (*m/f*) or none (*m/f/n*)	-ες (*m/f*) or -α (*n*)
G	-ος	-ων
D	-ι	-σι(ν)
A	-ν or -α (*m/f*) or none (*n*)	-ας (*m/f*) or -α (*n*)

The pattern of declension will be consistent for the various types of third declension nouns. If πόλις forms its dative plural as πόλεσι, then the dative plural form of δύναμις will be δυνάμεσι. The following feminine, masculine, and neuter words demonstrate some representative patterns for third declension nouns:

	Singular	Plural	Singular	Plural
N	ἡ πόλις	αἱ πόλεις	ἡ μήτηρ	αἱ μητέρες
G	τῆς πόλεως	τῶν πόλεων	τῆς μητρός	τῶν μητέρων
D	τῇ πόλει	ταῖς πόλεσι(ν)	τῇ μητρί	ταῖς μητράσι(ν)
A	τὴν πόλιν	τὰς πόλεις	τὴν μητέρα	τὰς μητέρας
N	ὁ βασιλεύς	οἱ βασιλεῖς	τὸ ἔθνος	τὰ ἔθνη
G	τοῦ βασιλέως	τῶν βασιλέων	τοῦ ἔθνους	τῶν ἐθνῶν
D	τῷ βασιλεῖ	τοῖς βασιλεῦσι(ν)	τῷ ἔθνει	τοῖς ἔθνεσι(ν)
A	τὸν βασιλέα	τοὺς βασιλεῖς	τὸ ἔθνος	τὰ ἔθνη

	Singular	Plural		Singular	Plural
N	ἡ χείρ	αἱ χεῖρες		ἡ σάρξ	αἱ σάρκες
G	τῆς χειρός	τῶν χειρῶν		τῆς σαρκός	τῶν σαρκῶν
D	τῇ χειρί	ταῖς χερσί(ν)		τῇ σαρκί	ταῖς σαρξί(ν)
A	τὴν χεῖρα	τὰς χεῖρας		τὴν σάρκα	τὰς σάρκας
N	τὸ ὕδωρ	τὰ ὕδατα		τὸ φῶς	τὰ φῶτα
G	τοῦ ὕδατος	τῶν ὑδάτων		τοῦ φωτός	τῶν φώτων
D	τῷ ὕδατι	τοῖς ὕδασι(ν)		τῷ φωτί	τοῖς φωσί(ν)
A	τὸ ὕδωρ	τὰ ὕδατα		τὸ φῶς	τὰ φῶτα

The student should bear in mind several salient points in order to master the third declension. The nominative singular is still the lexical form, but it is the *genitive singular* that reveals the noun stem of third declension nouns. Even though this stem occasionally mutates in ways that seem mysterious (χείρ, χειρός > χερσί), the genitive singular form will guide students through most of the complexities of the third declension. All third declension nouns have the same endings, but complex interactions among the constitutent consonants and vowels result in surprising forms. For instance, stems that end in κ form their nominative singular with a ξ at the end because the stem's concluding κ combines with the nominative singular ending -ς.

Masculine and feminine nouns alike follow the patterns of the third declension. Students will not be able to make educated guesses about a noun's gender simply because it belongs to the third declension. Some subgroups of third declension nouns are relatively predictable, however. Nouns that end with ις are usually feminine, nouns that end with μα are neuter, nouns that end with ος are neuter, and nouns with ευς are masculine.

Students will not be able to account for all the various transformations of third declension nouns. A certain amount of basic information must be memorized and the typical transformations must be learned to account for idiosyncratic forms.

Study Checklist

The forms of third declension nouns

Vocabulary

Nouns

ἀνήρ, ἀνδρός, ὁ   man, husband (like μήτηρ)

βασιλεύς, -έως, ὁ   king

γυνή, -αικός, ἡ   woman, wife (like σάρξ)

ἔθνος, -ους, τό   gentile, nation

μήτηρ, -τρός, ἡ   mother

πατήρ, -τρός, ὁ   father (like μήτηρ)

πίστις, -εως, ἡ   faith (like πόλις)

πόλις, -εως, ἡ   city

πούς, ποδός, ὁ   foot (like σάρξ)

πῦρ, -ός, τό   fire (like ὕδωρ)

σάρξ, σαρκός, ἡ   flesh

ὕδωρ, -ατος, τό   water

φῶς, φωτός, τό   light

χάρις, -ιτος, ἡ   grace (like χείρ; accusative singular χάριν; dative plural χάρισι)

χείρ, χειρός, ἡ   hand

Exercises

Translate from Greek to English.

1. ἀπεκρίθη ἡ γυνὴ καὶ εἶπεν αὐτῷ, οὐκ ἔχω ἄνδρα. λέγει αὐτῇ ὁ Ἰησους· καλῶς εἶπας ὅτι ἄνδρα οὐκ ἔχω· *πέντε γὰρ ἄνδρας ἔσχες καὶ νῦν ὁ ἀνήρ οὐκ ἔστιν σου ἀνήρ. (cp. John 4:17–18)

2. καὶ εἶπεν αὐτοῖς ὅτι Οὕτως ἔγραφη *παθεῖν τὸν Χριστὸν καὶ ἀναστῆναι ἐκ νεκρῶν τῇ *τρίτῃ ἡμέρᾳ, καὶ κηρυχθῆναι ἐπὶ τῷ ὀνόματι αὐτοῦ *μετάνοιαν εἰς *ἄφεσιν ἁμαρτιῶν. (cp. Luke 24:46–47)

3. θέλω δὲ ὑμᾶς εἰδέναι ὅτι ἄνδρος ἡ κεφαλὴ ὁ Χριστός ἐστιν, κεφαλὴ δὲ γυναικὸς ὁ ἀνήρ, κεφαλὴ δὲ τοῦ Χριστοῦ ὁ θεός. (cp. 1 Corinthians 11:3)

4. ἐὰν ἔλθῃς ποδὶ, ὀφείλεις πορευθῆναι τὴν ὁδὸν τοῦτον πρὸς τὸ ἱερόν.

5. λέγω ἐν τῷ ὀνόματι τῆς ματρὸς τοῦ βασιλέως.

6. τοῦτο μόνον θέλω *μαθεῖν ἀφ᾽ ὑμῶν, ἐξ ἔργων νόμου τὸ πνεῦμα ἐλάβετε ἢ ἐξ *ἀκοῆς πίστεως; (Galatians 3:2)

7. παρίσταμεν ἐν τῷ τόπῳ τούτῳ διὰ τὴν ἀγάπην τοῦ θεοῦ καὶ τὴν χάριν.

8. ὁ δὲ εἶπεν πρὸς αὐτοὺς ὅτι καὶ ταῖς ἄλλαις πόλεσιν κηρύξασθαί με δεῖ τὴν βασιλείαν τοῦ θεοῦ, ὅτι ἐπὶ τοῦτο ἀπεστάλην. (cp. Luke 4:43)

9. θέλει ὁ ἀνὴρ οὗτος προσεύχεσθαι σὺν τῇ γυναικὶ αὐτοῦ, ἀλλ᾽ οὐ θέλει ἡ γυνὴ αὐτοῦ προσεύχεσθαι σὺν τῷ ἄνδρι αὐτῆς.

10. οἱ δὲ Σαμαρῖται ἐκ τῆς πόλεως ἐκείνης ἐπίστευσαν εἰς αὐτὸν διὰ τὸν λόγον τῆς γυναικός. (cp. John 4:39)

11. διδάσκαλε, Μωϋσῆς ἔγραψεν ἡμῖν ὅτι ἐὰν ἀδελφὸς ἀποθάνῃ καὶ γυνὴ αὐτοῦ μὴ σχῇ τέκνον, ἵνα λάβῃ ὁ ἀδελφὸς αὐτοῦ τὴν γυναικὰ καὶ *ἐξαναστήσῃ *σπέρμα τῷ ἀδελφῷ αὐτοῦ. (cp. Luke 20:43)

12. οὐ *δύναται δὲ ὁ ὀφθαλμὸς εἰπεῖν τῇ χειρί· *χρείαν σου οὐκ ἔχω, ἢ πάλιν ἡ κεφαλὴ τοῖς ποσίν· *χρείαν ὑμῶν οὐκ ἔχω. (cp. 1 Corinthians 12:21)

13. ὑμεῖς δὲ οὐκ ἐστὲ ἐν σαρκὶ ἀλλὰ ἐν πνεύματι, ὅτι τὸ πνεῦμα θεοῦ *οἴκει ἐν ὑμῖν. εἰ δὲ ἄνθρωπος πνεῦμα Χριστοῦ οὐκ ἔχει, οὗτος οὐκ ἔστιν αὐτοῦ. εἰ δὲ Χριστὸς ἐν ὑμῖν, τὸ σῶμα νεκρὸν διὰ ἁμαρτίαν τὸ δὲ πνεῦμα ζωὴ διὰ δικαιοσύνην. (cp. Romans 8:9–10)

14. μέλλω ἐλθεῖν εἰς τὴν πόλιν ἐκείνην ὥστε εἰπεῖν σὺν τῷ βασιλεῖ περὶ τοῦ εὐαγγελίου.

15. ἐὰν γὰρ ὁ ἄνθρωπος δῷ ὑμῖν *ποτήριον ὕδατος ἐν ὀνόματι Χριστοῦ, *ἀμὴν λέγω ὑμῖν ὅτι οὐ καταλύσει *μισθὸν αὐτοῦ. (cp. Mark 9:41)

16. δεῖ γραφεῖν σε τὸ ὄνομα σου ἐπὶ τῆς γραφῆς ταύτης καὶ παραδιδόναι αὐτὴν τῷ ἀδελφῷ μου.

17. εἰ οὖν ἐγὼ *ἔνιψα ὑμῶν τοὺς πόδας ὁ κύριος καὶ ὁ διδάσκαλος, καὶ ὑμεῖς ὀφείλετε *νίπτειν τοὺς πόδας ἄλλων. (cp. John 13:14)

18. ὁ ἀπόστολος προσηύξατο ὑπὲρ αὐτοὺς ὅτι ἤσθιον καὶ ἔπιον σὺν τοῖς κακοῖς ἀνθρώποις.

19. ἤλθομεν εἶναι σὺν σοί, οὐδὲ ἔδωκας ἡμᾶς ἄρτον φαγεῖν οὐδὲ ὕδατα πιεῖν.

20. ἀπεκρίθη Ἰησοῦς αὐτῷ, Ἐὰν μὴ *νίψω σε, οὐκ ἔχεις *μέρος μετ᾽ ἐμοῦ. λέγει αὐτῷ Σίμων Πέτρος, Κύριε, μὴ τοὺς πόδας μου μόνον ἀλλὰ καὶ τὰς χεῖρας καὶ τὴν κεφαλήν. (John 13:8–9)

Translate from English to Greek.

1. The words of my master were like the light of my life.

2. You (sg) ought to receive that woman into your house.

3. I handed over that message to the king, but he did not answer it.

4. She did not want to speak again with that man because she did not believe his words.

5. Through the grace of our Lord we stand now at this place and glorify him.

6. We saw your mother and father beside the temple.

7. I want to go into the city in order to sell my writing to the gentiles.

8. Our righteousness is not through the works of the law but through faith.

9. Their house was destroyed by fire, and now they ought to find another place.

10. Her father wanted to speak with her husband, but her mother hindered that.

11. If you (sg) give me your hand, you will not fall away from that path.

12. While he was raising his eyes, he saw his mother and father.

13. The child was brought out of the fire by his/her father.

14. Before the people heard the voice of the king, his servants proclaimed his law concerning the other nations.

15. If your father were present, your spirit would be raised again.

XVI

Perfect Tense

The two principal parts yet to be learned are the perfect active indicative and the perfect middle/passive indicative. The perfect tense differs in aspect and form from the other tenses, but it has certain characteristics that make it relatively easy to recognize.

Perfect Active Indicative

The perfect active indicative, the *fourth principal part* of the Greek verb, begins with the present stem. It reduplicates the initial consonant, attaches a κ suffix to the stem, and adds the secondary endings to complete the form. The reduplication is similar to that of the μι verbs, but in the perfect tense ε is used as the connecting vowel.

	Singular	*Plural*
1ST	λέ-λυκ-α	λε-λύκ-αμεν
2ND	λέ-λυκ-ας	λέ-λυκ-ατε
3RD	λέ-λυκ-ε(ν)	λέ-λυκ-ασι(ν), λε-λυκ-αν

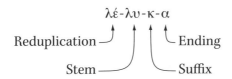

Not every verb is amenable to simple reduplication. Verb stems that begin with a vowel must obviously make some other provision for marking the perfect. Most of those verbs reduplicate by adding an ε to the initial stem vowel — that is, by omitting the non-existent reduplicated consonant and adding the ε connecting vowel directly to the stem. Verbs that begin with aspirated consonants (θ, φ, χ) are reduplicated with the non-aspirated forms of the consonants (τ, π, κ, respectively).

Similarly, certain consonants do not combine well with the perfect tense's κ suffix. Some consonants interact with the κ to produce compound consonants; some consonants disappear in favor of the κ; and sometimes the κ disappears in favor of the stem consonant (such forms are sometimes referred to as "second perfect" forms). All that being said, some perfect forms are simply irregular. The following illustrates how the perfect is formed:

Present Active	*Perfect Active*
ἐγγίζω	ἤγγικα *the reduplicated ε is added to the initial ε, and the ζ drops out*
θεραπεύω	τεθεράπευκα *the aspirated θ is reduplicated with τ*
γράφω	γέγραφα *the stem φ takes precedence over the perfect κ*
ἀκούω	ἀκήκοα *the second syllable is reduplicated here (Attic reduplication)*
πέμπω	πέπομφα *normal reduplication, stem π goes to φ rather than taking κ*

The perfect forms of μι verbs are formed fairly predictably from the stem; for instance, δίδωμι (stem δο-) forms the perfect δέδωκα.

Students should be alert for the non-indicative forms of the common perfect verb οἶδα. Οἶδα is actually derived from the same root as the aorist form εἶδον (the aorist principal part of ὁράω), and it means "I know" ("I am in a state of knowing"). The stem of οἶδα is εἰδ-; reduplication changes the initial εἰ to οἶ, but the perfect subjunctive of οἶδα is εἰδῶ (stem εἰδ- plus the ordinary subjunctive ending).

Perfect Middle/Passive Indicative

The perfect middle/passive principal part, the *fifth principal part*, is formed by reduplicating the present stem and adding the primary middle/passive endings, but without a connecting vowel.

	Singular	*Plural*
1ST	λέ-λυ-μαι	λε-λύ-μεθα
2ND	λέ-λυ-σαι	λέ-λυ-σθε
3RD	λέ-λυ-ται	λέ-λυ-νται

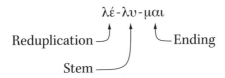

Just as the interactions between consonants at the end of the verb stem and the κ of the perfect active form are complex, so the interactions between stem consonants and the various consonants that begin the primary endings are all the more complex. For example, the perfect middle/passive principal part of γράφω is γέγραμμαι (the φ yields to the ending's initial μ), but the third person singular form of the γέγραμμαι is γέγραπται (the φ can coexist with the τ by shifting to its non-aspirated form). These changes will simply have to be learned on a case by case basis. Examine the list of principal parts to ascertain the perfect forms of the verbs with which you are already acquainted.

Use of the Perfect Tense

The perfect tense has both time and aspect. The aspect of the present tense is imperfective, indicating progressive action without regard to time; the aspect of the aorist tense is perfective, indicating that the action is viewed as an undifferentiated event without regard to time; the aspect of the perfect tense is *stative*, indicating a condition or a state of affairs as it stands in the present (this state may sometimes be the result of a prior action, but it may simply indicate that the author is emphasizing the present condition of the verb's subject).

The provisional translation of perfect verbs will have to be flexible depending on context, but students may start by translating λέλυκα, for example, as "I have loosed." Since the perfect usually expresses a present condition, students should be alert to the opportunity to translate perfect forms not only with the helping verb "to have," but often better with the verb "to be." The common use of γέγραπται should not be translated "it has been written," but "it *is* written"; similarly, John 12:23 (ἐλήλυθεν ἡ ὥρα) should be translated, "the hour is come," rather than "the hour has come." Οἶδα, "I know," clearly expresses present condition; it does not even *have* present or aorist forms. Students must pay attention to how they can best express the stative aspect of these forms.

Since the middle and passive voices of the perfect are identical in form, the student will have to discern whether to construe a given form as middle or passive. The usage of the verb will provide much help (some verbs do not appear in the middle voice, while others do not appear in the passive). Context will also help determine the voice of the verb. When usage and context leave the student at a loss to judge whether the verb is active or passive, then — as in the present and imperfect — the passive is to be preferred.

Pluperfect Tense

The pluperfect tense, which occurs infrequently in the New Testament, relocates the stative aspect of the perfect into past time. It is part of the perfect system and is formed from the perfect active and perfect middle/passive stems. Sometimes the pluperfect appears with both reduplication and an augment (ἐβέβλητο), but more often the augment falls away, in which case the pluperfect is most readily recognized by its distinctive use of the ει diphthong as a connecting vowel (cf. the form of πεπιστεύκεισαν, the third person plural pluperfect active indicative form of πιστεύω). Many of the pluperfect verbs in the New Testament are forms of either ἔρχομαι or οἶδα. The pluperfect may sometimes be used in a second class conditional sentence as the imperfect or aorist.

Study Checklist

Form of the perfect active and middle/passive indicative
Use of the perfect active and middle/passive indicative
The pluperfect
Learn the perfect form of every verb already introduced

Vocabulary

Verb

οἶδα *οἶδα, pluperfect ᾔδειν*   I know (perfect with present meaning; ᾔδειν functions as imperfect)

Nouns

ἀρχιερεύς, -έως, ὁ   high priest

δύναμις, -εως, ἡ   power

θάλασσα, -ης, ἡ   sea, lake

καιρός, ὁ   season, time

Adjectives

ἕκαστος, -η, -ον   each

ὅλος, -η, -ον   whole (always appears in predicative position)

Particles

ἀμήν   truly, indeed

ἰδού   behold, look

οὐδέ   and not; neither... nor (in οὐδέ ... οὐδέ ... constructions)

Exercises

Translate from Greek to English.

1. ἔλεγον οἱ Ἰουδαῖοι τῷ *Πιλάτῳ, οὐκ ὀφείλεις γράψαι· ὁ βασιλεὺς τῶν Ἰουδαίων, ἀλλ᾽ ὅτι ἐκεῖνος εἶπεν, βασιλεύς εἰμι τῶν Ἰουδαίων. ἀπεκρίθη ὁ *Πιλᾶτος· ὃ γέγραφα, γέγραφα. (as in John 19:21–22)

2. ἐγὼ ἐλήλυθα ἐν τῷ ὀνόματι τοῦ πατρός μου καὶ οὐ λαμβάνετέ με· ἐὰν ἄλλος ἔλθῃ ἐν τῷ ὀνόματί μου ἐκεῖνον λήμψεσθε. (cp. John 5:34)

3. ὁ δὲ εἶπεν· ὑμῖν δέδοται γνῶναι τὰ *μυστήρια τῆς βασιλείας τοῦ θεοῦ, τοῖς δὲ *λοιποῖς ἐν *παραβολαῖς. (Luke 8:10)

4. εἰλήφαμεν τὸ πνεῦμα τοῦ θεοῦ εἰς τὰς καρδίας ἡμῶν ἵνα κηρύξωμεν νῦν τὸ εὐαγγέλιον τοῖς ἄλλοις ἀνθρώποις. (Luke 8:10)

5. ἰδοὺ ἕστηκα ἐπὶ τὴν *θύραν καὶ *κρούω· ἐὰν ἀκούσῃ τῆς φωνῆς μου καὶ *ἀνοίξῃ τὴν θύραν, καὶ εἰσελεύσομαι πρὸς αὐτόν. (cp. Revelation 3:20)

6. περὶ δὲ τῆς ἡμέρας ἐκείνης καὶ ὥρας *οὐδεὶς οἶδεν, οὐδὲ οἱ ἄγγελοι τῶν οὐρανῶν οὐδὲ ὁ υἱός, εἰ μὴ ("except") ὁ πατὴρ μόνος. (Matthew 24:36)

7. εὑρήκαμεν τὸν κύριον καὶ πεπιστεύκαμεν ὅτι ὁ θεὸς ἀπέσταλκεν αὐτὸν ἡμῖν.

8. οὐκ ἐλήλυθα *καλέσαι (καλέω) δικαίους ἀλλὰ *ἁμαρτωλοὺς εἰς *μετάνοιαν. (Luke 5:32)

9. καὶ ἀπεκρίθη πρὸς αὐτὸν ὁ Ἰησοῦς, Γέγραπται ὅτι Οὐκ τὸν ἄρτον μόνον φάγεται ὁ ἄνθρωπος. (cp. Luke 4:4)

10. ὁ πάτηρ αὐτῆς πέποιθεν αὐτὸν ἄρχεσθαι δικαίαν ζωήν.

11. καὶ ἡμεῖς πεπιστεύκαμεν καὶ ἐγνώκαμεν ὅτι σὺ εἶ ὁ ἅγιος τοῦ θεοῦ. (John 6:69)

12. ἐγὼ δέδωκα αὐτοῖς τὸν λόγον σου, καὶ ὁ κόσμος θέλει ἀποκτεῖναι αὐτούς, ὅτι οὐκ εἰσὶν ἐκ τοῦ κόσμου καθὼς ἐγὼ οὐκ εἰμὶ ἐκ τοῦ κόσμου. (cp. John 17:14)

13. βεβλέφαμεν τὴν ζωὴν καὶ ἀκηκόαμεν καὶ *ἀπαγγέλομεν ὑμῖν τὴν ζωὴν ἵνα ὑμεῖς *κοινωνίαν ἔχητε μεθ᾽ ἡμῶν. καὶ ἡ *κοινωνία δὲ μετὰ τοῦ πατρὸς καὶ μετὰ τοῦ υἱοῦ Ἰησοῦ Χριστοῦ. (cp. 1 John 1:2–3)

14. ὁ τόπος οὗτος ἐδόθη ἡμῖν ἵνα προσευξώμεθα τῷ δικαίῳ καὶ τῷ πονηρῷ.

15. εἰ ἐγνώκατέ με, καὶ τὸν πατέρα μου γνώσεσθε· καὶ ἀπ᾽ *ἄρτι γινώσκετε αὐτὸν καὶ *ἑωράκατε (ὁράω) αὐτόν. (John 14:7)

16. καὶ ἐγένετο μετὰ τὸν εἰπεῖν τὸν Ἰησοῦς τοὺς λόγους τούτους, εἶπεν τοῖς μαθηταῖς αὐτοῦ, Οἴδατε ὅτι μετὰ *δύο ἡμέρας τὸ *πάσχα γίνεται, καὶ ὁ υἱὸς τοῦ ἀνθρώπου παραδίδοται εἰς τὸν ἀρχιερεῖς. (cp. Matthew 26:1–2)

17. ἀλλὰ τοῦτον οἴδαμεν *πόθεν ἐστίν· ὁ δὲ Χριστὸς ὅταν ἔρχηται οὐ γινώσκομεν *πόθεν ἐστίν. (cp. John 7:27)

18. βέβλησαι εἰς τὰς χεῖρας τοῦ θεοῦ καὶ λήμψεταί σε εἰς τὴν βασιλείαν αὐτοῦ.

19. μετὰ τὸ θεραπεῦσαι τὸν προφήτην τὴν γυναικὰ αὐτὴ ἀπῆλθεν εἰς τὴν γῆν αὐτῆς ὥστε καταλύσαι τοὺς κακοὺς ἀνθρώπους καὶ ἀπολύσαι τοὺς δούλους.

20. ἔλεγον οὖν αὐτῷ, Ποῦ ἐστιν ὁ πατήρ σου; ἀπεκρίθη Ἰησοῦς, Οὐδὲ ἐμὲ οἴδατε οὐδὲ τὸν πατέρα μου· εἰ ἐμὲ ᾔδειτε, καὶ τὸν πατέρα μου ἂν ᾔδειτε. (cp. John 8:19)

Translate from English to Greek.

1. This writing is written by the hand of my father.

2. We knew that you (pl) had faith in Jesus the Messiah.

3. I truly say to you (pl) that if a person does not want to leave her sins, she will not become my disciple.

4. The good news is proclaimed to every nation by the power of the Spirit.

5. People have seen the fire by the sea, and they have come to hear Jesus' voice.

6. I know that if the apostle began to speak, he would take the whole day.

7. We have seen good seasons and bad seasons. Let us, therefore, pray for God's grace in our lives.

8. You (pl) ought to know that Jesus is raised by God's power.

9. After that man had been brought before the high priest, he was sent to the king.

10. I do not know this man, and I have not seen him before this time.

11. Our writing is first sent to the master, and after that to the high priest.

12. The hour is come. Let us go to the temple and speak with the high priest.

13. We have found the faith among the gentiles.

14. They know that the water from that sea is good to drink.

15. Each woman and each man is saved by God's grace from the power of death.

XVII

Relative Pronouns

The relative pronoun relates a noun in a subordinate clause to an antecedent noun that appears in the main clause of a sentence. In the preceding sentence, the phrase "that appears in the main clause of a sentence" is a subordinate clause linked to the main clause by the relative pronoun "that." The relative pronoun is usually translated as "who" (for personal nouns), "that," or "which" — with appropriate adjustments for case differences ("to whom," "of which," and so on).

	Singular			Plural		
	M	*F*	*N*	*M*	*F*	*N*
N	ὅς	ἥ	ὅ	οἵ	αἵ	ἅ
G	οὗ	ἧς	οὗ	ὧν	ὧν	ὧν
D	ᾧ	ᾗ	ᾧ	οἷς	αἷς	οἷς
A	ὅν	ἥν	ὅ	οὕς	ἅς	ἅ

Conveniently, the relative pronoun reflects the form of the definite article without the initial τ. The exceptions are ἥ, which does not have an initial τ in the first place, and ὅς which lacks an initial τ and adds the final ς characteristic of second declension nouns.

The Greek relative pronoun typically agrees with its antecedent in gender and number; its case is derived from the role it plays in a clause.

ἐλάβετε πνεῦμα υἱοθεσίας ἐν ᾧ κράζομεν· Αββα ὁ πατήρ.	We have a spirit of adoption in which we cry: "Abba, Father!" (Romans 8:15)

The relative pronoun ᾧ is neuter and singular, in agreement with its antecedent, πνεῦμα, but it is in the dative case since it is the object of the preposition ἐν.

In some situations the relative pronoun does *not* receive its case from its function in a clause; rather, the relative pronoun adopts the case of another nearby noun — usually the antecedent, especially when the antecedent is in the genitive case. This phenomenon, common in the New Testament, is known as *attraction of the relative pronoun* because the relative pronoun is "attracted" to the case of another word.

Interrogative Pronouns

The interrogative pronoun serves in questions that inquire after an unknown noun. Thus, it is usually to be translated as "who?" or "what?" or "to whom?" (adjusted to reflect the appropriate case).

	Singular			*Plural*	
	M/F	N		M/F	N
N	τίς	τί		τίνες	τίνα
G	τίνος	τίνος		τίνων	τίνων
D	τίνι	τίνι		τίσι(ν)	τίσι(ν)
A	τίνα	τί		τίνας	τίνα

There is no distinction between masculine and feminine forms of the interrogative pronoun. Students should bear in mind that interrogative pronouns will *always* carry an acute accent. Note that the interrogative pronoun τί can also be used to mean "why?"

τίς προσεύχεται;	Who is praying?
τίνι προσεύχεται;	For what is he praying?
τί πέμπει;	What is she sending?
τί δέχεται τὰ ἔθνη;	Why is he receiving the Gentiles?

Although the form of the τί in the third example is possibly ambiguous, the fact that πέμπω is a transitive verb — that is, it takes a direct object — suggests that the τί should be construed as the direct object of πέμπει. If the τί is construed as a "why?" the result is the awkward query "Why is he sending?" (sending what?). Such a sentence is possible, but could be judged appropriate only if the context provided additional information that clarified who was sending and what she or he might be sending.

Indefinite Pronouns

	Singular		Plural	
	M/F	N	M/F	N
N	τις	τι	τινές	τινά
G	τινός	τινός	τινῶν	τινῶν
D	τινί	τινί	τισί(ν)	τισί(ν)
A	τινά	τι	τινάς	τινά

The indefinite pronoun is spelled the same way as the interrogative pronoun. They differ only in the way they are accented. Whereas the interrogative pronoun always takes an acute accent, the indefinite pronoun is enclitic and usually will not take an accent. If it is accented at all, the indefinite pronoun takes its accent on the ultima.

The indefinite pronoun can be used conventionally as a pronoun. It can also serve as an adjective. When the indefinite pronoun is used adjectivally, it can be translated several ways. For example, ἐγένετο ... ἱερεύς τις (Luke 1:5) means "there was a certain priest" or "there was some priest" ("some" functioning in the American colloquial sense of "Some guy asked me to dance").

A related form is the *indefinite relative pronoun*. The indefinite relative pronoun combines forms of the relative pronoun with the indefinite pronoun; it is translated "whoever," "whomever," "whatever," and so on. Since the indefinite relative pronoun simply combines two familiar forms, the student need not memorize it separately.

	Singular			Plural		
	M	F	N	M	F	N
N	ὅστις	ἥτις	ὅ τι	οἵτινες	αἵτινες	ἅτινα
G	οὗτινος	ἧστινος	οὗτινος	ὧντινων	ὧντινων	ὧντινων
D	ᾧτινι	ᾗτινι	ᾧτινι	οἷστισι	αἷστισι	οἷστισι
A	ὅντινα	ἥντινα	ὅ τι	οὕστινας	ἅστινας	ἅτινα

Of these forms, the nominative forms are by far the most common. Observe that in the neuter nominative and accusative forms, the component words remain separate.

Reflexive Pronouns

In Hellenistic Greek one way to express action with respect to the subject of a clause is by using a reflexive pronoun. Hence the reflexive pronoun has no nominative form; it occurs only in the genitive, dative, and accusative. The lexical form of these pronouns is the genitive singular. The first person pronoun means "myself" ("of myself," "to myself," "myself"); the second person pronoun, "yourself"; the third person pronoun, "himself," "herself," "itself."

	Singular			*Plural*		
	M	*F*	*N*	*M*	*F*	*N*
			First Person			
G	ἐμαυτοῦ	ἐμαυτῆς		ἑαυτῶν	ἑαυτῶν	
D	ἐμαυτῷ	ἐμαυτῇ		ἑαυτοῖς	ἑαυταῖς	
A	ἐμαυτόν	ἐμαυτήν		ἑαυτούς	ἑαυτάς	
			Second Person			
G	σεαυτοῦ	σεαυτῆς		ἑαυτῶν	ἑαυτῶν	
D	σεαυτῷ	σεαυτῇ		ἑαυτοῖς	ἑαυταῖς	
A	σεαυτόν	σεαυτήν		ἑαυτούς	ἑαυτάς	
			Third Person			
G	ἑαυτοῦ	ἑαυτῆς	ἑαυτοῦ	ἑαυτῶν	ἑαυτῶν	ἑαυτῶν
D	ἑαυτῷ	ἑαυτῇ	ἑαυτῷ	ἑαυτοῖς	ἑαυταῖς	ἑαυτοῖς
A	ἑαυτόν	ἑαυτήν	ἑαυτό	ἑαυτούς	ἑαυτάς	ἑαυτά

The plural form is peculiar inasmuch as it appears in the same form for all three persons. The neuter form would be the same in the first and second person if it occurred in those persons.

Reciprocal Pronouns

The reciprocal pronoun expresses the object of mutual action (English uses "one another" to express this). The reciprocal pronoun is always plural and only appears in the oblique cases: ἀλλήλων ("of one another"), ἀλλήλοις ("to one another"), ἀλλήλους ("one another").

Study Checklist

The relative pronoun
Agrees with antecedent in gender and number; case depends on use
Attraction of the relative pronoun

The interrogative pronoun (always takes acute accent)
Use of τί for "why?"

The indefinite pronoun (enclitic)
Adjectival use
Indefinite relative pronoun

The reflexive pronoun
The reciprocal pronoun

Vocabulary

Pronouns

ἀλλήλων   of one another

ἑαυτοῦ, -ῆς, -οῦ   of himself, herself, itself

ἐμαυτοῦ, -ῆς   of myself

ὅς, ἥ, ὅ   who, which (relative pronoun)

ὅστις, ἥτις, ὅ τι   whoever, whatever

σεαυτοῦ, -ῆς,   of yourself

τίς, (τί)   who? (what?)

τις, (τι)   someone, (something)

Verbs

καταβαίνω *καταβαίνω, καταβήσομαι, κατέβην, καταβέβηκα, —, —*
I descend, I go down

ὑπάγω *ὑπάγω, ὑπάξω, ὑπήγαγον, —, ὑπῆγμαι, ὑπήχθην*   I depart

χαίρω *χαίρω, χαρήσομαι, ἐχαίρησα, κεχάρηκα, κεχάρημαι, ἐχάρην*
I rejoice

Nouns

αἰών, -ῶνος, ὁ   age

δαιμόνιον, τό   demon

Adjectives

ἴδιος, -α, -ον   one's own

ἕτερος, -α, -ον   other, different

Exercises

Translate from Greek to English.

1. παρέδωκα γὰρ ὑμῖν ἐν πρώτοις, ὅ καὶ ἔλαβον, ὅτι Χριστὸς ἀπέθανεν ὑπὲρ τῶν ἁμαρτιῶν ἡμῶν κατὰ τὰς γραφάς καὶ ὅτι ἐγήγερται τῇ ἡμέρᾳ τῇ *τρίτῃ κατὰ τὰς γραφάς. (as in 1 Corinthians 15:3–4)

2. καὶ ὁ λόγος σὰρξ ἐγένετο καὶ *ἐσκήνωσεν ἐν ἡμῖν, καὶ ἑωράκαμεν τὴν δόξαν αὐτοῦ, δόξαν ὡς μόνον υἱὸν παρὰ πατρός, *πλήρης χάριτος καὶ ἀληθείας. (as in John 1:14)

3. ἀμὴν ἀμὴν λέγω σοι ὅτι ὃ οἴδαμεν λέγομεν καὶ ὃ ἀκηκόαμεν *μαρτυροῦμεν, καὶ τὴν *μαρυρίαν ἡμῶν οὐ λαμβάνετε. (as in John 3:11)

4. ἔλεγον οἱ μαθηταὶ πρὸς ἀλληούς, τίνα φάγονται οἱ ἄνθρωποι οὗτοι; ἄρτους οὐκ ἔχουσιν.

5. τί *διελογίζου ἐν τῇ καρδίᾳ σου τὸ *πρᾶγμα τοῦτο; οὐκ *ἐψεύσω ἀνθρώποις ἀλλὰ τῷ θεῷ. (cp. Acts 5:4)

6. ἡ πίστις, ἐὰν μὴ ἔχῃ ἔργα, νεκρά ἐστιν καθ' ἑαυτήν. (James 2:17)

7. εἶπεν οὖν ὁ Ἰησοῦς τοῖς δώδεκα, Μὴ καὶ ὑμεῖς θέλετε ὑπάγειν; (John 6:67)

8. ἀπεκρίθη αὐτῷ Σίμων Πέτρος, Κύριε, πρὸς τίνα ἀπελευσόμεθα; λόγους ζωῆς αἰωνίου ἔχεις. (as in John 6:68)

9. καὶ ἡμεῖς πεπιστεύκαμεν καὶ ἐγνώκαμεν ὅτι σὺ εἶ ὁ ἅγιος τοῦ θεοῦ. (John 6:69)

10. ταῦτά σοι γράφω ἵνα εἰδῇς *πῶς δεῖ ἐν οἴκῳ θεοῦ *ἀναστρέφεσθαι, ἥτις ἐστὶν ἐκκλησία θεοῦ. (as in 1 Timothy 3:14–15)

11. ἐχάρησαν οὖν οἱ μαθηταί, εἶδον γὰρ τὸν κύριον. (as in John 20:20)

12. Τί οὖν ἐροῦμεν; εὑρήκαμεν *Ἀβραὰμ τὸν *προπάτορα ἡμῶν κατὰ σάρκα; τί γὰρ ἡ γραφὴ λέγει; Ἐπίστευσεν δὲ * Ἀβραὰμ τῷ θεῷ, καὶ *ἐλογίσθη αὐτῷ εἰς δικαιοσύνην. (cp. Romans 4:1, 3)

13. Ὃ ἦν ἀπ' ἀρχῆς, ὃ ἀκηκόαμεν, ὃ βεβλέφομεν τοῖς ὀφθαλμοῖς ἡμῶν, ὃ *ἐθεασάμεθα καὶ αἱ χεῖρες ἡμῶν *ἐψηλάφησαν, περὶ τοῦ λόγου τῆς ζωῆς ... (cp. 1 John 1:1)

14. ἐὰν μή τις *μένῃ ἐν ἐμοί, ἐξεβλήθη ὡς τὸ *κλῆμα ... καὶ *συνάγουσιν αὐτὰ καὶ εἰς τὸ πῦρ βάλλουσιν. (cp. John 15:6)

15. Ταῦτα ἐμοὶ παρεδόθη ὑπὸ τοῦ πατρός μου, καὶ οὐδεὶς γινώσκει τὸν υἱὸν εἰ μὴ ὁ πατήρ, οὐδὲ τὸν πατέρα τις γινώσκει εἰ μὴ ὁ υἱὸς καὶ ᾧ ἐὰν θέλῃ ὁ υἱὸς αὐτὸν *ἀποκαλύψαι. (cp. Matthew 11:27)

16. ἡ *νὺξ *ἀπῆλθον, ἡ δὲ ἡμέρα ἐλήλυθεν. ἐκβάλλωμεν οὖν τὰ ἔργα τοῦ *σκότους, δεχώμεθα δὲ τοὺς λόγους τοῦ φωτός. (cp. Romans 13:12)

17. οὕτως οὖν καὶ ἐν τῷ νῦν καιρῷ *λεῖμμα κατὰ χάριν γέγονεν· εἰ δὲ χάριτι, *οὐκέτι ἐξ ἔργων. (cp. Romans 11:5–6)

18. Στέφανος δὲ χάριτι καὶ δυνάμει *ἔπραξεν σημεῖα ἐν τῷ λαῷ. (Acts 6:8)

19. τίνες δὲ τῶν ἀποστόλων ἵστασαν ἐν τοῖς ἀνθρώποις παρὰ τὴν θαλάσσην.

20. καί τις ἀνὴρ ἠνέχθη ἑκάστην ἡμέραν τῇ πόλιν θεραπεύεσθαι ὑπὸ τοῦ προφήτου.

Translate from English to Greek.

1. When he placed his hand on the foot of his brother, who was coming from the city, the man believed with his eyes and received peace.

2. Because they are being tempted, the head of the assembly wishes to depart from the evil messengers who do not proclaim life.

3. The king of this world goes from place to place as he wishes, but he does not have the power which the Lord has.

4. I have placed my joy in you (pl) so that you may know that I am present with you wherever you go.

5. If the holy prophet finds the sign of the kingdom before the crowd, he will save the life of the sister.

6. The same beloved women, who teach by the authority of the hour, pray for one another and gather together at night.

7. The Son of God, who comes from heaven, speaks well of this world, but he also teaches of another world which is coming.

8. You (sg) have joy because the Lord has healed you, but you will be tempted to receive it from the evil one who wishes to establish his kingdom.

9. We handed over to you (pl) what was sent to us by the good messenger who is from our assembly.

10. The one who establishes a good foundation for himself stands in righteousness before the people.

11. The children who are being taught by the good teacher are being sent into the world to release the slaves of sin.

12. The crowds are not persuaded by the high priest that they should destroy the temple so that he may hinder the good news of the kingdom.

13. What the eye has seen, the mouth speaks to the kingdom in order that we may go down the mountain and see for ourselves.

14. The commandment which comes from the Lord says to forgive on the sabbath those people who are in the assembly of the synagogue.

15. The woman sells the beautiful garments which she finds on the mountain to the temple so that the high priest may place fruit in the hands of other people.

XVIII

Participles

A participle is a verbal modifier (adjective/adverb). As such, it has several verbal characteristics (tense, voice, and participial mood) and several adjectival characteristics (gender, case, and number). The Greek participle is a flexible and elusive part of speech. It will not be possible to give a precise account of how to tell each participle's function. Students will have to develop a sense for how each participle functions based on its syntax, its context, and so on. The next three lessons will introduce the present, aorist, and perfect participles (respectively); they will also introduce adjectival, modal, and verbal uses of the participle. The relation of the tenses of the participles to the functions given in each chapter is purely fortuitous; each tense of the participle can function adjectivally, modally, and verbally, and each function can employ present, aorist, or perfect participles.

It is impossible to overemphasize the importance of grasping the Greek participle; this is the make-or-break point in understanding New Testament Greek. Though the challenge of tackling so versatile a phenomenon is imposing, the subsequent chapters will provide helpful guidelines to aid the student without oversimplifying this subtle locution.

Present Active Participles

The present active participle is declined as an adjective.

	Singular			*Plural*		
	M	*F*	*N*	*M*	*F*	*N*
N	λύων	λύουσα	λῦον	λύοντες	λύουσαι	λύοντα
G	λύοντος	λυούσης	λύοντος	λυόντων	λυουσῶν	λυόντων
D	λύοντι	λυούσῃ	λύοντι	λύουσι(ν)	λυούσαις	λύουσι(ν)
A	λύοντα	λύουσαν	λῦον	λύοντας	λυούσας	λύοντα

Μι verbs vary slightly from these patterns. The nominative and genitive illustrate the declension patterns for δίδωμι, ἵστημι, and τίθημι. The present participle of ἀφίημι is uncommon and does not appear in the New Testament.

	Singular			Plural		
	M	*F*	*N*	*M*	*F*	*N*
N	διδούς	διδοῦσα	διδόν	ἱστάς	ἱστᾶσα	ἱστάν
G	διδόντος	διδούσης	διδόντος	ἱστάντος	ἱστάσης	ἱστάντος
N	τιθείς	τιθεῖσα	τιθέν	ἀφιείς	ἀφιεῖσα	ἀφιέν
G	τιθέντος	τιθείσης	τιθέντος	ἀφιέντος	ἀφιείσης	ἀφιέντος

Εἰμί's participle follows the present active participial declension:

	Singular			Plural		
	M	*F*	*N*	*M*	*F*	*N*
N	ὤν	οὖσα	ὄν	ὄντες	οὖσαι	ὄντα
G	ὄντος	οὔσης	ὄντος	ὄντων	οὐσῶν	ὄντων
D	ὄντι	οὔσῃ	ὄντι	οὖσι(ν)	οὔσαις	οὖσι(ν)
A	ὄντα	οὖσαν	ὄν	ὄντας	οὔσας	ὄντα

The declension of the present middle/passive participle is simpler. The middle participle has a characteristic -μεν- syllable, and its endings are familiar from the first and second noun declensions.

	Singular			Plural		
	M	*F*	*N*	*M*	*F*	*N*
N	λυόμενος	λυομένη	λυόμενον	λυόμενοι	λυόμεναι	λυόμενα
G	λυομένου	λυομένης	λυομένου	λυομένων	λυομένων	λυομένων
D	λυομένῳ	λυομένη	λυομένῳ	λυομένοις	λυομέναις	λυομένοις
A	λυόμενον	λυομένην	λυόμενον	λυομένους	λυομένας	λυόμενα

Adjectival Uses of the Participle

The participle functions in several distinct ways, and a relatively simple use of the participle is as an adjective. The participle can function in each of the three ways that ordinary adjectives can — attributively, predicatively, and substantively.

The attributive use of the participle follows the pattern of attributive adjectives. The attributive participle is governed by an article that it shares with the noun, except in special cases, such as anarthrous proper nouns, in which cases the participle is governed by the article that the noun *would* take. The participle agrees with its noun in gender, case, and number.

ὁ λέγων μαθητής   the speaking disciple

ὁ μαθητής ὁ λέγων   the speaking disciple

In most cases, *adjectival participles are best translated by converting the participle into a relative clause* ("the disciple who is speaking" in the example given above). Of course, the attributive participle can, like the attributive adjective, appear without any article to agree with an anarthrous noun; for instance, μαθητής λέγων means "a speaking disciple" or "a disciple who is speaking."

The participle frequently functions substantively, just as an adjective would. In that case, the participle agrees with the implied noun it would be modifying (usually "person," or "man," or "woman"). The substantive participle is also governed by an article, but the substantive participle does not modify a noun that is syntactically explicit.

ὁ λέγων   the speaking one, *or* the one
who speaks, *or* the speaker

Just as an adjective can function predicatively, so can a participle. The predicative participle may be associated with the noun it modifies without a verb by situating the participle in the predicative position. It may also appear with a verb of being.

Ζῶν γὰρ ὁ λόγος τοῦ θεοῦ ...   For the word of God *is living*...
(Hebrews 4:12)

Participles: Tense, Time, and Translation

It is important to remember that the tense of a participle expresses the author's perspective on the action, *not* a time relation to other elements of the syntax. When the participle is used adjectivally, the distinction of aspects can be very difficult to bring out in translation, especially if the translator is aiming at idiomatically smooth English. A present participle may mean "one who is in the process of speaking," and an aorist participle may mean "one who characteristically speaks," but both would fairly be translated "the speaker" or "the one who was speaking." (The use of "was" in this sample translation depends on the assumption that the events narrated in the New Testament are events of the past; in another context, "the one who is speaking" might do just as well.)

Ἀφίημι *and* Τίθημι

These two μι verbs appear frequently in the New Testament. They might confuse students since their forms are not immediately recognizable.

	Singular	*Plural*		*Singular*	*Plural*
		Present Active Indicative			
1ST	τίθημι	τίθεμεν		ἀφίημι	ἀφίομεν, ἀφίεμεν
2ND	τίθης	τίθετε		ἀφεῖς	ἀφίετε
3RD	τίθησι(ν)	τιθέασι(ν)		ἀφίησι(ν)	ἀφιᾶσι(ν), ἀφίουσι(ν)
INF	τιθέναι			ἀφιέναι	
PART	τιθείς, τιθεῖσα, τιθέν			ἀφιείς, ἀφιεῖσα, ἀφιέν	
		Present Active Subjunctive			
1ST	τιθῶ	τιθῶμεν		ἀφιῶ	ἀφιῶμεν
2ND	τιθῇς	τιθῆτε		ἀφιῇς	ἀφιῆτε
3RD	τιθῇ	τιθῶσι(ν)		ἀφιῇ	ἀφιῶσι(ν)

continues

	Singular	Plural	Singular	Plural

Present Middle / Passive Indicative

	Singular	Plural	Singular	Plural
1ST	τίθεμαι	τιθέμεθα	ἀφίεμαι	ἀφιέμεθα
2ND	τίθεσαι	τίθεσθε	ἀφίεσαι	ἀφίεσθε
3RD	τίθεται	τίθενται	ἀφίεται	ἀφίονται
INF	τίθεσθαι		ἀφίεσθαι	
PART	τιθέμενος, -η, -ον		ἀφιέμενος, -η, -ον	

Imperfect Active Indicative

1ST	ἐτίθην	ἐτίθεμεν	ἤφιον	ἠφίομεν
2ND	ἐτίθες	ἐτίθετε	ἤφιες	ἠφίετε
3RD	ἐτίθει	ἐτίθεσαν	ἤφιε(ν)	ἤφιον

Imperfect Middle / Passive Indicative

1ST	ἐτιθέμην	ἐτιθέμεθα	ἀφιέμην	ἀφιέμεθα
2ND	ἐτίθεσο	ἐτίθεσθε	ἀφίεσο	ἀφίεσθε
3RD	ἐτίθετο	ἐτίθεντο	ἀφίετο	ἀφίεντο

First Aorist Active Indicative

1ST	ἔθηκα	ἐθήκαμεν	ἀφῆκα	ἀφήκαμεν
2ND	ἔθηκας	ἐθήκατε	ἀφῆκας	ἀφήκατε
3RD	ἔθηκε(ν)	ἔθηκαν	ἀφῆκεν	ἀφῆκαν
INF	θεῖναι		ἀφεῖναι	

Aorist Active Subjunctive (Second Aorist)

1ST	θῶ	θῶμεν	ἀφῶ	ἀφῶμεν
2ND	θῇς	θῆτε	ἀφῇς	ἀφῆτε
3RD	θῇ	θῶσι(ν)	ἀφῇ	ἀφῶσι(ν)

	Singular	Plural		Singular	Plural

Aorist Middle Indicative

1ST	ἐθέμην	ἐθέμεθα
2ND	ἔθου	ἔθεσθε
3RD	ἔθετο	ἔθεντο

Aorist Passive Indicative

1ST	ἐτέθην	ἐτέθημεν		ἀφέθην	ἀφέθημεν
		and so on			

Future Active Indicative

1ST	θήσω	θήσομεν		ἀφήσω	ἀφήσομεν
		and so on			

Future Passive Indicative

1ST	τεθήσομαι	τεθησόμεθα	ἀφεθήσομαι	ἀφεθησόμεθα
		and so on		

Perfect Active Indicative

1ST	τέθεικα	τεθείκαμεν		ἀφεῖκα	ἀφείκαμεν
		and so on			

Perfect Middle/Passive Indicative

1ST	τέθειμαι	τεθείμεθα		ἀφέωμαι	ἀφεώμεθα
		and so on			

Study Checklist

Form of the present active participle
Adjectival uses of the participle: attributive; substantive; and predicative
Tense of the participle *does not* express time
Forms of ἀφίημι and τίθημι

Vocabulary

Nouns

γραμματεύς, -έως, ὁ   scribe
ἐντολή, ἡ   commandment
θέλημα, -ατος, τό   will
ἱμάτιον, τό   garment
καρπός, ὁ   fruit
νύξ, νυκτός, ἡ   night

ὄρος, -ους, τό   mountain
πλοῖον, τό   boat
ῥῆμα, -ατος, τό   word
συναγωγή, ἡ   synagogue
χαρά, ἡ   joy

Verbs

ἀφίημι *ἀφίημι, ἀφήσω, ἀφῆκα, ἀφεῖκα, ἀφεῖμαι, ἀφέθην*   I leave, I forgive

κράζω *κράζω, κράξω, ἔκραξα, κέκραγα, —, —*   I cry out

συνάγω *συνάγω, συνάξω, συνήγαγον, —, συνῆγμαι, συνήχθην*   I gather together

τίθημι *τίθημι, θήσω, ἔθηκα, τέθεικα, τέθειμαι, ἐτέθην*   I put, I place

Exercises

Translate from Greek to English.

1. ἀπέκριθη ἐκεῖνος· ὁ ἄνθρωπος ὁ λεγόμενος Ἰησοῦς ἐθεράπευσέν ἐμε.

2. καὶ λέγει τῇ ἐκκλησίᾳ περὶ τοῦ ἀνδρὸς τοῦ τὴν *ξηρὰν χεῖρα ἔχοντος· ἔλθῃ εἰς τὸ *μέσον. (cp. Mark 3:3)

3. φωνὴ κράζουσα ἐν τῇ ἐρήμῳ, Ὁ κύριος ἐρχόμενος. *ἑτοιμάσωμεν τὴν ὁδὸν κυρίου.

4. καὶ ἤκουσεν ὁ βασιλεὺς *Ἡρῷδης, *φανερὸν γὰρ ἐγένετο τὸ ὄνομα αὐτοῦ, καὶ ἔλεγον ὅτι Ἰωάννης ὁ βαπτίζων ἐγήγερται ἐκ νεκρῶν. (Mark 6:14)

5. οὗτός ἐστιν ὁ ἄρτος ὁ ἐκ τοῦ οὐρανοῦ *καταβαίνων ἵνα τις ἐξ αὐτοῦ φάγῃ καὶ μὴ ἀποθάνῃ. (John 6:50)

6. ἐγὼ δὲ λέγω ὑμῖν ὅτι ὁ βλέπων γυναῖκα πρὸς τὸ *ἐπιθυμῆσαι αὐτὴν *ἤδη *ἐμοίχευσεν αὐτὴν ἐν τῇ καρδίᾳ αὐτοῦ. (cp. Matthew 5:28)

7. καὶ αὕτη ἐστιν ἡ ἐντολὴ αὐτοῦ, ἵνα πιστεύσωμεν τῷ ὀνόματι τοῦ υἱοῦ αὐτοῦ Ἰησοῦ Χριστοῦ. (1 John 3:23)

8. ἐὰν γὰρ ἀφῆτε τοῖς ἀνθρώποις τὰ *παραπτώματα αὐτῶν, ἀφήσει καὶ ὑμῖν ὁ πατὴρ ὑμῶν ὁ ἐν τοῖς οὐρανοῖς. (as in Matthew 6:14)

9. *τέλος γὰρ νόμου Χριστός ἐστιν εἰς δικαιοσύνην τῷ πιστεύοντι. (as in Romans 10:4)

10. ὁ γὰρ ἄρτος τοῦ θεοῦ ἐστιν ὁ καταβαίνων ἐκ τοῦ οὐρανοῦ καὶ ζωὴν διδοὺς τῷ κόσμῳ. (John 6:33)

11. *ἐλπίζω ἐπὶ τὸν *σταύρον τοῦ κυρίου καὶ ἐπὶ τῷ θεῷ τῷ ἐγείροντι τοὺς νεκρούς.

12. πνεύματα γὰρ δαιμονίων οἴσουσιν σημεῖα, ἃ ἐξέρχεται ἐπὶ τοὺς βασιλεῖς τοῦ κόσμου συναγαγεῖν αὐτοὺς εἰς τὸν *πόλεμον τῆς ἡμέρας τοῦ θεοῦ. (as in Revelation 16:14)

13. ἐν γὰρ τῇ σοφίᾳ τοῦ θεοῦ οὐκ ἔγνω ὁ κόσμος διὰ τῆς σοφίας αὐτοῦ τὸν θεόν. *εὐδόκησεν ὁ θεὸς διὰ τῆς *μωρίας τοῦ *κηρύγματος σῶσαι τοὺς πιστεύοντας. (cp. 1 Corinthians 1:21)

14. *Γνωρίζω γὰρ ὑμῖν, ἀδελφοί, τὸ εὐαγγέλιον τὸ κηρυσσόμενον ὑπ᾽ ἐμοῦ ὅτι οὐκ ἔστιν κατὰ ἄνθρωπον· οὐδὲ γὰρ ἐγὼ παρὰ ἀνθρώπου ἔλαβον αὐτὸ οὐδὲ ἐδιδάχθην, ἀλλὰ δι᾽ *ἀποκαλύψεως Ἰησοῦ Χριστοῦ. (cp. Galatians 1:11–12)

15. πώρωσις ἀπὸ *μέρους τῷ Ἰσραὴλ γέγονεν *ἄχρι οὗ τὸ πλήρωμα τῶν ἐθνῶν εἰσέλθῃ, καὶ οὕτως Ἰσραὴλ σωθήσεται. (cp. Romans 11:25–26)

16. καὶ ὁ ἐρχόμενος ἐκήρυσσεν εἰρήνην ὑμῖν τοῖς *μακρὰν καὶ εἰρήνην τοῖς *ἐγγύς. (cp. Ephesians 2:17)

17. Αὐτοὶ γὰρ οἴδατε, ἀδελφοί, τὴν *εἴσοδον ἡμῶν τὴν πρὸς ὑμᾶς ὅτι οὐ *κενὴ γέγονεν. (1 Thessalonians 2:1)

18. ὑμεῖς γὰρ *μιμηταὶ ἐγενήθητε, ἀδελφοί, τῶν ἐκκλησιῶν τοῦ θεοῦ τῶν οὐσῶν ἐν τῇ Ἰουδαίᾳ ἐν Χριστῷ Ἰησοῦ, ὅτι τὰ αὐτὰ *ἐπάθετε καὶ ὑμεῖς ὑπὸ τῶν ἰδίων *συμφυλετῶν καθὼς καὶ αὐτοὶ ὑπὸ τῶν Ἰουδαίων. (1 Thessalonians 2:14)

19. αὐτοὶ γὰρ *ἀκριβῶς οἴδατε ὅτι ἡ ἡμέρα κυρίου ὡς *κλέπτης ἐν νυκτὶ οὕτως ἔρχεται. (1 Thessalonians 5:2)

20. Χαίρω τῷ θεῷ μου … ὁ ἀκούων σου τὴν ἀγάπην καὶ τὴν πίστιν ἣν ἔχεις πρὸς τὸν κύριον Ἰησοῦν καὶ εἰς τοὺς ἁγίους. (cp. Philemon 4–5)

Translate from English to Greek.

1. After the evil master died, the slaves were released by the holy apostle in order that they might establish a just kingdom on the earth.

2. Who has taken the last bread from the people and has given it to the high priest?

3. A certain man went to the city to sell his land, but because it was the sabbath the crowds were not wanting the land.

4. The prophet who descended from heaven to proclaim the word of the Lord has established himself by his righteousness and love.

5. Whoever saves those other men and women from the nations will receive grace from our Lord.

6. Do the scriptures say that the demons will rule the world forever, or will the Lord of righteousness destroy them by the power of his hand?

7. I departed from the sea so that I might enter the city at the last season.

8. We are about to eat and drink in the assembly because we have been loosed from the flesh by the power of the Spirit.

9. Let us not hinder the work of the Holy Spirit, who hears us and teaches us the path of peace.

10. For if God sent to us the messenger himself, our souls would be saved from the power of sin.

11. You (pl) have been persuaded that you have life because of your laws, but I do not find love for one another in your hearts.

12. The brothers of wisdom pray for the people who have fallen from the path of light.

13. The children of peace knew that the hour of sin was present, but they did not stand upon their faith.

14. The disciples who believed their master proclaimed peace to the assembly, which healed the slaves according to the scriptures.

15. But just as the people want to hear the good news from the son of glory, they will not believe any one who tests them.

XIX

Aorist Participles

The *first aorist active participle* omits the ε- augment and adds endings with a characteristic -σα- connecting syllable. It is declined as follows:

	Singular			Plural		
	M	*F*	*N*	*M*	*F*	*N*
N	λύσας	λύσασα	λῦσαν	λύσαντες	λύσασαι	λύσαντα
G	λύσαντος	λυσάσης	λύσαντος	λυσάντων	λυσασῶν	λυσάντων
D	λύσαντι	λυσάσῃ	λύσαντι	λύσασι(ν)	λυσάσαις	λύσασι(ν)
A	λύσαντα	λύσασαν	λῦσαν	λύσαντας	λυσάσας	λύσαντα

The *second aorist active participle* applies the same endings as the present active participle to the unaugmented second aorist stem.

	Singular			Plural		
	M	*F*	*N*	*M*	*F*	*N*
N	λαβών	λαβοῦσα	λαβόν	λαβόντες	λαβοῦσαι	λαβόντα
G	λαβόντος	λαβούσης	λαβόντος	λαβόντων	λαβουσῶν	λαβόντων
D	λαβόντι	λαβούσῃ	λαβόντι	λαβοῦσι(ν)	λαβούσαις	λαβοῦσι(ν)
A	λαβόντα	λαβοῦσαν	λαβόν	λαβόντας	λαβούσας	λαβόντα

The *first aorist middle participle* applies the aorist connecting syllable -σα- to the unaugmented aorist stem and adds the present middle -μεν- endings.

	Singular			Plural		
M	*F*	*N*	*M*	*F*	*N*
N λυσάμενος	λυσαμένη	λυσάμενον	λυσάμενοι	λυσάμεναι	λυσάμενα
G λυσαμένου	λυσαμένης	λυσαμένου	λυσαμένων	λυσαμένων	λυσαμένων
D λυσαμένῳ	λυσαμένῃ	λυσαμένῳ	λυσαμένοις	λυσαμέναις	λυσαμένοις
A λυσάμενον	λυσαμένην	λυσάμενον	λυσαμένους	λυσαμένας	λυσάμενα

The *second aorist middle participle* applies the connecting vowel o and the present middle -μεν- endings to the unaugmented second aorist stem.

	Singular			Plural		
M	*F*	*N*	*M*	*F*	*N*
N λαβόμενος	λαβομένη	λαβόμενον	λαβόμενοι	λαβόμεναι	λαβόμενα
G λαβομένου	λαβομένης	λαβομένου	λαβομένων	λαβομένων	λαβομένων
D λαβομένῳ	λαβομένῃ	λαβομένῳ	λαβομένοις	λαβομέναις	λαβομένοις
A λαβόμενον	λαβομένην	λαβόμενον	λαβομένους	λαβομένας	λαβόμενα

The *aorist passive participle* adds the following endings to the aorist passive principal part and omits the ε- augment:

	Singular			Plural		
M	*F*	*N*	*M*	*F*	*N*
N λυθείς	λυθεῖσα	λυθέν	λυθέντες	λυθεῖσαι	λυθέντα
G λυθέντος	λυθείσης	λυθέντος	λυθέντων	λυθεισῶν	λυθέντων
D λυθέντι	λυθείσῃ	λυθέντι	λυθεῖσι(ν)	λυθείσαις	λυθεῖσι(ν)
A λυθέντα	λυθεῖσαν	λυθέν	λυθέντας	λυθείσας	λυθέντα

Adverbial Uses of the Participle

The adverbial participle describes *how* the main verb occurred, or *why* the main verb occurred, or *when* the main verb occurred, or *what else* was involved in the main verb's occurrence.

The *temporal participle* expresses an action prior to, contemporaneous with, or subsequent to the action of the main verb. While most participles *can* be construed as temporal participles, students should try to reserve temporal translations for situations in which the temporal usage is clearly most appropriate.

> προσῆλθον αὐτῷ διδάσκοντι   The high priests came to him *while*
> οἱ ἀρχιερεῖς ...   *he was teaching* ... (Matthew 21:23)

The *causal participle* expresses the reason for the action of the main verb. It is most commonly translated by shifting the participle to a finite form and prefacing it with "because," "since," or "for."

> Ἰωσὴφ ... δίκαιος ὢν καὶ μὴ   Joseph, *because he was* just and
> θέλων αὐτὴν δειγματίσαι ...   *did not want* to disgrace her ...
>   (Matthew 1:19)

The *concessive participle* expresses a factor that counts against the likelihood of the main verb. Thus, it expresses a concession, and it is typically translated by shifting the participle to a finite form and introducing it with "though," "even though," "although," or "despite."

> πολλὴν ἐν Χριστῷ παρρησίαν   *though I have* much boldness
> ἔχων ἐπιτάσσειν σοι ...   in Christ to command you ...
>   (Philemon 8)

The *modal participle* expresses the manner in which the action of the main verb took place. It adds specificity or focus to the main action, without suggesting a second or separate action — or put another way, it indicates the same action, characterized differently. The modal participle is best translated by preserving the participial form in English and allowing the participle to modify the main verb.

> ... καὶ ἐλάλει εὐλογῶν   ... and he spoke, *blessing* God.
> τὸν θεόν.   (Luke 1:64)

The participle of attendant circumstance is quite similar to the modal participle, except that the participle of attendant circumstance tends to express additional distinct actions attendant upon the main verb. The participle of attendant circumstance is best translated by shifting the participle to a finite form and joining it to the main verb with "and."

καὶ περιῆγεν τὰς κώμας   And he went on around the
κύκλῳ διδάσκων.   villages *and taught* (Mark 6:6b).

Students should bear in mind that these categories overlap and cross one another; therefore, there may be several defensible ways of construing a particular participle. Some interpreters may take one participle as modal, whereas others may regard it as a participle of attendant circumstance; some will interpret participle as causal, while others regard it as concessive. As students become comfortable with Greek, they will find it easier to distinguish cases in which context makes the role of the participle relatively clear from more ambiguous constructions. If students are uncertain about which usage best suits a particular construction, they should simply weigh the alternatives to see which produces the most coherent, plausible translation. This is a dimension of Greek syntax for which there are no rules. Memorization cannot take the place of literary sensitivity, though practice will help the student refine that sensitivity.

Participles: Tense, Time, and Translation

Again, it is important to remember that the tense of a participle expresses a characterization of the action, *not* a time relation to other elements of the syntax. The time of a participle relative to the rest of a clause is often best determined by simply observing logical priority when the action of one verb cannot plausibly have begun before another has ended. At other times, the author may supply explicit time markers (such as "now," "then," "the next day," and so on). If neither a relation of logical priority is apparent, nor any explicit time marker, the reader will have to ascertain how the participle and its main verb relate to one another. *Usually*, the word order of a sentence will indicate the sequence of events: verbs that represent earlier events tend to appear earlier in the sentence, and later events appear later. *Usually*, an aorist participle, whose aspect expresses action viewed as an entire event, will represent an action that takes place before the main verb. Indeed, aorist participles usually occur earlier in the sentence's word order, as the previous generalizations would suggest. Finally, a venerable tradition teaches that aorist participles indicate action before the time of the main verb, whereas present participles indicate action concurrent with the main verb. This guide is helpful, though not authoritative. These guidelines apply as generalizations, but the overriding rule for translating participles is that *context is decisive.*

Study Checklist

The form of the aorist participle
First aorist active and middle participles
Second aorist active and middle participles
Aorist passive participles

Adverbial uses of the participle: temporal, causal, concessive, modal, attendant circumstance

Vocabulary

Nouns

γλῶσσα, ἡ	tongue, language	λίθος, ὁ	stone
ἐλπίς, -ίδος, ἡ	hope	παιδίον, τό	child
ἐπαγγελία, ἡ	promise	παραβολή, ἡ	parable
θρόνος, ὁ	throne	χρόνος, ὁ	time

Adjectives

δεξιός, -ά, -όν   right (directional)

λοιπός, -ή, -όν   remaining; the rest (as a substantive); finally (used adverbially in the accusative case)

μέσος, -η, -ον   middle, amidst

Exercises

Translate from Greek to English.

1. Ἰωσὴφ ὁ ἀνὴρ αὐτῆς, δίκαιος ὤν, οὐκ ἤθελεν αὐτὴν *δειγματίσαι. (cp. Matthew 1:19)

2. ἠκολούθει γὰρ ὁ ὄχλος τοῦ λαοῦ κράζοντες ὅτι δεῖ ἆραι αὐτόν. (as in Acts 21:36; the plural participle κράζοντες goes with the singular noun ὁ ὄχλος in what is called a *constructio ad sensum.* Although the noun is itself singular, it refers to a plural entity and the participle reflects the crowd's plurality.)

3. καὶ ἀπολύσας τοὺς ὄχλους *ἀνέβη εἰς τὸ ὄρος κατ' ἰδίαν προσεύξασθαι. (Matthew 14:23)

4. οἶδα δὲ ὅτι ἐρχόμενος πρὸς ὑμᾶς ἐν *πληρώματι *εὐλογίας Χριστοῦ ἐλεύσομαι. (Romans 15:29)

5. οἱ δὲ ἀκούσαντες ἐχάρησαν καὶ *ἐπηγγείλαντο αὐτῷ *ἀργύριον δοῦναι. (Mark 14:11a)

6. ἀπὸ τότε ἤρξατο ὁ Ἰησοῦς κηρύσσειν καὶ λέγειν· *ἐγγύς ἐστιν ἡ βασιλεία. (as in Matthew 4:17)

7. καὶ σημεῖον ἔλαβεν *περιτομῆς *σφραγῖδα τῆς δικαιοσύνης τῆς πίστεως τῆς ἐν τῇ *ἀκροβυστίᾳ, εἰς τὸ εἶναι αὐτὸν πατερὰ τῶν πιστευόντων δι' *ἀκροβυστίας, εἰς τὸ *λογισθῆναι καὶ αὐτοῖς τὴν δικαιοσύνην. (as in Romans 4:11)

8. ἰδού, ὁ *ἀμνὸς τοῦ θεοῦ ὁ αἴρων τὴν ἁμαρτίαν τοῦ κόσμου. (cp. John 1:29)

9. Καὶ ὅτε εἶδον αὐτόν, ἔπεσα πρὸς τοὺς πόδας αὐτοῦ ὡς νεκρός· καὶ ἔθηκεν τὴν χεῖρα αὐτοῦ τὴν δεξιὰν ἐπ' ἐμὲ λέγων· ἐγώ εἰμι ὁ πρῶτος καὶ ὁ ἔσχατος. (as in Revelation 1:17)

10. νῦν ἀπολύεις τὸν δοῦλόν σου, δέσποτα, κατὰ τὸ ῥῆμά σου ἐν εἰρήνῃ· ὅτι εἶδον οἱ ὀφθαλμοί μου τὸ σωτήριόν σου ὃ ἡτοίμασας κατὰ πρόσωπον τῶν λαῶν, φῶς εἰς ἀποκάλυψιν ἐθνῶν καὶ δόξαν λαοῦ σου Ἰσραήλ. (as in Luke 2:29–32)

11. γέγραπται· ἔδωκεν αὐτοῖς ὁ θεὸς πνεῦμα *κατανύξεως, ὀφθαλμοὺς τοῦ μὴ βλέπειν καὶ *ὦτα τοῦ μὴ ἀκούειν. (as in Romans 11:8)

12. πορευθέντες οὖν *μαθητεύσετε τὰ ἔθνη, βαπτίζοντες αὐτοὺς εἰς τὸ ὄνομα τοῦ πατρὸς καὶ τοῦ υἱοῦ καὶ τοῦ ἁγίου πνεύματος, διδάσκοντες αὐτοὺς τὸν λόγον τοῦ κυρίου. (cp. Matthew 28:19–20)

13. ἦτε τῷ καιρῷ ἐκείνῳ *χωρὶς Χριστοῦ, *ξένοι τῶν διαθηκῶν τῆς ἐπαγγελίας, ἐλπίδα μὴ ἔχοντες καὶ *ἄθεοι ἐν τῷ κόσμῳ. (cp. Ephesians 2:12)

14. *παράγων παρα τὴν θάλασσαν, εἶδεν Σίμωνα καὶ Ἀνδρέαν· καὶ ἀφέντες τὰ *δίκτυα ἠκολούθησαν αὐτῷ. (as in Mark 1:16, 17)

15. ὅτε δὲ ἦλθεν τὸ *πλήρωμα τοῦ χρόνου, ἀπέστειλεν ὁ θεὸς τὸν υἱὸν αὐτοῦ, *γενόμενον ἐκ γυναικός, *γενόμενον ὑπὸ νόμον, ἵνα τὴν υἱοθεσίαν λάβωμεν. (cp. Galatians 4:4–5)

16. λέγει αὐτῇ ὁ Ἰησοῦς, Οὐκ εἶπόν σοι ὅτι ἐὰν πιστεύσῃς ὄψῃ τὴν δόξαν τοῦ θεου; ἦραν οὖν τὸν λίθον. (as in John 11:40–41)

17. ὁ δὲ Ἰησοῦς ἦρεν τοὺς ὀφθαλμοὺς καὶ εἶπεν, Πάτερ, εὐχαριστῶ σοι ὅτι ἤκουσάς μου. (as in John 11:41)

18. καὶ ἐκ τῆς συναγωγῆς ἐξελθόντες ἦλθον εἰς τὴν οἰκίαν Σίμωνος μετὰ Ἰακώβου, καὶ ἐθεράπευσεν τὴν μητέρα αὐτοῦ. (as in Mark 1:29)

19. ἡ μήτηρ αὐτοῦ καὶ οἱ ἀδελφοὶ αὐτοῦ καὶ *ἔξω στήκοντες ἀπέστειλαν πρὸς αὐτόν. (cp. Mark 3:31)

20. ὁ δὲ ἐξελθὼν ἤρξατο κηρύσσειν τοῖς ἀνθρώποις τὴν βασιλείαν τοῦ θεοῦ. (cp. Mark 1:45)

Translate from English to Greek.

1. While Jesus spoke to the crowd in parables, the high priests were wishing to kill him.

2. After the hour came, the messenger from heaven spoke to the king about the laws of God.

3. Although the remaining children wanted to learn the scriptures, they did not have a teacher who could teach them.

4. The beautiful garments of the scribes hinder the eyes of the people who are about to be led down an evil path.

5. The holy man who was handed over to die healed the souls of the righteous scribes and gave to them the promise of the kingdom of God.

6. Although the demons have power to tempt the brothers, the Lord sits on his throne of glory and rules with his right hand.

7. Because he cried out with his voice, the assembly heard him and prayed for him so that God might save him from sin.

8. The people came from other cities and spoke with other tongues which we did not know.

9. While he is coming in the evening, the Son of God is proclaiming life and peace in the day.

10. The same wilderness in which we found God does not give bread to others who enter.

11. In the midst of the assembly, the woman who was forgiven stood and spoke the word of the Lord to the people who would not listen to the Lord.

12. The Jews entered into the city believing in a law which leads to death.

13. Jesus came through the cities teaching and preaching the kingdom.

14. After the Christ was raised from the dead, his disciples gathered together at night because they were about to proclaim Jesus as the Christ in the day.

15. The man believed the beginning of the wisdom of the teacher, but he did not find truth in the last place.

X X

Perfect Participles

The *perfect active participle* retains the reduplication and the κ suffix of the perfect active indicative, but adds a different set of endings.

	Singular			*Plural*	
M	*F*	*N*	*M*	*F*	*N*
N λελυκώς	λελυκυῖα	λελυκός	λελυκότες	λελυκυῖαι	λελυκότα
G λελυκότος	λελυκυίας	λελυκότος	λελυκότων	λελυκυιῶν	λελυκότων
D λελυκότι	λελυκυίᾳ	λελυκότι	λελυκόσι(ν)	λελυκόσι(ν)	λελυκόσι(ν)
A λελυκότα	λελυκυῖαν	λελυκός	λελυκότας	λελυκυίας	λελυκότα

As with the perfect active active indicative, some forms of the participle do not tolerate the κ suffix; rather, they take the participial endings directly on their perfect stems. For instance, ἔρχομαι forms the perfect indicative ἐλήλυθα, and its perfect participle is ἐληλυθώς. The most common perfect participle is that of οἶδα, which may confuse students if they forget that the perfect active participle of οἶδα is εἰδώς (formed predictably from the εἰδ- stem).

The *perfect middle/passive participle* adds the familiar middle/passive participial endings to the perfect middle/passive stem.

	Singular			*Plural*	
M	*F*	*N*	*M*	*F*	*N*
N λελυμένος	λελυμένη	λελυμένον	λελυμένοι	λελυμέναι	λελυμένα
G λελυμένου	λελυμένης	λελυμένου	λελυμένων	λελυμένων	λελυμένων
D λελυμένῳ	λελυμένῃ	λελυμένῳ	λελυμένοις	λελυμέναις	λελυμένοις
A λελυμένον	λελυμένην	λελυμένον	λελυμένους	λελυμένας	λελυμένα

As might be expected, the consonant changes observed in the first person singular perfect middle/passive indicative, where the verb stem contacts the μ of the tense ending, apply also in the perfect middle/passive participle, where the verb stem comes into contact with the μ of the participial endings. For example, γράφω forms the perfect middle/passive γέγραμμαι, and the perfect middle/passive participle becomes γεγραμμένος.

Verbal Uses of the Participle

The participle frequently occurs in constructions where it functions as a verbal adjective.

The genitive absolute is a participial phrase wherein the participle and an associated noun or pronoun appear in the genitive case. The participle is translated as a finite verb with a noun or pronoun as its subject. In a strict absolute clause, the noun of the absolute clause has no syntactical relationship with any other part of the sentence — that is, it does not reappear in the main clause as a subject or object. The genitive absolute is typically interpreted as a temporal clause beginning with "while," "after," "during," or "before."

> καθίσαντος αὐτοῦ προσῆλθαν   *When he sat down,* his disciples
> αὐτῷ οἱ μαθηταὶ αὐτοῦ ...   came to him ... (Matthew 5:1b)

In this example, the subject of the genitive absolute appears twice in the main clause. This is an imprecise grammatical construction, but it is common in Hellenistic Greek.

Participles can appear as *complements* to finite verbs such as ἄρχομαι, which require some verbal form to complete them. In some cases, however, participles complement verbs of perception (βλέπω, ὁράω, ἀκούω).

> οὐ παύομαι εὐχαριστῶν   I do not stop *giving thanks*
> ὑπὲρ ὑμῶν ...   for you ... (Ephesians 1:16)

The participle also appears in *periphrastic constructions* with εἰμί. The imperfect forms of εἰμί with participles form a periphrastic imperfect.

> Ἦν ... ὁ Ἰωάννης βαπτίζων   John *was baptizing*
> ἐν Αἰνὼν ...   in Aenon ... (John 3:23)

This could just as well have been expressed ἐβάπτιζεν ὁ Ἰωάννης. Both the imperfect and the periphrastic construction express "was baptizing."

Further uses of participles will be treated in lesson XXVII. Students are now acquainted with many different uses of the participle, and they may feel overwhelmed by the possibilities. The following "decision tree" may be of some help in determining how a participle functions in its context.

Is the participle governed by an article?

Yes *Adjectival uses*

> Is the participle modifying a specific noun?
>
> **Yes,** *probably an attributive use of the participle.*
> **No,** *probably a substantive use of the participle.*

No *Check to make sure that this is not an anarthrous adjectival participle.*

> Is the participle agreeing with a noun in the genitive case?
>
> **Yes,** *this may well be a genitive absolute.*
>
> **No,** *check for a form of εἰμί.*
>
> > Is this participle the object of εἰμί?
> >
> > **Yes** Is the εἰμί-participle combination functioning as a main verb?
> >
> > > **Yes,** *probably a periphrastic construction.*
> > > **No,** *probably a predicative (adjectival) use of the participle.*
> >
> > **No** *This is probably one of the adverbial uses of the participle. Try each of the following to see which usage makes the best sense.*
> >
> > > Temporal, *"when,"* etc. *Is the clause emphasizing the participle's time?*
> > >
> > > Causal, *"because." Is the participle providing a reason for the main verb?*
> > >
> > > Concessive, *"though." Does the participle work against the main verb?*
> > >
> > > Modal. *Does the participle further specify the action of the main verb?*
> > >
> > > Attendant Circumstance. *Does the participle express another action attendant upon the main verb?*

Study Checklist

Forms of the perfect active participle
Forms of the perfect middle/passive participle

Verbal uses of the participle
Genitive absolute constructions
Verbal complements
Periphrastic constructions

Vocabulary

Nouns

ἔτος, -ους, τό   year

κρίσις, -εως, ἡ   judgment

σωτηρία, ἡ   salvation

φόβος, ὁ   fear

φυλακή, ἡ   guard; prison; watch (as a unit of time)

χρεία, ἡ   need

Verbs

ἀπαγγέλλω *ἀπαγγέλλω, ἀπαγγελῶ, ἀπήγγειλα, —, —, ἀπηγγέλην*
I announce, I report

εὐαγγελίζω *εὐαγγελίζω, —, εὐαγγέλισα, —, εὐηγγέλισμαι, εὐηγγελίσθην*
I bring good news, I evangelize

κάθημαι *κάθημαι, καθήσομαι, —, —, —, —*   I sit

καθίζω *καθίζω, καθίσεω, ἐκάθισα, κεκάθικα, —, —*   I seat, I sit

κρίνω *κρίνω, κρινῶ, ἔκρινα, κέκρινα, κέκριμαι, ἐκρίθην*   I judge

μένω *μένω, μενῶ, ἔμεινα, μεμένηκα, —, —*   I remain, I abide

παραλαμβάνω *παραλαμβάνω, παραλήμψομαι, παρέλαβον, —, —,*
παρελήμφθην I receive

σπείρω *σπείρω, —, ἔσπειρα, —, ἔσπαρμαι, ἐσπάρην*   I sow

Adjectives

μακάριος, -ία, -ιον   blessed

τυφλός, -ή, -όν   blind

Exercises

Translate from Greek to English.

1. μετὰ ταῦτα εἶδον, καὶ ἰδοὺ ὄχλος, ἐκ τῶν ἐθνῶν καὶ λαῶν καὶ γλωσσῶν, ἑστῶτες παρὰ τὸν θρόνον καὶ κράζουσιν φωνῇ μεγάλῃ λέγοντες· ἡ σωτηρία τῷ θεῷ ἡμῶν τῷ καθημένῳ ἐπὶ τῷ θρόνῳ. (cp. Revelation 7:9–10)

2. τὸ δὲ ῥῆμα τοῦ κυρίου μένει εἰς τὸν αἰῶνα. τοῦτο δέ ἐστιν τὸ ῥῆμα τὸ εὐαγγελισθὲν εἰς ὑμᾶς. (1 Peter 1:25)

3. ἀπέστειλα αὐτοὺς εἰς τὸν κόσμον ἵνα ἀποστείλωσιν ἀγαθὰ *δῶρα τῷ πεπιστεύκοτι ἐν τῷ ὀνόματι τοῦ Ἰησοῦ.

4. ἀποθανούμεθα ἐν ταῖς ἁμαρτίας ἡμῶν ἐὰν μὴ ἀποστείλωμεν τοὺς ἀρχιέρεις ἑαυτῶν εἰς τὴν *κώμην αὐτῶν.

5. ὁ *γεγεννήμενος ἐκ τοῦ θεοῦ ἁμαρτίαν οὐ *ποιεῖ, ὅτι σπέρμα δικαιοσύνης ἐν αὐτῷ μενεῖ. (cp. 1 John 3:9)

6. αὕτη ἐστιν ἡ *μαρτυρία τοῦ θεοῦ ὅτι μεμαρτύρηκεν περὶ τοῦ υἱοῦ αὐτοῦ, τοῦ ἄγοντος αὐτὰς εἰς τὴν ἀλήθειαν.

7. τὰ τέκνα ἐλήλυθεν τοῖς εἰσεληλύθοσιν εἰς πονηρόν.

8. καὶ *περιῆγεν ὁ Ἰησοῦς τὰς πόλεις καὶ τὰς **κώμας διδάσκων ἐν ταῖς συναγώγαις αὐτῶν καὶ κηρύσσων τὸ εὐαγγέλιον τῆς βασιλείας καὶ θεραπεύων *νόσον καὶ *μαλακίαν. (cp. Matthew 9:35)

9. καὶ εἰ ὁ *Σατανᾶς τὸν *Σατανᾶν ἐκβάλλει, ἐφ᾽ ἑαυτὸν *ἐμερίσθη· πῶς οὖν σταθήσεται ἡ βασιλεία αὐτοῦ; (Matthew 12:26)

10. ἀποκριθεὶς δὲ αὐτῷ ὁ Πέτρος εἶπεν, Κύριε, εἰ σὺ εἶ, κέλευσόν ("command") με ἐλθεῖν πρός σε ἐπὶ τὰ ὕδατα. (Matthew 14:28)

11. καὶ ἀνεῴχθη αὐτῷ βιβλίον τοῦ προφήτου Ἠσαΐου, καὶ δεξάμενος τὸ βιβλίον εὗρεν τὸν τόπον οὗ ἦν γεγραμμένον. (cp. Luke 4:17)

12. ἐγένετο δὲ ἐν τῷ τὸν ὄχλον στῆναι αὐτῷ καὶ ἀκούειν τὸν λόγον τοῦ θεοῦ καὶ αὐτὸς ἦν ἑστὼς παρὰ τὴν *λίμνην *Γεννησαρέτ, καὶ εἶδεν *δύο πλοῖα ἑστῶτα παρὰ τὴν *λίμνην· (cp. Luke 5:1–2)

13. καὶ εὑροῦσα συγάγηγα τὰς *φίλας καὶ *γείτονας λέγουσα,
    *Συγχάρητέ ("rejoice with") μοι, ὅτι εὗρον τὴν *δραχμὴν ἣν *ἀπώλεσα.
    (cp. Luke 15:9)

14. ὑμεῖς κατὰ τὴν σάρκα κρίνετε, ἐγὼ οὐ κρίνω *οὐδένα. καὶ ἐὰν κρίνω
    δὲ ἐγώ, ἡ *κρίσις μου *ἀληθινή ἐστιν, ὅτι μόνος οὐκ εἰμί, ἀλλ᾽ ἐγὼ
    καὶ ὁ πέμψας με πατήρ. (cp. John 8:15–16)

15. *Γνωρίζομεν δὲ ὑμῖν, ἀδελφοί, τὴν χάριν τοῦ θεοῦ τὴν δεδομένην
    ἐν ταῖς ἐκκλησίαις τῆς *Μακεδονίας. (2 Corinthians 8:1)

16. τούτῳ *καταλείψει ἄνθρωπος τὸν πατέρα καὶ τὴν μητέρα καὶ
    *προσκολληθήσεται πρὸς τὴν γυναῖκα αὐτοῦ, καὶ ἔσονται οἱ *δύο
    εἰς σάρκα *μίαν. (cp. Ephesians 5:31)

17. Τέκνα μου, ταῦτα γράφω ὑμῖν ἵνα μὴ *ἁμάρτητε. καὶ ἐάν τις
    *ἁμάρτῃ, *παράκλητον ἔχομεν πρὸς τὸν πατέρα, Ἰησοῦν Χριστὸν
    δίκαιον· (as in 1 John 2:1)

18. Γράφω ὑμῖν, *τεκνία, ὅτι ἀφέωνται ὑμῖν αἱ ἁμαρτίαι διὰ τὸ ὄνομα
    αὐτοῦ. (1 John 2:12)

19. Ὑμεῖς δέ, ἀγαπητοί, ὀφείλετε *μιμνήσκεσθαι τὰ ῥήματα τὰ
    *προειρημένα ὑπὸ τῶν ἀποστόλων τοῦ κυρίου ἡμῶν Ἰησοῦ Χριστοῦ.
    (as in Jude 17)

20. Καὶ εἶδον ἐπὶ τὴν δεξιὰν τοῦ καθημένου ἐπὶ τοῦ θρόνου *βιβλίον
    γεγραμμένον *ἔσωθεν καὶ *ὄπισθεν. (Revelation 5:1)

Translate from English to Greek.

1. When she had received judgment from her master, the prophet spoke to her about salvation from God.

2. The blessed king was proclaiming hope for the people who had entered into the city from the desert.

3. While the men judged the small scribes, the women brought them into the assembly and gave them fruit to eat.

4. A certain man exited the city, and he went to another city because the year of the Lord was about to begin.

5. By faith we believe that God is coming again, and he will give bread and fruit to the people who have need, but he will judge the evil ones.

6. While the guard sat in the temple, the messenger went to the high priest who was teaching the children.

7. If you (pl) abide in the words which the Lord spoke to you, the Lord will sow in you faith and righteousness.

8. Although the king sat on the throne to judge, he gave commands to the people as he wished.

9. Let us rejoice in the Lord, for we have been saved and placed on a foundation in Jesus Christ which will not be destroyed.

10. Some women went out to sow hope in the people because they (masculine) had fear of a day of judgment.

11. But now the prophet's words proclaim the good news that the Christ was raised from the dead.

12. After having entered the city, let us bring good news to men and women who do not have life in Christ.

13. Because the blind did not see the beautiful writings, they heard them from the apostles, and they believed in the Lord.

14. The people established peace because the Lord gave to them power over the evil ones who were destroying the world.

15. Her disciples carried the gospel of joy and glory to the nations who did not know.

XXI

Imperative Mood

Whereas the indicative mood is the mood of assertion, and the subjunctive mood is the mood of contingency, the imperative mood is the mood of command.

βλέπετε τοὺς κύνας ...　　*Look* [out for] the dogs ...
(Philippians 3:2)

The imperative appears only in the second person in English: "Go to bed!" The Greek imperative also includes a third person. This presents a problem that translators have addressed by rendering third person imperatives with the locution "Let them ..." or "Let her/him ...." Students may note that the English imperative verb "let" is itself a second person form. The force of the expression "Let them eat cake" is not, however, addressed to a second person audience, but to the third person group. The import of "Let them eat cake" is "They should eat cake," a third person formulation. Inasmuch as English lacks a third person imperative, the "let" idiom serves as an equivalent.

ἐλθέτω ἡ βασιλεία σου.　　*Let* your kingdom *come.*
(Luke 11:2)

The imperative appears principally in the present and aorist, active, middle, and passive voices. The perfect imperative is rare, and it will not be covered in this textbook. The *present active* and *middle passive imperatives* add the following endings to the present stem.

	Active		Middle/Passive	
	singular	*plural*	*singular*	*plural*
2ND	λῦ-ε	λύ-ετε	λύ-ου	λύ-εσθε
3RD	λυ-έτω	λυ-έτωσαν	λυ-έσθω	λυ-έσθωσαν

λῦ-ε
Stem ┘ └ Imperative Ending

λύ-ου
Stem ┘ └ Imperative Ending

Attentive students will immediately notice that the second person plural form of the present active imperative is identical to the second person plural present active indicative. Therefore, students must rely on context to help them discern which forms are imperatives and which are indicatives. In most cases, the distinction is clear.

The *aorist imperative* first drops the ε- augment from its indicative forms, then adds the following endings to the active, middle, and passive forms:

| | *Aorist Active* | | | *Aorist Middle* | |
	singular	*plural*		*singular*	*plural*
2ND	λῦσ-ον	λύσ-ατε		λῦσ-αι	λύσ-ασθε
3RD	λυσ-άτω	λυσ-άτωσαν		λυσ-άσθω	λυσ-άσθωσαν

$$\underset{\text{Stem}}{\underbrace{\lambda\hat{\upsilon}\sigma}}\text{-}\underset{\text{Imperative Ending}}{\underbrace{o\nu}} \qquad \underset{\text{Stem}}{\underbrace{\lambda\hat{\upsilon}\sigma}}\text{-}\underset{\text{Imperative Ending}}{\underbrace{\alpha\iota}}$$

λῦσ-ον
Stem — Imperative Ending   λῦσ-αι
Stem — Imperative Ending

| | *Passive Imperative* | |
	singular	*plural*
2ND	λύθ-ητι	λύθ-ητε
3RD	λυθ-ήτω	λυθ-ήτωσαν

λύθ-ητι
Stem — Imperative Ending

| | *Present Active Imperative, εἰμί* | |
	singular	*plural*
2ND	ἴσθι	ἔστε
3RD	ἔστω	ἔστωσαν

	Δίδωμι		῞Ιστημι		Τίθημι	
	singular	*plural*	*singular*	*plural*	*singular*	*plural*

Present Active Imperative

	singular	*plural*	*singular*	*plural*	*singular*	*plural*
2ND	δίδου	δίδοτε	ἴστη	ἴστατε	τίθει	τίθετε
3RD	διδότω	διδότωσαν	ἱστάτω	ἱστάτωσαν	τιθέτω	τιθέτωσαν

Present Middle / Passive Imperative

	singular	*plural*	*singular*	*plural*	*singular*	*plural*
2ND	δίδοσο	δίδοσθε	ἴστασο	ἴστασθε	τίθεσο	τίθεσθε
3RD	διδόσθω	διδόσθωσαν	ἱστάτω	ἱστάτωσαν	τιθέσθω	τιθέσθωσαν

Aorist Active Imperative

	singular	*plural*	*singular*	*plural*	*singular*	*plural*
2ND	δός	δότε	στῆθι	στῆτε	θές	θέτε
3RD	δότω	δότωσαν	στήτω	στήτωσαν	θέτω	θέτωσαν

Aorist Middle Imperative

	singular	*plural*	*singular*	*plural*
2ND	δοῦ	δόσθε	θοῦ	θέσθε
3RD	δόσθω	δόσθωσαν	θέσθω	θέσθωσαν

Again, students should observe the second person singular aorist middle imperative's similarity to the present active infinitive. Since the infinitive and the imperative have such different syntactical functions, however, the context ought to suffice to eliminate ambiguity.

The *second aorist active* and *middle imperative* are formed by adding the present active imperative endings to the second aorist stem without the ε- augment.

	Active		Middle	
	singular	*plural*	*singular*	*plural*
2ND	λάβ-ε	λάβ-ετε	λαβ-οῦ	λάβ-εσθε
3RD	λαβ-έτω	λαβ-έτωσαν	λαβ-έσθω	λαβ-έσθωσαν

Uses of the Imperative

The Greek imperative is used in ways quite similar to the English imperative. Indeed, while there are several categories of uses of the imperative, they amount simply to commanding and forbidding.

The tenses in the imperative carry no time value, but do express aspect. The difference in aspect is very slight, however, and may be impossible to render in English. An aorist imperative tends to indicate a command that a certain specific action be done; the aorist imperative focuses on the specificity of the commanded action, without implying anything about its duration or its becoming a habit. A present imperative indicates a command to do an action customarily, or constantly. It focuses on the commanded action as a process, a disposition, or a custom. This distinction does not *always* apply, though, so students should not emphasize aspectual differences unless the context reinforces the aspectual distinction.

Negative commands show the following pattern: prohibitions in the aorist tense typically appear in the subjunctive mood, as explained in Lesson XI; prohibitions in the present tense usually appear in the imperative mood.

Mén

The postpositive particle μέν is often untranslatable. It is sometimes used to mark a phrase that contrasts with another phrase, which is, in turn, marked by δέ. This μέν ... δέ construction may be translated as "on the one hand ... on the other hand," though it is not necessary to translate this μέν and δέ at all.

Study Checklist

Forms of the present active and middle/passive imperative
Forms of the aorist active, middle, and passive imperative
Uses of the imperative
Uses of μέν

Vocabulary

Particles

μέν   on the one hand (or untranslatable postpositive particle)

οὔτε   neither; nor (in an οὔτε ... οὔτε construction)

πῶς   how? (interrogative particle)

τε   and (weaker than καί; postpositive)

Adjective

ὅσος, -η, ον   as much as

Preposition

ἐνώπιον   before (with genitive when used as preposition)

Conjunctions

ἄχρι, ἄχρις   until; as far as (as preposition with genitive)

δίο   therefore

ἕως   until; as far as (as preposition with genitive)

Adverbs

ἐκεῖ   there

ἔξω   without; outside of (as preposition with genitive)

ἔτι   still, yet

εὐθύς, εὐθέως   immediately

ἤδη   already

οὗ   where

ὧδε   here, to here

Exercises

Translate from Greek to English.

1. μὴ *θησαυρίζετε ὑμῖν *θησαυροὺς ἐπὶ τῆς γῆς. (Matthew 6:19)

2. μὴ δῶτε τὸ ἅγιον τοῖς *κυσίν, μηδὲ βάλητε τοὺς *μαργαρίτας ὑμῶν ἐνώπιον τῶν *χοίρων. (as in Matthew 7:6)

3. καὶ ἀποκριθεὶς ὁ Ἰησοῦς εἶπεν αὐτοῖς, Πορευθέντες ἀπαγγείλατε *Ἰωάννῃ ἃ ἀκούετε καὶ βλέπετε. (Matthew 11:4)

4. οὗτός ἐστιν περὶ οὗ γέγραπται, Ἰδοὺ ἐγὼ ἀποστέλλω τὸν ἄγγελόν μου πρὸ προσώπου σου, ὃς *κατασκευάσει τὴν ὁδόν σου *ἔμπροσθέν σου. (Matthew 11:10)

5. Χαίρετε ἐν κυρίῳ *πάντοτε· πάλιν ἐρῶ, χαίρετε. (Philippians 4:4)

6. ἤκουον δὲ αὐτοῦ ἄχρι τούτου τοῦ λόγου καὶ *ἐπῆραν τὴν φωνὴν αὐτῶν λέγοντες, αἶρε ἀπὸ τῆς γῆς τοῦτον τὸν ἄνδρα. (as in Acts 22:22)

7. ὁ δὲ Ἰωάννης ἐκώλυεν αὐτὸν λέγων, Ἐγὼ χρείαν ἔχω ὑπὸ σοῦ βαπτισθῆναι, καὶ σὺ ἔρχῃ πρός με; (as in Matthew 3:14)

8. μὴ *εἰδωλολάτραι γίνεσθε ὥς τινες αὐτῶν, καθὼς γέγρταπται· Ἐκάθισεν ὁ λαὸς φαγεῖν καὶ πεῖν, καὶ ανέστησαν *παίζειν. (cp. 1 Corinthians 10:7)

9. ἐν τούτῳ ἐδοξάσθη ὁ πατήρ μου, ἵνα καρπὸν φέρητε καὶ γένησθε ἐμοὶ μαθηταί. (cp. John 15:8)

10. Ἀσπάσασθε τοὺς ἀδελφοὺς ἐν *φιλήματι ἁγίῳ. (cp. 1 Thessalonians 5:26)

11. Τὸ λοιπὸν προσεύχεσθε, ἀδελφοί, περὶ ἡμῶν, ἵνα ὁ λόγος τοῦ κυρίου *τρέχῃ καὶ δοξάζηται καθὼς καὶ πρὸς ὑμᾶς. (2 Thessalonians 3:1)

12. *Μνημόνευε Ἰησοῦν Χριστὸν ἐγηγερμένον ἐκ νεκρῶν, ἐκ *σπέρματος Δαυίδ, κατὰ τὸ εὐαγγέλιόν μου. (2 Timothy 2:8)

13. ὅτι τὸ εὐαγγέλιον ἡμῶν οὐκ ἐγενήθη εἰς ὑμᾶς ἐν λόγῳ μόνον ἀλλὰ καὶ ἐν δυνάμει καὶ ἐν πνεύματι ἁγίῳ, καθὼς οἴδατε *οἷοι ἐγενήθημεν ἐν ὑμῖν δι᾽ ὑμᾶς. (cp. 1 Thessalonians 1:5)

14. ὁ κύριος αὐτὸν ἤγαγεν ἐκ τῆς φυλακῆς καὶ εἶπεν· Ἀπαγγείλατε Ἰακώβῳ καὶ τοῖς ἀδελφοῖς ταῦτα. καὶ ἐξελθὼν ἐπορεύθη εἰς ἕτερον τόπον. (cp. Acts 12:17)

15. Πάτερ ἡμῶν ὁ ἐν τοῖς οὐρανοῖς, *ἁγιασθήτω τὸ ὄνομά σου, ἐλθέτω ἡ βασιλεία σου, γενηθήτω τὸ θέλημά σου, ὡς ἐν οὐρανῷ καὶ ἐπὶ γῆς. (Matthew 6:9b–10)

16. Τὸν ἄρτον ἡμῶν τὸν *ἐπιούσιον δὸς ἡμῖν *σήμερον· καὶ ἄφες ἡμῖν τὰ *ὀφειλήματα ἡμῶν, ὡς καὶ ἡμεῖς ἀφήκαμεν τοῖς *ὀφειλέταις ἡμῶν. (Matthew 6:11–12)

17. καὶ μὴ εἰσενέγκῃς ἡμᾶς εἰς *πειρασμόν, ἀλλὰ *ῥῦσαι ἡμᾶς ἀπὸ τοῦ πονηροῦ, ὅτι σοῦ ἐστιν ἡ βασιλεία καὶ ἡ δύναμις καὶ ἡ δόξα εἰς τοὺς αἰῶνας. (Matthew 6:13; the words from ὅτι on are of dubious textual authority)

18. Τί τὸ *ὄφελος, ἀδελφοί μου, ἐὰν πίστιν λέγῃ τις ἔχειν, ἔργα δὲ μὴ ἔχῃ; μὴ *δύναται ἡ πίστις σῶσαι αὐτόν; (James 2:14)

19. ὑμῖν δὲ λέγω τοῖς λοιποῖς τοῖς ἐν *Θυατείροις, ὅσοι οὐκ ἔχουσιν τὴν *διδαχὴν ταύτην, οἵτινες οὐκ ἔγνωσαν τὰ *βαθέα τοῦ *Σατανᾶ, ὡς λέγουσιν. (Revelation 2:24)

20. Μὴ *πολλοὶ διδάσκαλοι γίνεσθε, ἀδελφοί μου, εἰδότες ὅτι *μεῖζον *κρίμα λημψόμεθα. (James 3:1)

Translate from English to Greek.

1. Let her write these words which I am speaking to you (pl) so that they may be given to the remaining people in the age which is coming.

2. Do not hinder (pl) the blind to be healed by the holy prophet who is coming into the city.

3. After he prayed in the temple, the high priest departed for the sea.

4. If you (sg) entered the wilderness, your eyes would see and your ears would hear well the voice of the spirit.

5. Remain (pl) with the children by the sea in order that you may receive the salvation which the Lord will bring to them and to you.

6. Let them believe the last prophet because he speaks the truth to the people.

7. Come (sg) to the assembly which has been healed by the only apostle of the kingdom of peace.

8. Proclaim (pl) life to the ones who are dying just as you proclaim it to the whole world.

9. Do not judge (pl) the world except as God judges the world so that salvation may come to the people.

10. She was faithful to the commandments of the Lord while she had the writings of the apostles and the prophets who came before her.

XXII

Contract Verbs

There is a category of Greek verbs that have stems ending in the short vowels α, ε, or o. Whereas stems that end in either a consonant or a long vowel simply add a connecting vowel and tense ending, stems that end in short vowels combine, or *contract*, with the connecting vowel before adding the tense endings. This is the same phenomenon encountered when verbs that begin with α, ε, or o take an augment. The two short vowels contract into one long vowel (or diphthong). The oddity of contract verbs is restricted to the formation of their present system. The remaining principal parts are formed predictably by lengthening the stem vowel and adding the tense endings.

Students should note, however, that the lexical form of these verbs is the uncontracted form, even though that form will never be seen in actual use. For instance, although the first person singular present active indicative form of a verb may be ποιῶ, the lexical form is ποιέω. Keeping the lexical form uncontracted helps those who consult a lexicon understand why the word they are looking up takes the particular forms it does.

Contract Verbs in -εω

Contract verbs whose stems end in -εω show the same pattern of contraction that we saw with respect to augmentation:

ε + ε = ει	ε + ο = ου	ε + ω = ω
ε + ου = ου	ε + η = η	ε + η = η

In other words, short ε added to short vowels forms a diphthong, either ει or ου; ε added to long vowels or diphthongs is absorbed into the long vowel/diphthong.

Present Active Indicative

	singular	plural
1ST	ποιῶ	ποιοῦμεν
2ND	ποιεῖς	ποιεῖτε
3RD	ποιεῖ	ποιοῦσι(ν)
INF	ποιεῖν	

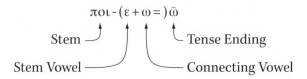

$$\pi ο ι\text{-}(\varepsilon + \omega =)\,\hat{\omega}$$

Stem — Stem Vowel — Connecting Vowel — Tense Ending

Present Middle/Passive Indicative

	singular	plural
1ST	ποιοῦμαι	ποιούμεθα
2ND	ποιῇ	ποιεῖσθε
3RD	ποιεῖται	ποιοῦνται
INF	ποιεῖσθαι	

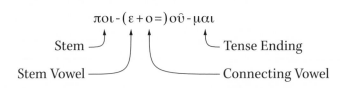

$$\pi ο ι\text{-}(\varepsilon + ο =)\,ο\hat{υ}\text{-}μαι$$

Stem — Stem Vowel — Connecting Vowel — Tense Ending

	Singular	Plural		Singular	Plural
	Imperfect Active Indicative			*Imperfect Middle/Passive Indicative*	
1ST	ἐποίουν	ἐποιοῦμεν		ἐποιούμην	ἐποιούμεθα
2ND	ἐποίεις	ἐποιεῖτε		ἐποιοῦ	ἐποιεῖσθε
3RD	ἐποίει	ἐποίουν		ἐποιεῖτο	ἐποιοῦντο

	Singular	Plural	Singular	Plural
	Present Active Subjunctive		*Present Middle/Passive Subjunctive*	
1ST	ποιῶ	ποιῶμεν	ποιῶμαι	ποιώμεθα
2ND	ποιῇς	ποιῆτε	ποιῇ	ποιῆσθε
3RD	ποιῇ	ποιῶσι(ν)	ποιῆται	ποιῶνται
	Present Active Imperative		*Present Middle/Passive Imperative*	
2ND	ποίει	ποιεῖτε	ποιοῦ	ποιεῖσθε
3RD	ποιείτω	ποιείτωσαν	ποιείσθω	ποιείσθωσαν

The future principle part of ποιέω is ποιήωσω; the aorist principal part is ἐποίησα; the perfect active is πεποίηκα; the perfect middle/passive, πεποίημαι; and the aorist passive, ἐποιήθην. Note how the stem vowel (ε) lengthens, which is the only adjustment that takes place.

Two-Ending Adjectives

Some adjectives have identical masculine and feminine forms, but nevertheless have different neuter endings. This means that it will often be difficult or impossible to ascertain the gender of an adjective's referent from the form of the adjective. Two common examples of this sort of adjective are αἰώνιος, the adjective meaning "eternal," and ἁμαρτωλός, an adjective meaning "sinful" (or when used substantively, "sinful person," "sinner").

	Singular		Plural	
	M/F	N	M/F	N
N	ἁμαρτωλός	ἁμαρτωλόν	ἁμαρτωλοί	ἁμαρτωλά
G	ἁμαρτωλοῦ	ἁμαρτωλοῦ	ἁμαρτωλῶν	ἁμαρτωλῶν
D	ἁμαρτωλῷ	ἁμαρτωλῷ	ἁμαρτωλοῖς	ἁμαρτωλοῖς
A	ἁμαρτωλόν	ἁμαρτωλόν	ἁμαρτωλούς	ἁμαρτωλά

Study Checklist

Forms of contract verbs in -εω (learn all principal parts)
Two-ending adjectives

Vocabulary

Verbs

αἰτέω *αἰτέω, αἰτήσω, ᾔτησα, ᾔτηκα, ᾔτημαι, ᾐτήθην*   I ask;
I request (middle)

ἀκολουθέω *ἀκολουθέω, ἀκολουθήσω, ἠκολούθησα, ἠκολούθηκα,
ἠκολούθημαι, ἠκολουθήθην*   I follow

δοκέω *δοκέω, δόξω, ἔδοξα, —, —, —*   I think, I seem

ζητέω *ζητέω, ζητήσω, ἐζήτησα, —, —, ἐζητήθην*   I seek

θεωρέω *θεωρέω, θεωρήσω, ἐθεώρησα, τεθεώρηκα, —, —*   I look at,
I behold

καλέω *καλέω, καλέσω, ἐκάλεσα, κέκληκα, κέκλημαι, ἐκλήθην*   I call (note
unexpected principal parts)

λαλέω *λαλέω, λαλήσω, ἐλάλησα, λελάληκα, λελάλημαι, ἐλαλήθην*   I speak,
I say

μαρτυρέω *μαρτυρέω, μαρτυρήσω, ἐμαρτύρησα, μεμαρτύρηκα,
μεμαρτύρημα, ἐμαρτύρηθην*   I testify, I witness

παρακαλέω *παρακαλέω, παρακαλέσω, παρεκάλεσα, παρακέκληκα,
παρακέκλημαι, παρεκλήθην*   I exhort, I counsel, I comfort

περιπατέω *περιπατέω, περιπατήσω, περιεπάτησα, —, —, περιεπατήθην*
I walk (metaphor for "I live")

ποιέω *ποιέω, ποιήσω, ἐποίησσα, πεποίηκα, πεποίημαι, —*   I do, I make

τηρέω *τηρέω, τηρήσω, ἐτήρησα, τετήρηκα, τετήρημαι, ἐτηρήθην*   I keep

φοβέομαι *φοβέομαι, —, —, —, —, ἐφοβήθην*   I am frightened

Adjectives

αἰώνιος, -ον   eternal

ἁμαρτωλός, -όν   sinful (used substantively, "sinner")

Exercises

Translate from Greek to English.

1. ἐὰν μείνητε ἐν ἐμοὶ καὶ τὰ ῥήματά μου ἐν ὑμῖν μείνῃ, ὃ ἐὰν θέλητε αἰτήσασθε καὶ γενήσεται ὑμῖν. (John 15:7)

2. λαλήσας ὁ θεὸς τοῖς πατράσιν ἐν τοῖς προφήταις, ἐπ᾽ ἐσχάτου τῶν ἡμερῶν τούτων ἐλάλησεν ἡμῖν ἐν υἱῷ. (as in Hebrews 1:1–2)

3. οὕτως λαλεῖτε καὶ οὕτως ποιεῖτε ὡς διὰ νόμου *ἐλευθερίας μέλλοντες κρίνεσθαι. (James 2:12)

4. οἱ γὰρ ἄρχοντες οὐκ εἰσὶν φόβος τῷ ἀγαθῷ ἔργῳ ἀλλὰ τῷ κακῷ. θέλεις δὲ μὴ φοβεῖσθαι τὴν ἐξουσίαν; τὸ ἀγαθὸν ποίει. (Romans 13:3)

5. Λέγω δέ, πνεύματι περιπατεῖτε καὶ *ἐπιθυμίαν σαρκὸς μὴ *τελέσητε. (cp. Galatians 5:16)

6. τοῦτο *φρονεῖτε ἐν ὑμῖν ὃ καὶ ἐν Χριστῷ Ἰησοῦ. (Philippians 2:5)

7. εἰ οὖν ἠγέρθητε σὺν τῷ Χριστῷ, τὰ *ἄνω ζητεῖτε, οὗ ὁ Χριστός ἐστιν ἐν δεξιᾷ τοῦ θεοῦ καθήμενος· τὰ *ἄνω *φρονεῖτε, μὴ τὰ ἐπὶ τῆς γῆς. (cp. Colossians 3:1–2)

8. Διὰ τοῦτο καὶ ἡμεῖς, ἀφ᾽ ἧς ἡμέρας ἠκούσαμεν, οὐ *παυόμεθα ὑπὲρ ὑμῶν προσευχόμενοι καὶ αἰτούμενοι. (Colossians 1:9)

9. ἄρα οὖν, ἀδελφοί, στήκετε, καὶ *κρατεῖτε τὰς *παραδόσεις ἃς ἐδιδάχθητε *εἴτε διὰ λόγου εἴτε δι᾽ *ἐπιστολῆς ἡμῶν. (2 Thessalonians 2:15)

10. Οὗτός ἐστιν ὁ ἐλθὼν δι᾽ ὕδατος καὶ αἵματος, Ἰησοῦς Χριστός· οὐκ ἐν τῷ ὕδατι μόνον ἀλλ᾽ ἐν τῷ ὕδατι καὶ ἐν τῷ αἵματι· καὶ τὸ πνεῦμά ἐστιν τὸ μαρτυροῦν, ὅτι τὸ πνεῦμά ἐστιν ἡ ἀλήθεια. (1 John 5:6)

11. μὴ γὰρ *οἰέσθω ὁ ἄνθρωπος ἐκεῖνος ὅτι λήμψεταί τι παρὰ τοῦ κυρίου. (James 1:7)

12. μὴ λαλεῖτε κατὰ ἀλλήλων, ἀδελφοί· ὁ λαλῶν κατὰ ἀδελφοῦ ἢ κρίνων τὸν ἀδελφὸν αὐτοῦ λαλεῖ κατὰ νόμου καὶ κρίνει νόμον· εἰ δὲ νόμον κρίνεις, οὐκ εἶ ποιῶν νόμον ἀλλὰ κρίνων. (cp. James 4:11)

13. οἴδατε ὅτι ὡς πατὴρ ἐν μέσῳ τὰ τέκνα αὐτοῦ ἐγενήθημεν, παρακαλοῦντες ὑμᾶς καὶ μαρτυρόμενοι εἰς τὸ περιπατεῖν ὑμᾶς ἀξίως τοῦ θεοῦ. (as in 1 Thessalonians 2:11–12)

14. καὶ ὃ ἐὰν αἰτῶμεν λαμβάνομεν ἀπ᾽ αὐτοῦ, ὅτι τὰς ἐντολὰς αὐτοῦ τηροῦμεν καὶ τὰ ἀρεστὰ ἐνώπιον αὐτοῦ ποιοῦμεν. (1 John 3:22)

15. οὕτως λαλεῖτε καὶ οὕτως ποιεῖτε ὡς διὰ νόμου *ἐλευθερίας μέλλοντες κρίνεσθαι. (James 2:12)

16. μακάριοι οἱ εἰρηνοποιοί, ὅτι αὐτοὶ υἱοὶ θεοῦ *κληθήσονται. (Matthew 5:9)

17. καὶ εὐθὺς ἀναβαίνων ἐκ τοῦ ὕδατος εἶδεν σχιζόμενος τοὺς οὐρανοὺς καὶ τὸ πνεῦμα ὡς περιστερὰν καταβαῖνον εἰς αὐτόν. (Mark 1:10)

18. καὶ ἐδίδασκεν αὐτοὺς ἐν παραβολαῖς *πολλά, καὶ ἔλεγεν αὐτοῖς ἐν τῇ διδαχῇ αὐτοῦ, Ἀκούετε. ἰδοὺ ἐξῆλθεν ὁ σπείρων σπεῖραι. καὶ ἐγένετο ἐν τῷ σπείρειν ὃ μὲν ἔπεσεν παρὰ τὴν ὁδόν, καὶ ἦλθεν τὰ *πετεινὰ καὶ ἔφαγεν αὐτό. (cp. Mark 4:2–4)

19. ἐργάζεσθε μὴ τὸν ἄρτον τὸν *ἀπολλύμενον ἀλλὰ τὸν ἄρτον τὸν μένοντα εἰς ζωὴν αἰώνιον, ὃν ὁ υἱὸς τοῦ ἀνθρώπου ὑμῖν δώσει· ἐπὶ γὰρ τούτου δέδωκεν τὴν ἐπαγγελίαν αὐτοῦ ὁ θεός. (cp. John 6:27)

20. ὃς ἐὰν οὖν λύσῃ *μίαν τῶν ἐντολῶν τούτων τῶν μικρῶν, καὶ διδάξει οὕτως τοὺς ἀνθρώπους, μικρὸς κληθήσεται ἐν τῇ βασιλείᾳ τῶν οὐρανῶν· ὃς δ᾽ ἂν ποιήσῃ καὶ διδάξῃ, οὗτος *μέγας κληθήσεται ἐν τῇ βασιλείᾳ τῶν οὐρανῶν. (cp. Matthew 5:19)

Translate from English to Greek.

1. We beheld the Son of God descending from the heavens, and we cried out because we were frightened.

2. The men make bread each day for the women who take it to the blind.

3. Walk in the light as Jesus, and the peace of God will comfort you (sg).

4. Speaking to the crowd about the children, the apostle was testifying on behalf of them because of their sin.

5. Let them seek the good things which come from God, who made the land and the sky.

6. The men and the women from the city followed Jesus as he walked beside the sea in order that they might be healed by him.

7. While Jesus walked, the blind ones called to him and cried out, saying, "Lord, heal us."

8. The child asks her teacher about the day because she wants to know.

9. While the woman was seeking the foundation of hope, the high priest was hindering the people to enter into the temple.

10. The people were baptized in the sea by the holy one of God, who places joy in their hearts.

XXIII

Optative Mood

The optative mood mediates between the subjunctive, which expresses contingency, and the imperative, which expresses volition. The optative, then, is the mood that expresses wishing or conjecturing. The function of the optative overlaps to a great extent with the subjunctive, and thus the subjunctive gradually supplanted the optative in Hellenistic Greek.

The optative mood occurs about 65 times in the New Testament. Roughly a quarter of those happen when Paul answers his rhetorical questions with the phrase μὴ γένοιτο ("Let it not be!"). Another dozen optatives are εἴη, the third person singular present active optative form of εἰμί, "may she/he/it be." These two examples illustrate the distinctive feature of the optative — a diphthong using ι as the connecting vowel. The optative mood, then, uses a diphthong formed with ι and appends the secondary endings to the verb stem without any augments, since this is a non-indicative form. The first person singular form of the optative typically retains the archaic -μι ending (familiar from εἰμί and μι verbs).

	Singular	*Plural*
	Present Active Optative	
1ST	λύ-οιμι	λύ-οιμεν
2ND	λύ-οις	λύ-οιτε
3RD	λύ-οι	λύ-οιεν
	Εἰμί	
1ST	εἴην	εἴημεν
2ND	εἴης	εἴητε
3RD	εἴη	εἴησαν

	Singular	Plural

Present Middle/Passive Optative

1ST	λυ-οίμην	λυ-οίμεθα
2ND	λύ-οιο	λύ-οισθε
3RD	λύ-οιτο	λύ-οιντο

First Aorist Active Optative

1ST	λύσ-αιμι	λύσ-αιμεν
2ND	λύσ-αις	λύσ-αιτε
3RD	λύσ-αι	λύσ-αιεν

First Aorist Middle Optative

1ST	λυσ-αίμην	λυσ-αίμεθα
2ND	λύσ-αιο	λύσ-αισθε
3RD	λύσ-αιτο	λύσ-αιντο

First Aorist Passive Optative

1ST	λυθ-είην	λυθ-είημεν
2ND	λυθ-είης	λυθ-είητε
3RD	λυθ-είη	λυθ-είησαν

Second Aorist Active Optative

1ST	βάλ-οιμι	βάλ-οιμεν
2ND	βάλ-οις	βάλ-οιτε
3RD	βάλ-οι	βάλ-οιεν

Second Aorist Middle Optative

1ST	βαλ-οίμην	βαλ-οίμεθα
2ND	βάλ-οιο	βάλ-οισθε
3RD	βάλ-οιτο	βάλ-οιντο

Second Aorist Passive Optative

(not found in the NT)

Uses of the Optative

The optative mood has three main functions in the New Testament. It appears in the context of *wishes*, usually declarative or exclamatory, such as Paul's characteristic μὴ γένοιτο. Another example:

> χάρις ὑμῖν καὶ εἰρήνη   *May* grace and peace *be multiplied*
> πληθυνθείη.   for you. (1 Peter 1:2)

The optative appears in *deliberative* clauses, usually either directly or indirectly interrogative, often with ἄν.

> διελογίζετο ποταπὸς   She was wondering what kind of
> εἴη ὁ ἀσπασμὸς οὗτος   greeting this *might be.* (Luke 1:29)

The optative appears in *future less probable* (fourth class) conditional sentences. The future less probable conditional expresses the author's assumption that the conditional sentence is hypothetical, but unlikely to be fulfilled. This usage is complicated by the fact that there is no complete example of a future less probable conditional in the New Testament. The form of a future less probable conditional requires εἰ with an optative verb in the protasis and ἄν with an optative verb in the apodosis. The New Testament preserves several partial future less probable conditionals in which either the protasis or the apodosis is given.

> εἰ καὶ *πάσχοιτε* διὰ δικαιοσυνήν,   If indeed you *were to suffer* on account
> [εἴητε] μακάριοι.   of righteousness, [you would be] blessed.
> (1 Peter 3:14)

Third Declension Adjectives

Some adjectives are called "third declension" adjectives because their paradigms diverge from other declensions in ways similar to the paradigms for third declension nouns.

		Singular		Plural	
		M/F	N	M/F	N
N		ἀληθής	ἀληθές	ἀληθεῖς	ἀληθῆ
G		ἀληθοῦς	ἀληθοῦς	ἀληθῶν	ἀληθῶν
D		ἀληθεῖ	ἀληθεῖ	ἀληθέσι(ν)	ἀληθέσι(ν)
A		ἀληθῆ	ἀληθές	ἀληθεῖς	ἀληθῆ

	Singular			Plural		
	M	F	N	M	F	N
N	εὐθύς	εὐθεῖα	εὐθύ	εὐθεῖς	εὐθεῖαι	εὐθέα
G	εὐθέος	εὐθείας	εὐθέος	εὐθέων	εὐθειῶν	εὐθέων
D	εὐθεῖ	εὐθείᾳ	εὐθεῖ	εὐθέσι(ν)	εὐθείαις	εὐθέσι(ν)
A	εὐθύν	εὐθεῖαν	εὐθύ	εὐθεῖς	εὐθείας	εὐθέα

Study Checklist

Forms of the optative

Uses of the optative
Wishes or hopes
Deliberative (questions)
Future less probable conditional

The form and meaning of the future less probable conditional
Εἰ + optative in protasis, optative + ἄν in apodosis
Hypothetical and unlikely to be fulfilled

Third declension adjectives

Vocabulary

Verbs

εὐλογέω εὐλογέω, εὐλογήσω, εὐλόγησα, εὐλόγηκα, εὐλόγημαι, εὐλογήθην
I bless

εὐχαριστέω εὐχαριστέω, εὐχαριστήσῶ, εὐχαρίστησα, —, —, εὐχαριστήθην
I give thanks

κατοικέω κατοικέω, —, κατῴκησα, —, —, — I inhabit

κρατέω κρατέω, κρατήσω, ἐκράτησα, κεκράτηκα, κεκράτημαι, —
I grasp

προσκυνέω προσκυνέω, προσκυνήσω, προσεκύνησα,
προσκεκύνηκα, —, — I worship

προσφέρω προσφέρω, προσοίσω, προσήνεγκα/προσήνεγκον/προσένεικα,
προσενήνοχα, —, προσηνέχθην/προσηνείχθην I bring to, I offer

ὑπάρχω ὑπάρχω, ὑπάρξομαι, ὑπηρξάμην, —, —, — I am, I subsist (τὰ
ὑπάρχοντα [nominative plural participle] "one's belongings")

φωνέω φωνέω, φωνήσω, ἐφώνησα, —, —, ἐφωνήθην I sound, I call out

Adjectives

ἀληθής, -ές true

εὐθύς, -εῖα, -ύ straight (the adjectival form developed alongside the
adverbial form; see lesson XXI)

Exercises

Translate from Greek to English.

1. *ἐνένευον δὲ τῷ πατρὶ αὐτοῦ, τί ἂν θέλοι καλεῖσθαι αὐτό.
(cp. Luke 1:62)

2. οὗτοι δὲ οἱ ἄνθρωποι ἦσαν ἐν *Βεροίᾳ, οἵτινες ἐδέξαντο τὸν λόγον
μετὰ πάσης *προθυμίας, καθ᾽ ἡμέραν *ἀνακρίνοντες τὰς γραφὰς
εἰ ἔχοι ταῦτα οὕτως. (cp. Acts 17:11)

3. ἀλλ᾽ εἰ καὶ *πάσχοιτε διὰ δικαιοσύνην, μακάριοι. τὸν δὲ φόβον
αὐτῶν μὴ φοβηθῆτε. (1 Peter 3:14)

4. αὐτοὶ δὲ *ἐπλήσθησαν *ἀνοίας, καὶ *ἐλάλουν πρὸς ἀλλήλους τί ἂν
ποιήσαιεν τῷ Ἰησοῦ. (cp. Luke 6:11)

5. ὁ δὲ θεὸς τῆς ἐλπίδος *πληρώσαι ὑμᾶς χαρᾶς καὶ εἰρήνης ἐν τῷ πιστεύειν ὑμᾶς, εἰς τὸ *περισσεύειν ὑμᾶς ἐν τῇ ἐλπίδι ἐν δυνάμει πνεύματος ἁγίου. (cp. Romans 15:13)

6. αὐτὸς δὲ ὁ θεὸς καὶ πατὴρ ἡμῶν καὶ ὁ κύριος ἡμῶν Ἰησοῦς *εὐλογήσαι τὴν ὁδὸν ἡμῶν πρὸς ὑμᾶς. (cp. 1 Thessalonians 3:11)

7. παρακαλέσαι ὑμῶν τὰς καρδίας καὶ *στηρίξαι ἐν ἑκάστῳ ἔργῳ καὶ λόγῳ ἀγαθῷ. (2 Thessalonians 2:17)

8. Ὁ δὲ κύριος *κατευθύναι ὑμῶν τὰς καρδίας εἰς τὴν ἀγάπην τοῦ θεοῦ καὶ εἰς τὴν *ὑπομονὴν τοῦ Χριστοῦ. (2 Thessalonians 3:5)

9. καὶ ἀποκριθεὶς εἶπεν αὐτῇ, *Μηκέτι εἰς τὸν αἰῶνα ἐκ σοῦ *μηδεὶς καρπὸν φάγοι. καὶ ἤκουον οἱ μαθηταὶ αὐτοῦ. (Mark 11:14)

10. Γέγραπται γὰρ ἐν *βίβλῳ *ψαλμῶν, Γενηθήτω ἡ οἰκία αὐτοῦ ἔρημος καὶ μὴ ἔστω ὁ *κατοικῶν ἐν αὐτῇ, καί, Τὴν *ἐπισκοπὴν αὐτοῦ λαβέτω ἕτερος. (cp. Acts 1:20)

11. οὐ *παύομαι *εὐχαριστῶν ὑπὲρ ὑμῶν *μνείαν ποιούμενος ἐπὶ τῶν *προσευχῶν μου, ἵνα ὁ θεὸς τοῦ κυρίου ἡμῶν Ἰησοῦ Χριστοῦ, ὁ πατὴρ τῆς δόξης, δώῃ ὑμῖν πνεῦμα σοφίας καὶ *ἀποκαλύψεως ἐν *ἐπιγνώσει αὐτοῦ. (Ephesians 1:16–17)

12. δώῃ αὐτῷ ὁ κύριος εὑρεῖν *ἔλεος παρὰ κυρίου ἐν ἐκείνῃ τῇ ἡμέρᾳ. (2 Timothy 1:18)

13. δοκοῦντος δὲ τοῦ λαοῦ καὶ *διαλογιζομένων τῶν ἀνθρώπων ἐν ταῖς καρδίαις αὐτῶν περὶ τοῦ Ἰωάννου, *μήποτε αὐτὸς εἴη ὁ Χριστός. (cp. Luke 3:15)

14. Ὡς δὲ ἐν ἑαυτῷ *διηπόρει ὁ Πέτρος τί ἂν εἴη τὸ *ὅραμα ὃ εἶδεν, ἰδοὺ οἱ ἄνδρες οἱ ἀπεσταλμένοι ὑπὸ τοῦ *Κορνηλίου *διερωτήσαντες τὴν οἰκίαν τοῦ *Σίμωνος *ἐπέστησαν ἐπὶ τὸν *πυλῶνα. (Acts 10:17)

15. Οἶδά σου τὰ ἔργα, ὅτι οὔτε *ψυχρὸς εἶ οὔτε *ζεστός. (Revelation 3:15)

16. καὶ προσεύξασθε ὑπὲρ ἐμοῦ, ἵνα μοι δοθῇ λόγος ἐν *ἀνοίξει τοῦ στόματός μου, ἐν *παρρησίᾳ *γνωρίσαι τὸ *μυστήριον τοῦ εὐαγγελίου. (cp. Ephesians 6:19)

17. *ἔλεος ὑμῖν καὶ εἰρήνη καὶ ἀγάπη *πληθυνθείη. (Jude 2)

18. ὁ δὲ ἀποκριθεὶς εἶπεν, Γέγραπται, Οὐκ ἐπ᾽ ἄρτῳ μόνῳ *ζήσεται ὁ ἄνθρωπος, ἀλλ᾽ ἐπὶ τοῖς ῥήματι τοῖς πορευομένοις διὰ στόματος θεοῦ. (cp. Matthew 4:4)

19. *καταρτίσαι ὑμᾶς ἐν ἑκάστι ἀγαθῷ εἰς τὸ ποιῆσαι τὸ θέλημα αὐτοῦ, ποιῶν ἐν ἡμῖν τὸ *εὐάρεστον ἐνώπιον αὐτοῦ διὰ Ἰησοῦ Χριστοῦ, ᾧ ἡ δόξα εἰς τοῦ αἰῶνας [τῶν αἰώνων]· ἀμήν. (Hebrews 13:21)

20. *νόει ὃ λέγω· δώσει γάρ σοι ὁ κύριος *σύνεσιν ἐν πᾶσιν. (2 Timothy 2:7)

Translate from English to Greek.

1. Let us worship the Lord in his temple while he gives us life and peace.

2. The high priest blessed what the crowd offered before he prayed for them.

3. The people who inhabit the earth do not know that God has placed them on the earth.

4. We exist to worship God, who gives us our belongings.

5. You (pl) cannot grasp salvation by yourself, but only as God gives it to you.

6. If you (sg) spoke a true word, we could find the true path of righteousness.

7. We saw the light in the house, but we had fear concerning who was there.

8. At the right time, the Christ entered into the world and died for the people, but the people did not see his love.

9. You all called from the sea, but we did not hear you.

10. We cry out in the night because we are not near the city.

XXIV

More Contract Verbs

Many of the most common contract verbs end in -εω, but a considerable number end in -αω and -οω. Bear in mind that: the peculiarities of the contract are restricted to the present system; the stem vowel lengthens for the non-present forms; a contract verb in the present system does not entail any peculiarities in meaning or translation.

Contract Verbs in -αω and -οω

Contract verbs whose stems end in -αω and -οω exhibit the following patterns of contraction:

$$\alpha + \eta = \alpha \qquad \alpha + ου = ω \qquad \alpha + ει = ᾳ \ (or\ ᾱ)$$
$$\alpha + ε = \alpha \qquad \alpha + ο = ω \qquad \alpha + ω = ω \qquad \alpha + \eta = \alpha$$

$$ο + \eta = οι \qquad ο + ου = ου \qquad ο + ει = οι \ (or\ ου)$$
$$ο + ε = ου \qquad ο + ο = ου \qquad ο + ω = ω \qquad ο + \eta = ω$$

These contraction patterns are somewhat more complicated than the -εω patterns. The ει contraction pattern, wherein the customary contraction, ᾳ or οι, is disrupted for infinitives, where the contraction changes to long α and ου. For the rest, ο with short vowels usually forms ου; ο with long vowels forms ω; and ο with ι-diphtongs forms οι. The process operates somewhat differently with α. When α contracts with ε or η, it forms a long α; with ο, ου, or ω, an ω; and with ι-diphthongs, α becomes ᾳ.

Present Active Indicative

	singular	plural	singular	plural
1ST	ἀγαπῶ	ἀγαπῶμεν	πληρῶ	πληροῦμεν
2ND	ἀγαπᾷς	ἀγαπᾶτε	πληροῖς	πληροῦτε
3RD	ἀγαπᾷ	ἀγαπῶσι(ν)	πληροῖ	πληροῦσι(ν)
INF	ἀγαπᾶν		πληροῦν	

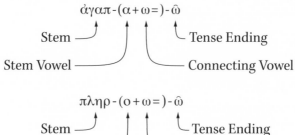

Present Middle / Passive Indicative

	singular	plural		singular	plural
1ST	ἀγαπῶμαι	ἀγαπώμεθα		πληροῦμαι	πληρούμεθα
2ND	ἀγαπᾷ	ἀγαπᾶσθε		πληροῖ	πληροῦσθε
3RD	ἀγαπᾶται	ἀγαπῶνται		πληροῦται	πληροῦνται
INF	ἀγαπᾶσθαι			πληροῦσθαι	

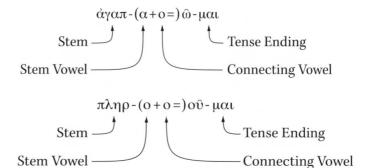

Present Active Subjunctive

	singular	plural		singular	plural
1ST	ἀγαπῶ	ἀγαπῶμεν		πληρῶ	πληρῶμεν
2ND	ἀγαπᾷς	ἀγαπᾶτε		πληροῖς	πληρῶτε
3RD	ἀγαπᾷ	ἀγαπῶσι(ν)		πληροῖ	πληρῶσι(ν)

	Singular	Plural		Singular	Plural

Present Middle/Passive Subjunctive

1ST	ἀγαπῶμαι	ἀγαπώμεθα		πληρῶμαι	πληρώμεν
2ND	ἀγαπᾷ	ἀγαπᾶσθε		πληροῖ	πληρῶσθε
3RD	ἀγαπᾶται	ἀγαπῶνται		πληρῶται	πληρῶνται

Present Active Imperative

| 2ND | ἄγαπα | ἀγαπᾶτε | | πλήρου | πληροῦτε |
| 3RD | ἀγαπάτω | ἀγαπάτωσαν | | πληρούτω | πληρούτωσαν |

Present Middle/Passive Imperative

| 2ND | ἀγαπῶ | ἀγαπᾶσθε | | πληροῦ | πληροῦσθε |
| 3RD | ἀγαπάσθω | ἀγαπάσθωσαν | | πληρούσθω | πληρούσθωσαν |

Imperfect Active Indicative

1ST	ἠγάπων	ἠγαπῶμεν		ἐπλήρουν	ἐπληροῦμεν
2ND	ἠγάπας	ἠγαπᾶτε		ἐπλήρους	ἐπληροῦτε
3RD	ἠγάπα	ἠγάπων		ἐπλήρου	ἐπλήρουν

Imperfect Middle/Passive Indicative

1ST	ἠγαπώμην	ἠγαπώμεθα		ἐπληρούμην	ἐπληρούμεθα
2ND	ἠγαπῶ	ἠγαπᾶσθε		ἐπληροῦ	ἐπληροῦσθε
3RD	ἠγαπᾶτο	ἠγαπῶντο		ἐπληροῦτο	ἐπληροῦντο

The future principle part of ἀγαπάω is ἀγαπήσω, of πληρόω is πληρώσω; the aorist principal parts are ἠγάπησα and ἐπλήρωσα; the perfect active parts are ἠγάπηκα and πεπλήρωκα; the perfect middle/passive, ἠγάπημαι and πεπλήρωμαι; and the aorist passive, ἠγαπήθην and ἐπληρώθην. Note how the stem vowels α and ο lengthen.

Unusual Adjectives

Some adjectives do not follow the familiar patterns. These forms must simply be learned. The paradigm of πᾶς, πᾶσα, πᾶν ("every, all"):

	Singular			Plural		
	M	F	N	M	F	N
N	πᾶς	πᾶσα	πᾶν	πάντες	πᾶσαι	πάντα
G	παντός	πάσης	παντός	πάντων	πασῶν	πάντων
D	παντί	πάσῃ	παντί	πᾶσι(ν)	πάσαις	πᾶσι(ν)
A	πάντα	πᾶσαν	πᾶν	πάντας	πάσας	πάντα

Translating πᾶς can be tricky. When it is used in the predicate position, πᾶς should usually be translated "all" (πᾶς ὁ νόμος, "all the law"). When used in the attributive position, πᾶς should be translated "whole" (ὁ πᾶς κόσμος, "the whole world"). With anarthrous nouns, πᾶς may be translated "every" (singular nouns) or "all" (plural nouns). When used in this way, πᾶς is the functional equivalent of a definite article, and students should not be surprised to encounter a construction such as πᾶς ἄνθρωπος ὁ περιπατῶν ἐν τῇ ἀληθείᾳ ("every person who walks in the truth") or πάντες ἄνθρωποι οἱ περιπατοῦντες ἐν τῇ ἀληθείᾳ ("all people who walk in the truth"). Finally, πᾶς can be used substantively to mean "every person" and πᾶν, "everything" (singular); πάντες to mean "all people" and πάντα, "all things." If students attend to the number of the adjective and to the function of the noun it modifies, there should be little ambiguity.

The singular of πολύς is usually translated "much," the plural as "many." As with πᾶς, observe the number of the adjective carefully.

	Singular			Plural		
	M	F	N	M	F	N
N	πολύς	πολλή	πολύ	πολλοί	πολλαί	πολλά
G	πολλοῦ	πολλῆς	πολλοῦ	πολλῶν	πολλῶν	πολλῶν
D	πολλῷ	πολλῇ	πολλῷ	πολλοῖς	πολλαῖς	πολλοῖς
A	πολύν	πολλήν	πολύ	πολλούς	πολλάς	πολλά

The paradigm of μέγας, μεγάλη, μέγα ("large, great"):

| | *Singular* | | | *Plural* | | |
	M	F	N	M	F	N
N	μέγας	μεγάλη	μέγα	μεγάλοι	μεγάλαι	μεγάλα
G	μεγάλου	μεγάλης	μεγάλου	μεγάλων	μεγάλων	μεγάλων
D	μεγάλῳ	μεγάλη	μεγάλῳ	μεγάλοις	μεγάλαις	μεγάλοις
A	μέγαν	μεγάλην	μέγα	μεγάλους	μεγάλας	μεγάλα

Study Checklist

Forms of contract verbs in -αω and -οω (learn all the principal parts)

Unusual adjectives

Translating πᾶς and πολύς

Vocabulary

Verbs

ἀγαπάω *ἀγαπάω, ἀγαπήσω, ἠγάπησα, ἠγάπηκα, ἠγάπημαι, ἠγαπήθην*
I love

γεννάω *γεννάω, γεννήσω, ἐγέννησα, γεγέννηκα, γεγέννημαι, ἐγεννήθην*
I beget

ἐπερωτάω *ἐπερωτάω, ἐπερωτήσω, ἐπερώτησα,* —, —, —   I ask, I entreat

ἐρωτάω *ἐρωτάω, ἐρωτήσω, ἠρώτησα, ἠρώτηκα,* —, —   I ask, I request

ζάω *ζάω, ζήσω, ἔζησα, ἔζηκα,* —, —   I live (irregular; its original form
was ζήω)

ὁράω *ὁράω, ὄψομαι, εἶδον, ἑώρακα,* —, *ὤφθην*   I see (irregular)

πληρόω *πληρόω, πληρώσω, ἐπλήρωσα, πεπλήρωκα, πεπλήρωμαι,*
ἐπληρώθην   I fill, I fulfill

σταυρόω *σταυρόω, σταυρώσω, ἐσταύρωσα, ἐσταύρωκα, ἐσταύρωμαι,*
ἐσταυρώθην   I crucify

τιμάω *τιμάω, τιμήσω, ἐτίμησα, τετίμηκα, τετίμημαι, ἐτιμήθην*   I honor

φανερόω *φανερόω, φανερώσω, ἐφανέρωσα, πεφανέρωκα, πεφανέρωμαι,*
ἐφανερώθην   I make manifest

φιλέω *φιλέω, φιλήσω, ἐφίλησα, πεφίληκα, πεφίλημαι, ἐφιλήθην*   I like

Adjectives

μέγας, μεγάλη, μέγα   great, large

πᾶς, πᾶσα, πᾶν   all, every

πολύς, πόλλη, πολύ   much, many

Conjunction

ὅπως   so as to (like ἵνα)

Exercises

Translate from Greek to English.

1. μακάριοι οἱ *πραεῖς (πραΰς), ὅτι αὐτοὶ *κληρονομήσουσιν τὴν γῆν... μακάριοι οἱ *καθαροὶ τῇ καρδίᾳ, ὅτι αὐτοὶ τὸν θεὸν *ὄψονται. (Matthew 5:5, 8)

2. οὕτως *λαμψάτω τὸ φῶς ὑμῶν *ἔμπροσθεν τῶν ἀνθρώπων, ὅπως ἴδωσιν ὑμῶν τὰ καλὰ ἔργα καὶ δοξάσωσιν τὸν πατέρα ὑμῶν τὸν ἐν τοῖς οὐρανοῖς. (Matthew 5:16)

3. ἐγώ εἰμι ὁ ἄρτος ὁ ζῶν ὁ ἐκ τοῦ οὐρανοῦ καταβάς· ἐάν τις φάγῃ ἐκ τούτου τοῦ ἄρτου ζήσει εἰς τόν αἰῶνα· καὶ ὁ ἄρτος δὲ ὃν ἐγὼ δώσω ἡ σάρξ μού ἐστιν ὑπὲρ τῆς τοῦ κόσμου ζωῆς. (John 6:51)

4. Καὶ ὅταν προσεύχησθε, οὐκ ἔσεσθε ὡς οἱ *ὑποκριταί· ὅτι φιλοῦσιν ἐν ταῖς συναγωγαῖς καὶ ἐν ταῖς *γωνίαις τῶν **πλατειῶν ἑστῶτες προσεύχεσθαι, ὅπως *φανῶσιν τοῖς ἀνθρώποις· ἀμὴν λέγω ὑμῖν, ἔχουσιν τὸν *μισθὸν αὐτῶν. (cp. Matthew 6:5)

5. ζητεῖτε δὲ πρῶτον τὴν βασιλείαν τοῦ θεοῦ καὶ τὴν δικαιοσύνην αὐτοῦ, καὶ ταῦτα πάντα *προστεθήσεται ὑμῖν. (Matthew 6:33)

6. οὐδὲ γὰρ ὁ πατὴρ κρίνει *οὐδένα, ἀλλὰ τὴν κρίσιν πᾶσαν δέδωκεν τῷ υἱῷ, ἵνα πάντες *τιμῶσι τὸν υἱὸν καθὼς *τιμῶσι τὸν πατέρα. ὁ μὴ *τιμῶν τὸν υἱὸν οὐ *τιμᾷ τὸν πατέρα τὸν πέμψαντα αὐτόν. (John 5:22–23)

7. *ἐραυνᾶτε τὰς γραφάς, ὅτι ὑμεῖς δοκεῖτε ἐν αὐταῖς ζωὴν αἰώνιον ἔχειν· καὶ ἐκεῖναί εἰσιν αἱ μαρτυροῦσαι περὶ ἐμοῦ· καὶ οὐ θέλετε ἐλθεῖν πρός με ἵνα ζωὴν ἔχητε. (John 5:39–40)

8. ἐλήλυθεν γὰρ Ἰωάννης ὁ *βαπτιστὴς μὴ ἐσθίων ἄρτον μήτε πίνων οἶνον, καὶ λέγετε, Δαιμόνιον ἔχει. (Luke 7:33)

9. καὶ ὅ τι ἂν αἰτήσητε ἐν τῷ ὀνόματί μου τοῦτο ποιήσω, ἵνα δοξασθῇ ὁ πατὴρ ἐν τῷ υἱῷ· ἐάν τι αἰτήσητέ με ἐν τῷ ὀνόματί μου ἐγὼ ποιήσω. (John 14:13–14)

10. ἀπεκρίθη Ἰησοῦς καὶ εἶπεν αὐτῷ, Ἐάν τις ἀγαπᾷ με τὸν λόγον μου τηρήσει, καὶ ὁ πατήρ μου ἀγαπήσει αὐτόν, καὶ πρὸς αὐτὸν ἐλευσόμεθα καὶ *μονὴν παρ᾽ αὐτῷ ποιησόμεθα. (John 14:23)

11. ὁ μὴ ἀγαπῶν με τοὺς λόγους μου οὐ τηρεῖ· καὶ ὁ λόγος ὃν ἀκούετε οὐκ ἔστιν ἐμοῦ, ἀλλὰ τοῦ πέμψαντός με πατρός. (cp. John 14:24)

12. μείνατε ἐν ἐμοί, *κἀγὼ ἐν ὑμῖν. καθὼς τὸ *κλῆμα οὐ δύναται καρπὸν φέρειν ἀφ᾽ ἑαυτοῦ ἐὰν μὴ μένῃ ἐν τῇ *ἀμπέλῳ, οὕτως οὐδὲ ὑμεῖς ἐὰν μὴ ἐν ἐμοὶ μένητε. (John 15:4)

13. ἐν τούτῳ ἐφανερώθη ἡ ἀγάπη τοῦ θεοῦ ἐν ἡμῖν, ὅτι τὸν υἱὸν αὐτοῦ τὸν *μονογενῆ ἀπέσταλκεν ὁ θεὸς εἰς τὸν κόσμον ἵνα ζήσωμεν δι᾽ αὐτοῦ. ἐν τούτῳ ἐστὶν ἡ ἀγάπη, οὐχ ὅτι ἡμεῖς ἠγαπήκαμεν τὸν θεόν, ἀλλ᾽ ὅτι αὐτὸς ἠγάπησεν ἡμᾶς καὶ ἀπέστειλεν τὸν υἱὸν αὐτοῦ *ἱλασμὸν περὶ τῶν ἁμαρτίων ἡμῶν. (1 John 4:9–10)

14. Ἀγαπητοί, οὐκ ἐντολὴν *καινὴν γράφω ὑμῖν, ἀλλ᾽ ἐντολὴν *παλαιὰν ἣν εἴχετε ἀπ᾽ ἀρχῆς· ἡ ἐντολὴ ἡ *παλαιά ἐστιν ὁ λόγος ὃν ἠκούσατε. πάλιν ἐντολὴν καινὴν γράφω ὑμῖν, ὅ ἐστιν ἀληθὲς ἐν αὐτῷ καὶ ἐν ὑμῖν, ὅτι ἡ *σκοτία *παράγεται καὶ τὸ φῶς τὸ ἀληθινὸν ἤδη φαίνει. (1 John 2:7–8)

15. Τεκνία, μὴ ἀγαπῶμεν λόγῳ μηδὲ τῇ γλώσσῃ ἀλλὰ ἐν ἔργῳ καὶ ἀληθείᾳ. (1 John 3:18)

16. Ἀγαπητοί, ἀγαπῶμεν ἀλλήλους, ὅτι ἡ ἀγάπη ἐκ τοῦ θεοῦ ἐστιν, καὶ πᾶς ὁ ἀγαπῶν ἐκ τοῦ θεοῦ γεγέννηται καὶ γινώσκει τὸν θεόν. ὁ μὴ ἀγαπῶν οὐκ ἔγνω τὸν θεόν, ὅτι ὁ θεὸς ἀγάπη ἐστίν. (1 John 4:7–8)

17. ἐγώ εἰμι ἡ *ἄμπελος, ὑμεῖς τὰ *κλήματα. ὁ μένων ἐν ἐμοὶ *κἀγὼ ἐν αὐτῷ οὗτος φέρει πολὺν καρπόν, ὅτι *χωρὶς ἐμοῦ οὐ δύνασθε ποιεῖν *οὐδέν. (John 15:5)

18. Ἀγαπητοί, εἰ οὕτως ὁ θεὸς ἠγάπησεν ἡμᾶς, καὶ ἡμεῖς ὀφείλομεν
ἀλλήλους ἀγαπᾶν. θεὸν οὐδεὶς *τεθέαται· ἐὰν ἀγαπῶμεν ἀλλήλους,
ὁ θεὸς ἐν ἡμῖν μένει καὶ ἡ ἀγάπη αὐτοῦ ἐν ἡμῖν *τετελειωμένη ἐστίν.
(cp. 1 John 4:11–12)

19. μὴ *σκοπούντων ἡμῶν τὰ βλεπόμενα ἀλλὰ τὰ μὴ βλεπόμενα·
τὰ γὰρ βλεπόμενα *πρόσκαιρα, τὰ δὲ μὴ βλεπόμενα αἰώνια.
(2 Corinthians 4:18)

20. ἡμεῖς ἀπὸ τοῦ νῦν οὐδένα οἴδαμεν κατὰ σάρκα· εἰ καὶ ἐγνώκαμεν
κατὰ σάρκα Χριστόν, ἀλλὰ νῦν οὐκέτι γινώσκομεν. ὥστε εἴ τις ἐν
Χριστῷ, *καινὴ *κτίσις· τὰ *ἀρχαῖα *παρῆλθεν, ἰδοὺ γέγονεν
*καινά. (2 Corinthians 5:16–17)

Translate from English to Greek.

1. You (pl) will not fulfill the whole law because of your sin, but you will know the God of the law because of his love.

2. If you (sg) wish to know the Lord, ask him for righteousness.

3. If they crucify the people, will they destroy the temple?

4. The love of God and the peace of Christ were manifested to us by the word of the prophet.

5. The large crowd walked to the temple in order to find salvation in the law, but they did not find it.

6. Many women gathered together against the power of their master.

7. O that great day, when Jesus was raised from the dead!

8. You all love your own ways which lead to evil.

9. While she begat a son, the husband died in the temple.

10. If we have no sin, we will crucify sinners.

XXV

Indirect Discourse

Students of the Greek New Testament are often perplexed by the way Greek represents conversation, thought, and perception. Sometimes Greek simply quotes a source, just as English would. This is known as *direct discourse*, and we have already seen much of this in the exercises.

εἶπεν αὐτῷ· σὺ εἶ ὁ ἐρχόμενος He said to him, "Are you the coming
ἢ ἕτερον προσδοκῶμεν; one, or shall we await another?"
(Matthew 11:3)

When Greek does not use this direct form for reporting discourse, it adopts one of a variety of ways of expressing the content of statements, thoughts, or perceptions. These patterns are conventionally categorized together as *indirect discourse*.

The simplest of these constructions uses ὅτι as a sort of quotation mark, and the discourse in its original form follows ὅτι. Sometimes it is easiest simply to omit the ὅτι when translating this sort of indirect discourse. If the ὅτι is preserved as "that," the sentence must be recast from its original content to reflect the indirect translation.

ὁ δὲ εἶπεν αὐτῷ *ὅτι* But he said to him, "Your brother has
ὁ ἀδελφός σου ἥκει... come..." *or* But he said to him *that* his
brother had come... (Luke 15:27)

καὶ ἀκούσας *ὅτι* Ἰησοῦς And when he heard *that* this was Jesus
ὁ Ναζαρηνός ἐστιν... the Nazarene... *or* And when he heard,
"This is Jesus the Nazarene"... (Mark 10:47)

When indirect discourse represents discourse that would not ordinarily take the indicative mood, chiefly commands or exhortation, ἵνα or ὅπως can be substituted for ὅτι.

Αὕτη ἐστὶν ἡ ἐντολὴ ἡ ἐμή, This is my commandment, *that* you
ἵνα ἀγαπᾶτε αλλήλους... love one another... (The commandment
is the imperative ἀγαπᾶτε αλλήλους)
(John 15:12)

The context will guide students in deciding whether to retain the indirect discourse or to construct the sentence as direct discourse. Apart from that decision, this form of indirect discourse should present few problems.

Another common way of expressing indirect discourse uses an infinitive after a verb of discourse. This structure may be hard to translate unless a finite form is substituted for the infinitive. Remember that the subject of the infinitive will be found in the accusative case.

ἀκούω σχίσματα ἐν ὑμῖν ὑπάρχειν ...	I hear that schisms *exist* among you... *or* I hear that *there are* schisms among you ... (1 Corinthians 11:18)
ὁ λέγων ἐν αὐτῷ μένειν...	The one who says "I *abide* in him"... *or* The one who says he [she] *abides* in him ... (1 John 2:6)

Some interpreters prefer to translate such constructions with the infinitive intact. For instance, they may substitute the gloss "I *claim*" for the more familiar translation of λέγω, "I say." Employing such an approach, the example of indirect discourse given above reads, "The one who claims to abide in him."

The third manner of expressing indirect discourse — using a participle to express the content of a thought or perception — is so familiar to English-speakers that they may have a hard time construing the Greek syntax. In this instance, as with the infinitive, the subject of the participle appears in the accusative.

εἶδεν Σίμωνα καὶ Ἀνδρέαν ... ἀμφιβάλλοντας ἐν τῇ θαλάσσῃ ...	He saw Simon and Andrew... *casting* in the sea ... (Mark 1:16)
Ἀκούομεν γάρ τινας περιπατοῦντας ἐν ὑμῖν ἀτάκτως ...	For we hear that some among you *are walking* in a disorderly way... (2 Thessalonians 3:11)

The first use is so close to an adjectival use of the participle that some scholars do not recognize it as an example of indirect discourse. It can appropriately be described as an anarthrous predicative use of the participle (see lesson XX). The surer instance of indirect discourse can be identified by the necessity of introducing "that" into the translation to mark the content of the indirect discourse.

A fourth construction for indirect discourse uses the interrogative pronoun as though it were a relative pronoun in a clause which represents a statement that could have been a question if it were quoted in direct discourse.

> οὔπω ἐφανερώθη τί ἐσόμεθα.   *What we will* be has not yet been revealed.
> (The indirect question is τί ἐσόμεθα;
> "What will we be?")(1 John 3:2)

All of the preceding constructions appear with verbs of speaking where we would typically anticipate seeing indirect discourse, but it is essential that the student remember that the Greek language treats *all* forms of perception and cognition as discourse. It is as though the Greek language presupposes that the eye tells the brain, "A bird up on the left; three women ahead; a book in my lap," and the brain thinks, "I will look up to see this bird," and then, "What sort of bird is it?" The thought or the perception is expressed as indirect discourse.

Study Checklist

Indirect Discourse
Using ὅτι, ἵνα, or ὅπως
Using infinitives
Using participles
Indirect Questions

Vocabulary

Verbs

ἀναβαίνω *ἀναβαίνω, ἀναβήσομαι, ἀνέβην, ἀναβέβηκα, —, —*   I go up

ἀνοίγω *ἀνοίγω, ἀνοίξω, ἀνέῳξα/ἠνέῳξα/ἤνοιξα, ἀνέῳγα, ἀνέῳγμαι/ἠνέῳγμαι, ἀνεῴχθην/ἠνεῴχθην/ἠνοίχθην*   I open

Adjective

τοιοῦτος, τοιαύτη, τοιοῦτο(ν)   such as (declined like οὗτος)

Preposition

ἔμπροσθεν   before (with the genitive), in front of

Particles

ἄρα   then, therefore

μήδε   and not, but not; μήδε ... μήδε, neither... nor

οὐχί   not

Adverbs

ὅπως   how, in what way; in order that (as a conjunction with the subjunctive), so that

οὐκέτι, μηκέτι   no longer

ποῦ   where? to where?

Exercises

Translate from Greek to English.

1. οἱ δὲ ἀρχιερεῖς καὶ ὅλον τὸ συνέδριον ἐζήτουν κατὰ τοῦ Ἰησοῦ μαρτυρίαν εἰς τὸ θανατῶσαι αὐτόν, καὶ οὐχ ηὕρισκον. (Mark 14:55)

2. καὶ σταυροῦσιν αὐτὸν καὶ *διαμερίζονται τὰ ἱμάτια αὐτοῦ βάλλοντες *κλῆρον ἐπ' αὐτὰ τίς τί ἄρῃ. ἦν δὲ ὥρα *τρίτη καὶ ἐσταύρωσαν αὐτόν. (Mark 15:24–25)

3. Καὶ ἔστιν αὕτη ἡ *ἀγγελία ἣν ἀκηκόαμεν ἀπ' αὐτοῦ καὶ *ἀναγγέλλομεν ὑμῖν, ὅτι ὁ θεὸς φῶς ἐστιν καὶ *σκοτία ἐν αὐτῷ οὐκ ἔστιν οὐδεμία. (1 John 1:5)

4. Ἐὰν εἴπωμεν ὅτι *κοινωνίαν ἔχομεν μετ' αὐτοῦ καὶ ἐν τῷ *σκότει περιπατῶμεν, *ψευδόμεθα καὶ οὐ ποιοῦμεν τὴν ἀλήθειαν. (1 John 1:6)

5. ἐὰν δὲ ἐν τῷ φωτὶ περιπατῶμεν ὡς αὐτός ἐστιν ἐν τῷ φωτί, *κοινωνίαν ἔχομεν μετ' ἀλλήλων καὶ τὸ αἷμα Ἰησοῦ τοῦ υἱοῦ αὐτοῦ *καθαρίζει ἡμᾶς ἀπὸ πάσης ἁμαρτίας. (1 John 1:7)

6. ἐὰν εἴπωμεν ὅτι ἁμαρτίαν οὐκ ἔχομεν, ἑαυτοὺς *πλανῶμεν καὶ ἡ ἀλήθεια οὐκ ἔστιν ἐν ἡμῖν. (1 John 1:8)

7. ἐὰν *ὁμολογῶμεν τὰς ἁμαρτίας ἡμῶν, πιστός ἐστιν καὶ δίκαιος ἵνα ἀφῇ ἡμῖν τὰς ἁμαρτίας καὶ *καθαρίσῃ ἡμᾶς ἀπὸ πάσης *ἀδικίας. ἐὰν εἴπωμεν ὅτι οὐχ ἡμαρτήκαμεν, *ψεύστην ποιοῦμεν αὐτὸν καὶ ὁ λόγος αὐτοῦ οὐκ ἔστιν ἐν ἡμῖν. (1 John 1:9–10)

8. ἀλλὰ τοῦτό ἐστιν τὸ εἰρημένον διὰ τοῦ προφήτου *Ἰωήλ, Καὶ ἔσται ἐν ταῖς ἐσχάταις ἡμέραις, λέγει ὁ θεός, *ἐκχεῶ ἀπὸ τοῦ πνεύματός μου ἐπὶ πᾶσαν σάρκα, καὶ *προφητεύσουσιν οἱ υἱοὶ ὑμῶν καὶ τὰ τεκνία ὑμῶν *ὁράσεις ὄψονται. (cp. Acts 2:16–17)

9. Πέτρος δὲ πρὸς αὐτούς, *Μετανοήσατε, καὶ βαπτισθήτω ἕκαστος ὑμῶν ἐπὶ τῷ ὀνόματι Ἰησοῦ Χριστοῦ εἰς *ἄφεσιν τῶν ἁμαρτιῶν ὑμῶν, καὶ *λήμψεσθε τὴν *δωρεὰν τοῦ ἁγίου πνεύματος. (cp. Acts 2:38)

10. ὑμῖν γάρ ἐστιν ἡ ἐπαγγελία καὶ τοῖς τέκνοις ὑμῶν καὶ πᾶσιν τοῖς εἰς *μακρὰν ὅσους ἂν *προσκαλέσηται κύριος ὁ θεὸς ἡμῶν. (Acts 2:39)

11. Ἐγένετο δὲ ἐν τῷ βαπτισθῆναι πάντα τὸν λαὸν καὶ Ἰησοῦ βαπτισθέντος καὶ προσευχομένου *ἀνεῳχθῆναι τὸν οὐρανὸν καὶ καταβῆναι τὸ πνεῦμα τὸ ἅγιον *σωματικῷ εἴδει ὡς περιστερὰν ἐπ᾽ αὐτόν, καὶ φωνὴν ἐξ οὐρανοῦ γενέσθαι, Σὺ εἶ ὁ υἱός μου ὁ ἀγαπητός, ἐν σοὶ *εὐδόκησα. (cp. Luke 3:21–22)

12. καὶ στήσαντες αὐτοὺς ἐν τῷ μέσῳ *ἐπυνθάνοντο, Ἐν ποίᾳ δυνάμει ἢ ἐν ποίῳ ὀνόματι ἐποιήσατε τοῦτο ὑμεῖς; (Acts 4:7)

13. τότε Πέτρος *πλησθεὶς πνεύματος ἁγίου εἶπεν πρὸς αὐτούς, *Ἄρχοντες τοῦ λαοῦ καὶ *πρεσβύτεροι, εἰ ἡμεῖς *σήμερον *ἀνακρινόμεθα ἐπὶ *εὐεργεσίᾳ ἀνθρώπου *ἀσθενοῦς ἐν τίνι οὗτος σέσωται. (Acts 4:8–9)

14. *γνωστὸν ἔστω πᾶσιν ὑμῖν καὶ παντὶ τῷ λαῷ *Ἰσραὴλ ὅτι ἐν τῷ ὀνόματι Ἰησοῦ Χριστοῦ τοῦ *Ναζωραίου, ὃν ὑμεῖς ἐσταυρώσατε, ὃν ὁ θεὸς ἤγειρεν ἐκ νεκρῶν, ἐν τούτῳ οὗτος παρέστηκεν ἐνώπιον ὑμῶν *ὑγιής. (Acts 4:10–11)

15. καὶ θεωρεῖ τὸν οὐρανὸν *ἀνεῳγμένον καὶ καταβαῖνον *σκεῦός τι ὡς *ὀθόνην μεγάλην *τέσσαρσιν *ἀρχαῖς *καθιέμενον ἐπὶ τῆς γῆς. (Acts 10:11)

16. Τῇ δὲ *ἐπαύριον ἀναστὰς ἐξῆλθεν σὺν αὐτοῖς, καί τινες τῶν ἀδελφῶν τῶν ἀπὸ *Ἰόππης συνῆλθον αὐτῷ. τῇ δὲ *ἐπαύριον εἰσῆλθεν εἰς τὴν *Καισάρειαν· ὁ δὲ *Κορνήλιος ἦν *προσδοκῶν αὐτούς, συγκαλεσάμενος τοὺς *συγγενεῖς αὐτοῦ καὶ τοὺς *ἀναγκαίους φίλους. (Acts 10:23b–24)

17. Τίνι γὰρ εἶπέν ποτε τῶν ἀγγέλων, Υἱός μου εἶ σύ, ἐγὼ *σήμερον γεγέννηκά σε; καὶ πάλιν, Ἐγὼ ἔσομαι αὐτῷ εἰς πατέρα, καὶ αὐτὸς ἔσται μοι εἰς υἱόν; (Hebrews 1:5)

18. καὶ πρὸς μὲν τοὺς ἀγγέλους λέγει, Ὁ ποιῶν τοὺς ἀγγέλους αὐτοῦ
πνεύματα, καὶ τοὺς *λειτουργοὺς αὐτοῦ πυρὸς *φλόγα· πρὸς δὲ τὸν
υἱόν, Ὁ θρόνος σου, ὁ θεός, εἰς τὸν αἰῶνα τοῦ αἰῶνος.
(Hebrews 1:7–8b)

19. ὅ τε γὰρ ἁγιάζων καὶ οἱ ἁγιαζόμενοι ἐξ ἑνὸς πάντες· δι' ἣν αἰτίαν
οὐκ *ἐπαισχύνεται ἀδελφοὺς αὐτοὺς καλεῖν, λέγων, *Ἀπαγγελῶ τὸ
ὄνομά σου τοῖς ἀδελφοῖς μου, ἐν μέσῳ ἐκκλησίας *ὑμνήσω σε.
(Hebrews 2:11–12)

20. καὶ πάλιν, Ἐγὼ ἔσομαι *πεποιθὼς ἐπ' αὐτῷ· καὶ πάλιν, Ἰδοὺ ἐγὼ καὶ
τὰ παιδία ἅ μοι ἔδωκεν ὁ θεός. (Hebrews 2:13)

Translate from English to Greek.

1. She said to the crowds, "If you give to the ones who do not have bread,
you will be disciples of Christ."

2. The prophet taught the children that Christ loves all people who
abide in him.

3. Having heard that the man destroyed the synagogue, the women went
up to the king in order to speak to him concerning it.

4. We heard that you (pl) open your assembly to all who believe
in Jesus' name.

5. When Jesus said, "I will go up into the heavens," the high priest of the
temple did not believe him.

6. The crowds saw the high priest offering bread to the Lord.

7. The teacher said in front of the children that he will no longer lead
them down the evil road.

8. Where are you (sg) going that you are carrying so much?

9. With an assembly such as the one in the city, the apostle did not want
to go to another.

10. Neither will I come to you (pl) nor will I speak to you because I did not
receive the writings of the commandments.

XXVI

Numbers

Numbers appear frequently in the Greek New Testament. Fortunately, most numbers are indeclinable — that is, their form remains the same in all cases, regardless of whether they are singular or plural. Unfortunately, several of the numbers decline somewhat unpredictably. Numbers above "four" are indeclinable; the number δύο, "two," is indeclinable, save that its dative form is δυσί(ν) for all genders. The number one, εἷς, has distinct forms for the cases and all three genders. Three and four (τρεῖς and τέσσαρες) are declined as two-ending adjectives, but instead of taking the second declension pattern that most two-ending adjectives follow, they are closer to third declension adjectives. Of course, εἷς is always singular, and the higher numbers are always plural, so there will be only one grammatical number for each cardinal number.

	Eἷς			*Δύο*
	M	*F*	*N*	*M/F/N*
N	εἷς	μία	ἕν	δύο
G	ἑνός	μιᾶς	ἑνός	δύο
D	ἑνί	μιᾷ	ἑνί	δυσί(ν)
A	ἕνα	μίαν	ἕν	δύο

	Τρεῖς		*Τέσσαρες*	
	M/F	*N*	*M/F*	*N*
N	τρεῖς	τρία	τέσσαρες	τέσσαρα
G	τριῶν	τριῶν	τεσσάρων	τεσσάρων
D	τρισί	τρισί	τέσσαρσι	τέσσαρσι
A	τρεῖς	τρία	τεσσάρας	τέσσαρα

The negative nouns οὐδείς and μηδείς (meaning "no one" and "nothing") are declined as εἷς; οὐδείς is used with the indicative mood, and μηδείς with non-indicative moods.

Ἀπόλλυμι

The verb ἀπολλύμι is a common, yet peculiar verb. Some forms of its present system follow the paradigm of a μι verb, and others follow the paradigm of an ω verb. Ἀπόλλυμι thus illustrates the more general tendency for ω verbs to supplant μι verbs.

Ἀπόλλυμι is conjugated as a regular μι verb whose stem ends in υ, with the following exceptions. The present active indicative third singular appears as ἀπόλλυει in John 12:25, rather than as the expected ἀπόλλυσι. The future active indicative can appear as ἀπολέσω or ἀπολῶ (with contraction of the connecting vowel: ἀπόλητε). The future middle is formed from the stem ἀπολε- (with contraction). The aorist active principal part of ἀπόλλυμι is ἀπωλέσα, but the only aorist active form that appears in the New Testament is the infinitive ἀπολέσαι.

The translation of ἀπόλλυμι is also complicated. In the active voice, it can mean "I destroy" or "I lose" (here, in the sense of "I lost my textbook"). In the middle voice, ἀπόλλυμι usually means "I perish" (or, for inanimate subjects, "spoils" or "goes bad").

The forms in which ἀπολλύμι appear in the New Testament are provided here. The forms in parentheses do not themselves appear, but are found in other Hellenistic texts. Note that the angel of the abyss in Revelation 9:11 is Ἀπολλύων, the Destroyer, the present active participial form of ἀπόλλυμι.

Present System
Active indicative: may appear with -ω endings (ἀπολλύει)
Middle indicative: regular μι verb forms
Active imperative: second singular form is ἀπόλλυε (not expected ἄπολλυ)
Middle participle: formed regularly (ἀπολλύμενος, and so on)
Imperfect passive: third plural form is ἀπώλλυντο

Future System
Active indicative: formed from ἀπολε- stem (with contraction *or* σ infix)
Middle indicative: formed from ἀπολε- stem (with contraction)

Aorist System
Active and middle indicative: formed regularly from ἀπώλεσα
Active and middle infinitives: ἀπολέσαι, ἀπολέσθαι (regular)

Active subjunctive: formed regularly
Middle subjunctive: formed regularly, with contraction
Active participle: formed regularly (ἀπολέσας, and so on)
Middle participle: formed from ἀπολομένος

Perfect System
Active participle: formed from stem ἀπολωλώς

Δύναμαι

The verb δύναμαι ("I am able") has one main complication and several additional twists. The complication is that the augmented forms of δύναμαι vary between ε- augments and η- augments, occasionally within the same text. There is no difference in meaning, but this inconsistency can be confusing. The twists involve the instances in which δύναμαι provides alternate forms for a single conjugation of the verb. Thus, δύνασαι and δύνῃ occur interchangeably for the present middle/deponent indicative second singular of δύναμαι. Note that δύναμαι typically takes an infinitive as its complement.

	Singular	Plural		Singular	Plural
Present Middle / Deponent Indicative			*Aorist Present / Deponent Indicative*		
1ST	δύναμαι	δυνάμεθα		ἠδυνήθην	ἠδυνήθημεν
2ND	δύνασαι *or* δύνῃ	δύνασθε *or* δύνασε		(ἠδυνήθης)	ἠδυνήθητε
3RD	δύναται	δύνανται		ἠδυνάσθη *or* ἠδυνήθη	ἠδυνήθησαν
INF	δύνασθαι				
PART	δυνάμενος, -η, -ον				
Imperfect Middle / Deponent Indicative			*Future Middle / Deponent Indicative*		
1ST	(ἐδυνάμην)	ἐδυνάμεθα		(δυνήσομαι)	δυνησόμεθα
2ND	(ἐδύνω)	ἐδύνασθε		δυνήσῃ	δυνήσεσθε
3RD	ἐδύνατο *or* ἠδύνατο	ἠδύναντο		δυνήσεται	δυνήσονται

δύνηται   present middle/deponent subjunctive third singular

δύνωνται   present middle/deponent subjunctive third plural

δυνηθῆτε   aorist present/deponent subjunctive second plural

δυναίμην   present middle/deponent optative first singular

δύναιντο   present middle/deponent optative third plural

Study Checklist

Forms of numbers

Forms of ἀπόλλυμι

Forms of δύναμαι

Vocabulary

Numbers

εἷς, μία, ἕν	one	πέντε	five	ἐννέα	nine
δύο	two	ἕξ	six	δέκα	ten
τρεῖς	three	ἑπτά	seven	ἕνδεκα	eleven
τέσσαρες	four	ὀκτώ	eight	δώδεκα	twelve

Verbs

ἀπόλλυμι *ἀπόλλυμι, ἀπολέσω/ἀπολῶ, ἀπώλεσα, ἀπολώλεκα/ἀπόλωλα,*
—, — I destroy, I lose [track of]; I perish (middle/deponent)

δύναμαι *δύναμαι, δυνήσομαι, —, —, —, ἠδυνήθην* I am able, I can

Nouns

μηδείς, μηδεμία, μηδέν   no one, nothing

οὐδείς, οὐδεμία, οὐδέν   no one, nothing

Exercises

Translate from Greek to English.

1. Οὐδεὶς δύναται δυσὶ κυρίοις *δουλεύειν· καὶ γὰρ τὸν ἕνα *μισήσει
   ἢ τὸν ἕτερον ἀγαπήσει· οὐ δύνασθε θεῷ *δουλεύειν καὶ *μαμωνᾷ.
   (cp. Matthew 6:24)

2. Καὶ συναγάγων τοὺς δώδεκα μαθητὰς αὐτοῦ ἔδωκεν αὐτοῖς
   ἐξουσίαν πνευμάτων *ἀκαθάρτων ὥστε ἐκβάλλειν αὐτὰ καὶ
   θεραπεύειν πᾶσαν νόσον καὶ πᾶσαν *μαλακίαν. Τῶν δὲ δώδεκα
   ἀποστόλων τὰ ὀνόματά ἐστιν ταῦτα. (cp. Matthew 10:1–2a)

3. καὶ ἔδωκαν *κλήρους αὐτοῖς, καὶ ἔπεσεν ὁ *κλῆρος ἐπὶ *Μαθθίαν, καὶ *συγκατεψηφίσθη μετὰ τῶν ἔνδεκα ἀποστόλων. (Acts 1:26)

4. ἓν σῶμα καὶ ἓν πνεῦμα, καθὼς καὶ ἐκλήθητε ἐν μιᾷ ἐλπίδι τῆς *κλήσεως ὑμῶν· εἷς κύριος, μία πίστις, ἓν *βάπτισμα· εἷς θεὸς καὶ πατὴρ πάντων, ὁ ἐπὶ πάντων καὶ διὰ πάντων καὶ ἐν πᾶσιν. (Ephesians 4:4–6)

5. Ἑνὶ δὲ ἑκάστῳ ἡμῶν ἐδόθη ἡ χάρις κατὰ τὸ *μέτρον τῆς *δωρεᾶς του Χριστοῦ. (Ephesians 4:7)

6. ᾧ μὲν γὰρ διὰ τοῦ πνεύματος δίδοται λόγος σοφίας, ἄλλῳ δὲ λόγος *γνώσεως κατὰ τὸ αὐτὸ πνεῦμα, ἑτέρῳ πίστις ἐν τῷ αὐτῷ πνεύματι, ἄλλῳ δὲ *χαρίσματα *ἰαμάτων ἐν τῷ ἑνὶ πνεύματι.(1 Corinthians 12:8–9)

7. τὸ γὰρ σῶμα ἕν ἐστιν καὶ *μέλη πολλὰ ἔχει, πάντα δὲ τὰ μέλη τοῦ σώματος πολλὰ ὄντα ἕν ἐστιν σῶμα, οὕτως καὶ ὁ Χριστός. (cp. 1 Corinthians 12:12)

8. Καὶ ἐλθόντος αὐτοῦ εἰς τὸ *πέραν εἰς τὴν χώραν τῶν *Γαδαρηνῶν *ὑπήντησαν αὐτῷ δύο *δαιμονιζόμενοι. (Matthew 8:28)

9. *Συγκαλεσάμενος δὲ τοὺς δώδεκα ἔδωκεν αὐτοῖς δύναμιν καὶ ἐξουσίαν ἐπὶ πάντα τὰ *δαιμόνια καὶ *νόσους θεραπεύειν, καὶ ἀπέστειλεν αὐτοὺς κηρύσσειν τὴν βασιλείαν τοῦ θεοῦ. (Luke 9:1–2a)

10. Καὶ ἐγένετο ἐν τῷ πορεύεσθαι εἰς *Ἰερουσαλὴμ καὶ αὐτὸς *διήρχετο διὰ μέσον *Σαμαρείας καὶ *Γαλιλαίας. καὶ εἰσερχομένου αὐτοῦ εἴς τινα *κώμην *ἀπήντησαν [αὐτῷ] δέκα *λεπροὶ ἄνδρες, οἳ ἔστησαν *πόρρωθεν. (Luke 17:11–12)

11. δεῖ οὖν τὸν *ἐπίσκοπον *ἀνεπίλημπτον εἶναι, μιᾶς γυναικὸς ἄνδρα. (1 Timothy 3:2a)

12. ἑπτὰ ἀδελφοὶ ἦσαν· καὶ ὁ πρῶτος ἔλαβεν γυναῖκα, καὶ ἀποθνήσκων οὐκ ἀφῆκεν σπέρμα. (Mark 12:20)

13. Καὶ εἶδον ὅτε ἤνοιξεν τὸ *ἀρνίον μίαν ἐκ τῶν ἑπτὰ *σφραγίδων, καὶ ἤκουσα ἑνὸς ἐκ τῶν τεσσάρων *ζῴων λέγοντος ὡς φωνὴ *βροντῆς, Ἔρχου. (Revelation 6:1)

14. Καὶ ἤκουσα μεγάλης φωνῆς ἐκ τοῦ ναοῦ λεγούσης τοῖς ἑπτὰ ἀγγέλοις, Ὑπάγετε καὶ *ἐκχέετε τὰς ἑπτὰ *φιάλας τοῦ *θυμοῦ τοῦ θεοῦ εἰς τὴν γῆν. (Revelation 16:1)

15. καὶ ἐγένετο ἡ πόλις ἡ μεγάλη εἰς τρία *μέρη, καὶ αἱ πόλεις τῶν ἐθνῶν ἔπεσαν. (Revelation 16:19a)

16. Καὶ ἦλθεν εἷς ἐκ τῶν ἑπτὰ ἀγγέλων τῶν ἐχόντων τὰς ἑπτὰ *φιάλας, καὶ ἐλάλησεν μετ᾽ ἐμοῦ λέγων, *Δεῦρο, δείξω σοι τὸ *κρίμα τῆς *πόρνης τῆς μεγάλης τῆς καθημένης ἐπὶ ὑδάτων πολλῶν. (Revelation 17:1)

17. καὶ τὰ δέκα *κέρατα ἃ εἶδες δέκα βασιλεῖς εἰσιν, οἵτινες βασιλείαν οὔπω ἔλαβον, ἀλλὰ ἐξουσίαν ὡς βασιλεῖς μίαν ὥραν λαμβάνουσιν μετὰ τοῦ *θηρίου. (Revelation 17:12)

18. ῞Ωσπερ γὰρ ἄνθρωπος ἀπερχόμενος ἐκάλεσεν τοὺς ἰδίους δούλους καὶ ἔδωκεν αὐτοῖς τὰ ὑπάρχοντα αὐτοῦ, καὶ ᾧ μὲν ἔδωκεν πέντε *τάλαντα, ᾧ δὲ δύο, ᾧ δὲ ἕν, ἑκάστῳ κατὰ ἰδίαν δύναμιν, καὶ ἀπῆλθεν. (cp. Matthew 25:14–15)

19. Ἐγένετο δὲ μετὰ τοὺς λόγους τούτους ὡσεὶ ἡμέραι ὀκτώ καὶ παραλαβὼν Πέτρον καὶ Ἰωάννην καὶ Ἰάκωβον ἀνέβη εἰς τὸ ὄρος προσεύξασθαι. (Luke 9:28)

20. καὶ ἔπεσεν ἐπὶ πρόσωπον παρὰ τοὺς πόδας αὐτοῦ εὐχαριστῶν αὐτῷ· καὶ αὐτὸς ἦν *Σαμαρίτης. ἀποκριθεὶς δὲ ὁ Ἰησοῦς εἶπεν, Οὐχὶ οἱ δέκα ἐκαθαρίσθησαν; οἱ δὲ ἐννέα ποῦ; (Luke 17:16–17)

Translate from English to Greek.

1. The people are not able to save themselves because they walk in sin.

2. If the king does not establish a kingdom for righteousness, the prophet will speak against him.

3. The crowd casts out the ones who bring evil into the city, and they perish in the wilderness.

4. After two years, the men entered the city and destroyed the twelve synagogues.

5. The blind people inhabited the house by the sea for seven days to pray.

6. While Jesus lived on the earth, the twelve disciples did not do the commandments because they did not know what to do.

7. The only son of the woman was raised from the dead by the prophet, and the woman gave him bread to eat.

8. No one loves the world like God.

9. When evening came, the people were tested by the evil spirits who walk on the earth.

10. You (sg) ought to sell your boat to the king.

XXVII

When the cases were introduced in lesson III, students learned the basic uses of the various grammatical cases. By this time, these should come readily to the student's recollection when observing a declined form. This lesson will illustrate some of the other uses for each case.

Nominative Case

The nominative occasionally appears when a noun is isolated and has no clear relation to a verb; for instance, in the titles of books and in the greetings of epistles. Such clauses are examples of the *independent nominative*. The greetings of Paul's letters are a good illustrations of this phenomenon, as are the titles of Acts and Revelation:

Πράξεις Ἀποστόλων   *Acts* of Apostles
Ἀποκάλυψις Ἰωάννου   *Revelation* of John

The nominative is frequently used when names are introduced. Here, the nominative serves the function that quotation marks do in English — it sets off the noun in question from its context and indicates that it is being used as a name, not as an ordinary element in the sentence. This is called the *nominative of appellation*. Some instances of this phenomenon could be construed as indirect discourse; others may conceal an implied verb of being. In Revelation 9:11, however, this usage is clear:

ὄνομα ἔχει Ἀπολλύων.   He has the name *"Apollyon."*
(Revelation 9:11)

Ἀπολλύων should otherwise be in the accusative to agree with ὄνομα.

The nominative sometimes appears in true *nominative absolutes* — that is, when the clause governed by the nominative noun has no syntactical connection with the main clause. Nominative absolutes also occur in exclamations, such as καλός, "good!"

ταῦτα ἃ θεωρεῖτε ἐλεύσονται   *These things* that you see, days
ἡμέραι ἐν αἷς οὐκ ἀφεθήσεται   will come in which stone will not
λίθος ἐπὶ λίθῳ ...   be left upon stone ... (Luke 21:6)

The nominative is sometimes used when the vocative would be more appropriate. This usage may reflect the beginnings of a change in the spelling of the vocative form, or it may be a form of the nominative absolute.

> ὁ κυριός μου καὶ ὁ θεός μου   *My Lord* and *my God*! (John 20:28)

Genitive Case

The genitive frequently indicates a selection from a group. English uses "of" in this sense also ("she's one of a kind"). This usage is known as the *partitive genitive.*

> τινες τῶν γραμματέων   some *of the scribes* (Mark 2:6)

Sometimes the genitive is used in a way closely related to the qualitative genitive. In this usage, the genitive is used not to *describe* so much as to *define* the referent of the genitive. While a qualitative genitive can generally be translated as though the genitive phrase were an adjective, this usage, the *epexegetical genitive*, can more appropriately be translated with a phrase such as "that is" or "namely."

> σημεῖον ἔλαβεν περιτομῆς...   He received a sign, namely,
> *circumcision*...(Romans 4:11)

In this example, περιτομῆς could hardly function qualitatively, for the sign in question is not a "circumcision-like" kind of sign. Instead, circumcision itself *is* the sign.

The genitive can be used with adverbial force to express time at which an action took place (*genitive of time*).

> ἦλθεν πρὸς αὐτὸν *νυκτός*...   He came to him *at night*...
> (John 3:2)

The genitive can be used to express quantities; it is most often used this way for prices (*genitive of quantity* or *price*).

> ἀγοράσωμεν δηναρίων   Shall we buy loaves *for two*
> διακοσίων ἄρτους...;   *hundred denarii*...? (Mark 6:37)

The genitive is a component in certain comparative expressions, which will be covered in greater depth in the next lesson.

Dative Case

The *dative of time* is used to express the point in time when an incident occurs. The dative of time applies the dative's *local* function to time rather than space.

<blockquote>

δεῖ αὐτὸν ... ἀποκτανθῆναι καὶ It is necessary that he ... die
τῇ τρίτῃ ἡμέρᾳ ἐγερθῆναι.   and *on the third day* be raised.
(Matthew 16:21)

</blockquote>

The dative case is commonly used for constructions in which the noun in the dative case specifies the pertinent interest, importance, or relevance of the main clause. This usage is often most easily translated with the phrase "with respect to" or "with reference to," and is thus called the *dative of respect*.

<blockquote>

ὃ γὰρ ἀπέθανεν, τῇ ἁμαρτίᾳ For the death he died, he died
ἀπέθανεν ἐφάπαξ ...   *with respect to sin*, once for all.
(Romans 6:10)

</blockquote>

The dative is sometimes used to express possession (hence, *possessive dative*), usually with a verb of being. This construction is closely related to the dative of advantage and the use of the dative for the indirect object.

<blockquote>

ἔσται χαρά σοι καὶ ἀγαλλίασις ...   *You* will have joy and exultation ...
(literally, "there will be *to you*
joy and exultation") (Luke 1:14)

</blockquote>

The dative case can be used for the direct object of certain verbs, especially for verbs of social relationship: for instance, ἀρέσκω, "I please"; διακονέω, "I serve (as a slave)"; δουλεύω, "I serve (as a slave)"; λατρεύω, "I serve, I worship"; προσκυνέω, "I reverence"; ὑπακούω, "I obey"; and others. When a preposition that takes the dative case is prefixed to a verb, that compound verb often takes its object in the dative case.

<blockquote>

μάρτυς γάρ μού ἐστιν ὁ θεός, For God is my witness, *whom* I
ᾧ λατρεύω ἐν τῷ πνεύματί μου ... serve with my spirit ... (Romans 1:9)

ἡ πίστις συνήργει *τοῖς*   Faith was working together with his
ἔργοις αὐτοῦ ...   [Abraham's] *works*... (James 2:22)

</blockquote>

Accusative Case

In lessons XIV and XXV we observed that when an infinitive or participle requires a distinct, explicit subject to express its verbal dimension, that subject is set in the *accusative of general reference*.

> ὁ δὲ Ἰησοῦς οὐκέτι οὐδὲν ἀπεκρίθη, Jesus no longer answered anything,
> ὥστε θαυμάζειν τὸν Πιλᾶτον. so that *Pilate* marvelled. (Mark 15:5)

Some constructions take two direct objects. In such cases, both objects are set in the accusative case, the *double accusative*.

> ὃς ἂν ποτίσῃ *ἕνα* τῶν μικρῶν Whoever gives *one* of these
> τούτων *ποτήριον ψυχροῦ* ... little ones *a cup* of cold drink ...
> (Matthew 10:42)

Sometimes an adjective or a noun phrase in the accusative case functions as an adverb. This usage, known as the *adverbial accusative*, was first mentioned with respect to adjectives in lesson VIII and has appeared in some exercises.

> *πρῶτον* λέγετε· εἰρήνη τῷ *First,* say: "Peace to this house."
> οἴκῳ τούτῳ. (Luke 10:5)

The accusative case also can mark extension in time or space (*accusative of extent*).

> ἐκεῖ ἔμειναν οὐ *πολλὰς ἡμέρας*. They remained there not
> *many days.* (John 2:12)

Use of Grammatical Categories

Students should always bear in mind that these grammatical labels describe various usages; they do not limit usage, nor do they constitute a comprehensive taxonomy of possible uses. Sometimes a student will recognize how a dative noun is being used without being able to fit the usage comfortably into a particular category, and at other times a given construction might fit equally well into several categories with little difference in meaning. The importance of these grammatical categories lies in their capacity to help students recognize and characterize common uses, and thus to understand the ways in which Greek syntax ordinarily works. *Usage defeats categorization.*

Study Checklist

Uses of the nominative
Independent nominative
Nominative of appellation
Nominative absolute

Uses of the genitive
Partitive genitive
Epexegetical genitive
Genitive of time
Genitive of price
Comparative genitive (next lesson)

Uses of the dative
Dative of time
Dative of respect
Possessive dative
Direct object of particular verbs

Uses of the accusative
Accusative of general reference
Double accusative
Adverbial accusative
Accusative of extent of time or space

Vocabulary

Verbs

ἁμαρτάνω   ἁμαρτάνω, ἁμαρτήσω, ἡμάρτησα / ἥμαρτον, ἡμάρτηκα,
ἡμάρτημαι, ἡμαρτήθην   I sin

δέω   δέω, δήσω, ἔδησα, δέδεκα, δέδεμαι, ἐδέθην   I bind

διώκω   διώκω, διώξω, ἐδίωξα, δεδίωχα, δεδίωγμαι, ἐδιώχθην   I pursue,
I persecute

ἐγγίζω   ἐγγίζω, ἐγγιῶ, ἤγγισα, ἤγγικα, —, —   I draw near

ἐπιγινώσκω   ἐπιγινώσκω, ἐπιγνώσομαι, ἐπέγνων, ἐπέγνωκα, —,
ἐπεγνώσθην   I recognize, I get to know

θαυμάζω   θαυμάζω, θαυμάσω, ἐθαύμασα, τεθαύμακα, τεθαύμασμαι,
ἐθαυμάσθην   I marvel, I am amazed

Nouns

ἀνάστασις, -εως, ἡ   resurrection

γενεά, ἡ   generation

θηρίον, τό   wild animal

θλίψις, -εως, ἡ   tribulation, oppression

μέρος, τό   part

ναός, ὁ   temple

σπέρμα, -ατος, τό   seed, offspring

τιμή, ἡ   honor

Exercise

Translate from Greek to English.

Ἀρχὴ τοῦ εὐαγγελίου Ἰησοῦ Χριστοῦ υἱοῦ θεοῦ. Καθὼς γέγραπται ἐν
τῷ *Ἠσαΐα τῷ προφήτῃ, Ἰδοὺ ἀποστέλλω τὸν ἄγγελόν μου πρὸ προσώπου
σου, ὃς *κατασκευάσει τὴν ὁδόν σου· φωνὴ *βοῶντος ἐν τῇ ἐρήμῳ,
*Ἑτοιμάσατε τὴν ὁδὸν κυρίου, *εὐθείας ποιεῖτε τὰς *τρίβους αὐτοῦ –
ἐγένετο Ἰωάννης ὁ βαπτίζων ἐν τῇ ἐρήμῳ καὶ κηρύσσων *βάπτισμα
*μετανοίας εἰς *ἄφεσιν ἁμαρτιῶν. καὶ *ἐξεπορεύετο πρὸς αὐτὸν πᾶσα
ἡ *Ἰουδαία *χώρα καὶ οἱ *Ἱεροσολυμῖται πάντες, καὶ ἐβαπτίζοντο
ὑπ᾽ αὐτοῦ ἐν τῷ *Ἰορδάνῃ *ποταμῷ *ἐξομολογούμενοι τὰς ἁμαρτίας
αὐτῶν. καὶ ἐκήρυσσεν Ἰωάννης λέγων, Ἔρχεται ὁ *ἰσχυρότερός
μου *ὀπίσω μου, οὗ οὐκ εἰμὶ *ἱκανὸς *κύψας λῦσαι τὸν *ἱμάντα τῶν
*ὑποδημάτων αὐτοῦ· ἐγὼ ἐβάπτισα ὑμᾶς ὕδατι, αὐτὸς δὲ βαπτίσει
ὑμᾶς ἐν πνεύματι ἁγίῳ. Καὶ ἐγένετο ἐν ἐκείναις ταῖς ἡμέραις ἦλθεν
Ἰησοῦς ἀπὸ *Ναζαρὲτ τῆς *Γαλιλαίας καὶ ἐβαπτίσθη εἰς τὸν
*Ἰορδάνην ὑπὸ *Ἰωάννου. καὶ εὐθὺς ἀναβαίνων ἐκ τοῦ ὕδατος εἶδεν
*σχιζομένους τοὺς οὐρανοὺς καὶ τὸ πνεῦμα ὡς *περιστερὰν
καταβαῖνον εἰς αὐτόν· καὶ φωνὴ ἐγένετο ἐκ τῶν οὐρανῶν, Σὺ εἶ ὁ υἱός
μου ὁ ἀγαπητός, ἐν σοὶ *εὐδόκησα. Καὶ εὐθὺς τὸ πνεῦμα αὐτὸν
ἐκβάλλει εἰς τὴν ἔρημον. καὶ ἦν ἐν τῇ ἐρήμῳ *τεσσεράκοντα ἡμέρας
πειραζόμενος ὑπὸ τοῦ *Σατανᾶ, καὶ ἦν μετὰ τῶν *θηρίων, καὶ οἱ
ἄγγελοι *διηκόνουν αὐτῷ. (cp. Mark 1:1–12)

XXVIII

Comparison

Greek syntax provides several ways to express comparisons. The most common comparative constructions use the comparative degree of the adjective. Other constructions use the comparative adverb μᾶλλον to express the comparison. Each of these has features that may trip up an interpreter, so students should stay alert for the characteristics of comparative structures.

Comparative Adjectives and Adverbs

English adjectives customarily form their comparative and superlative degrees by adding suffixes: cool, cooler, coolest. A typical Greek adjective forms its comparative degree by adding the suffix -τερ between the adjective stem, with either ο or ω as the connecting vowel, and the case endings: τίμιος, "costly"— positive degree; τιμιώτερος, "costlier"— comparative degree. Greek adverbs regularly form their comparative degree by using the accusative case of the comparative adjective as an adverbial accusative (lessons VIII and XXVII).

The superlative degree is uncommon in the New Testament. It is typically formed by adding the suffix -τατ, with ο or ω as the connecting vowel, or -ιστ to the adjective stem: τίμιος, "costly"— positive degree; τιμιώτατος, "costliest"— superlative degree. The best known instance of the superlative degree in the New Testament occurs when Luke addresses his reader as κράτιστε Θεόφιλε, "most excellent Theophilus" (Luke 1:3). Greek adverbs regularly form their superlative degree by using the accusative case of the superlative adjective as an adverbial accusative.

New Testament authors commonly use the comparative degree with superlative force, as when Jesus calls the mustard seed μικρότερον πάντων τῶν σπερμάτων, "smaller than all the seeds." The superlative degree commonly has elative force (meaning "exceedingly, extremely") rather than strictly superlative force.

Unusual Comparative Adjectives and Adverbs

Some of the most common adjectives and adverbs take unexpected forms in the comparative degree. Fortunately, the pattern of inflection for these unexpected forms is itself regular.

Positive	Comparative	Superlative
ἀγαθός	κρείσσων	κράτιστος
κακός	χείρων, ἥσσων	—
μέγας	μείζων	μέγιστος
μικρός	μικρότερος, ἐλάσσων	ἐλάχιστος
πολύς	πλείων, πλέων	πλεῖστος

Comparative adjectives ending in ων are declined as μείζων:

	Masculine/Feminine		Neuter	
	singular	*plural*	*singular*	*plural*
N	μείζων	μείζονες	μεῖζον	μείζονα
G	μείζονος	μειζόνων	μείζονος	μειζόνων
D	μείζονι	μείζοσι(ν)	μείζονι	μείζοσι(ν)
A	μείζονα	μείζονας	μεῖζον	μείζονα

The unexpected adverbial forms, which are not inflected, are:

Positive	Comparative	Superlative
εὖ ("good")	βέλτιον ("better")	—
κακῶς ("badly")	ἧσσον ("worse")	—
μάλα ("very")	μᾶλλον ("more")	μάλιστα ("most")
πολύ	πλεῖον, πλέον	—

Comparative Constructions

Comparisons can be formulated in Greek with several different constructions. An adjective in the comparative degree can be used with the object of the comparison set in the genitive case (the *genitive of comparison* or *comparative genitive*).

μείζων ἐστὶν ὁ θεὸς   God is greater *than* our
τῆς καρδίας ἡμῶν ...   hearts ... (1 John 3:20)

Other comparative constructions do not use the genitive case; rather they use the conjunction ἤ (ordinarily translated as "or") and then set the object of the comparison in the same case as the noun to which it is being compared. This construction is especially useful for comparing indeclinable forms, such as infinitives.

μείζων δὲ ὁ προφητεύων   The one who prophesies is
ἤ ὁ λαλῶν γλώσσαις ...   greater *than* the one who speaks
in tongues ... (1 Corinthians 14:5)

Nouns, phrases, and clauses may be compared by using the adverb μᾶλλον, "more," with ἤ, a construction that does not require a comparative adjective — indeed, it does not require an adjective at all.

μακάριόν ἐστιν *μᾶλλον*   It is *more* blessed to give
διδόναι *ἤ* λαμβάνειν.   *than* to receive. (Acts 20:35)

Study Checklist

The form of the comparative and superlative adjective
The form of the comparative and superlative adverb
The forms of unexpected comparatives and superlatives

Comparative structures
Comparative genitive
Comparative + ἤ
Μᾶλλον + ἤ

Vocabulary

Verbs

δικαιόω δικαιόω, δικαίωσω, ἐδικαίωσα, —, δεδικαίωμαι, ἐδικαιώθην
I justify, rectify, acquit

ἐργάζομαι ἐργάζομαι, —, ἐργασάμην/εἰργασάμην, —, εἴργασμαι,
εἰργάσθην   I work, I bring about

λογίζομαι λογίζομαι, —, ἐλογισάμην, —, —, ἐλογίσθην   I account,
I reckon

οἰκοδομέω οἰκοδομέω, οἰκοδομήσω, ᾠκοδόμησα, ᾠκοδόμηκα,
οἰκοδόμημαι/ᾠκοδόμημαι, οἰκοδομήθην/ᾠκοδομήθην   I build up

πλανάω πλανάω, πλανήσω, ἐπλάνησα, —, πεπλάνημαι, ἐπλανήθην
I lead astray

Adjectives

δεύτερος, -α, -ον   second

ἐμός, -ή, -όν   my, mine

ὅμοιος, -οία, -οιον   like

πρεσβύτερος, -α, -ον   older; an elder (as a substantive)

τρίτος, -η, -ον   third

Adverbs

μᾶλλον   more

σήμερον   today

Exercise

Translate from Greek to English.

Ὁ πρεσβύτερος *ἐκλεκτῇ *κυρίᾳ καὶ τοῖς τέκνοις αὐτῆς, οὓς ἐγὼ ἀγαπῶ
ἐν ἀληθείᾳ, καὶ οὐκ ἐγὼ μόνος ἀλλὰ καὶ πάντες οἱ ἐγνωκότες τὴν
ἀλήθειαν, διὰ τὴν ἀλήθειαν τὴν μένουσαν ἐν ἡμῖν, καὶ μεθ' ἡμῶν ἔσται
εἰς τὸν αἰῶνα. ἔσται μεθ' ἡμῶν χάρις *ἔλεος εἰρήνη παρὰ θεοῦ πατρός,
καὶ παρὰ Ἰησοῦ Χριστοῦ τοῦ υἱοῦ τοῦ πατρός, ἐν ἀληθείᾳ καὶ ἀγάπῃ.
Ἐχάρην *λίαν ὅτι εὕρηκα ἐκ τῶν τέκνων σου περιπατοῦντας ἐν
ἀληθείᾳ, καθὼς ἐντολὴν ἐλάβομεν παρὰ τοῦ πατρός. καὶ νῦν ἐρωτῶ σε,
*κυρία, οὐχ ὡς ἐντολὴν *καινὴν γράφων σοι ἀλλὰ ἣν εἴχομεν ἀπ'

ἀρχῆς, ἵνα ἀγαπῶμεν ἀλλήλους. καὶ αὕτη ἐστὶν ἡ ἀγάπη, ἵνα περιπατῶμεν
κατὰ τὰς ἐντολὰς αὐτοῦ· αὕτη ἡ ἐντολή ἐστιν, καθὼς ἠκούσατε
ἀπ᾽ ἀρχῆς, ἵνα ἐν αὐτῇ περιπατῆτε. ὅτι πολλοὶ *πλάνοι ἐξῆλθον εἰς τὸν
κόσμον, οἱ μὴ *ὁμολογοῦντες Ἰησοῦν Χριστὸν ἐρχόμενον ἐν σαρκί·
οὗτός ἐστιν ὁ *πλάνος καὶ ὁ *ἀντίχριστος. βλέπετε ἑαυτούς, ἵνα μὴ
ἀπολέσητε ἃ εἰργασάμεθα ἀλλὰ μισθὸν *πλήρη *ἀπολάβητε. πᾶς ὁ
προάγων καὶ μὴ μένων ἐν τῇ *διδαχῇ τοῦ Χριστοῦ θεὸν οὐκ ἔχει· ὁ μένων
ἐν τῇ *διδαχῇ, οὗτος καὶ τὸν πατέρα καὶ τὸν υἱὸν ἔχει. εἴ τις ἔρχεται
πρὸς ὑμᾶς καὶ ταύτην τὴν *διδαχὴν οὐ φέρει, μὴ λαμβάνετε αὐτὸν εἰς
οἰκίαν καὶ χαίρειν αὐτῷ μὴ λέγετε· ὁ λέγων γὰρ αὐτῷ χαίρειν
*κοινωνεῖ τοῖς ἔργοις αὐτοῦ τοῖς πονηροῖς. Πολλὰ ἔχων ὑμῖν γράφειν
οὐκ ἐβουλήθην διὰ *χάρτου καὶ *μέλανος, ἀλλὰ ἐλπίζω γενέσθαι πρὸς
ὑμᾶς καὶ στόμα πρὸς στόμα λαλῆσαι, ἵνα ἡ χαρὰ ἡμῶν πεπληρωμένη ᾖ.
Ἀσπάζεταί σε τὰ τέκνα τῆς ἀδελφῆς σου τῆς *ἐκλεκτῆς. (2 John 1–13)

XXIX

More Uses of Participles

Lessons XVII–XIX introduced the most prominent uses of the participle, but participles will be encountered in many other constructions as well. These are more controversial, less clearly defined, or less common categories for analyzing the use of participles. While interpreters will disagree over the precise applicability of these categories, students will certainly benefit from acquainting themselves with these examples of participial usage and from trying to imagine how they themselves would handle such constructions.

Sometimes the participle seems to represent a condition for the main clause, as though it were the protasis of a conditional sentence.

τί ὠφελεῖται ἄνθρωπος   What does it benefit a person,
κερδήσας τὸν κόσμον   *gaining* the world but losing
ἑαυτὸν δὲ ἀπολέσας;   oneself? (cp. Luke 9:25)

Here the "gaining" is the condition for the antithetical "losing." In the parallel passage, Matthew uses the phrase ἐὰν … κερδήσῃ where Luke has κερδήσας. The force of the first participle in Luke surely approximates that of the subjunctive verb in Matthew 16:26.

The participle can be used to indicate the means by which the main clause comes about (the *instrumental participle*).

τίς ἐξ ὑμῶν *μεριμνῶν*   Who among you *by worrying*
δύναται προσθεῖναι ἐπὶ τὴν   is able to add one cubit to his or her
ἡλικίαν αὐτοῦ πῆχυν ἕνα;   lifespan? (cp. Matthew 6:27)

The participle is sometimes used to express the purpose of the main clause. This usage is not especially common, and it is frequently associated with the future participle (for instance, Acts 8:27 states that the Ethiopian eunuch ἐληλύθει προσκυνήσων, "had come to worship"). This is known by various names: the *final* use, the *purposive* use, the *telic* use.

τοῦτο δὲ ἔλεγεν *πειράζων*   But this he said *to test* him …
αὐτόν …   (John 6:6)

There is debate over whether there is an *imperatival use* of the participle. Advocates of the imperatival use point to passages such as Romans 12:9–19 and 1 Peter 2:18, 3:1. Others explain these participles under another description: perhaps they are elliptical periphrastic constructions with the form of εἰμί omitted. Interpreters may accept or reject the category of the imperatival participle, but they must account for the participles in such constructions.

> τῇ ἐλπίδι *χαίροντες*,   *Rejoice in hope, endure*
> τῇ θλίψει *ὑπομένοντες*...   *tribulation ... (Romans 12:12)*

Φημί

A common word in the New Testament is the μι verb, φημί, which is synonymous with λέγω. It merits attention because the three present tense forms that appear in the New Testament (φημί, first person singular; φησίν, third person singular; and φασίν, third person plural) are enclitic. The third person singular, imperfect active form, ἔφη, is *not* enclitic. These four are the only forms of φημί found in the New Testament.

Study Checklist

More uses of the participle
Conditional use of the participle
Instrumental use of the participle
Final (purposive, telic) use of the participle
Imperatival use of the participle
Forms of φημί

Vocabulary

Adjectives

ἄξιος, -ία, -ον	worthy		ὀλίγος, -η, -ον	few
καινός, -ή, -όν	new			

Nouns

ἐπιθυμία, ἡ	desire		πρόβατον, τό	sheep
μνημεῖον, τό	tomb, monument		τέλος, -ους, τό	end, goal

Verbs

βούλομαι βούλομαι, —, —, —, —, ἐβουλόμην I wish, I would like

ἑτοιμάζω ἑτοιμάζω, ἑτοιμάσω, ἡτοίμασα, ἡτοίμακα, ἡτοίμασμαι, ἡτοιμάσθην I prepare

μισέω μισέω, μισήσω, ἐμίσησα, μεμίσηκα, μεμίσημαι, — I hate

φημί φησίν (present active indicative third singular); φασίν (present active indicative third plural); ἔφη (imperfect active indicative third singular) I say

Adverb

πάντοτε always

Preposition

χωρίς without (takes the genitive)

Exercise

Translate from Greek to English.

Εὐχαριστῶ τῷ θεῷ μου πάντοτε *μνείαν σου ποιούμενος ἐπὶ τῶν προσευχῶν μου, ἀκούων σου τὴν ἀγάπην καὶ τὴν πίστιν ἣν ἔχεις πρὸς τὸν κύριον Ἰησοῦν καὶ εἰς πάντας τοὺς ἁγίους, ὅπως ἡ *κοινωνία τῆς πίστεώς σου *ἐνεργὴς γένηται ἐν *ἐπιγνώσει παντὸς ἀγαθοῦ τοῦ ἐν ἡμῖν εἰς Χριστόν· χαρὰν γὰρ πολλὴν ἔσχον καὶ *παράκλησιν ἐπὶ τῇ ἀγάπῃ σου, ὅτι τὰ *σπλάγχνα τῶν ἁγίων *ἀναπέπαυται διὰ σοῦ, ἀδελφέ. Διό, πολλὴν ἐν Χριστῷ *παρρησίαν ἔχων *ἐπιτάσσειν σοι τὸ *ἀνῆκον, διὰ τὴν ἀγάπην μᾶλλον παρακαλῶ, τοιοῦτος ὢν ὡς Παῦλος *πρεσβύτης, νυνὶ δὲ καὶ *δέσμιος Χριστοῦ Ἰησοῦ– παρακαλῶ σε περὶ τοῦ ἐμοῦ τέκνου, ὃν ἐγέννησα ἐν τοῖς *δεσμοῖς *' Ὀνήσιμον, τόν ποτέ σοι *ἄχρηστον νυνὶ δὲ καὶ σοὶ καὶ ἐμοὶ *εὔχρηστον, ὃν *ἀνέπεμψά σοι, αὐτόν, τοῦτ' ἔστιν τὰ ἐμὰ *σπλάγχνα· ὃν ἐγὼ ἐβουλόμην πρὸς ἐμαυτὸν *κατέχειν, ἵνα ὑπὲρ σοῦ μοι *διακονῇ ἐν τοῖς *δεσμοῖς τοῦ εὐαγγελίου, χωρὶς δὲ τῆς σῆς *γνώμης οὐδὲν ἠθέλησα ποιῆσαι, ἵνα μὴ ὡς κατὰ *ἀνάγκην τὸ ἀγαθόν σου ᾖ ἀλλὰ κατὰ *ἑκούσιον. *τάχα γὰρ διὰ τοῦτο *ἐχωρίσθη πρὸς ὥραν ἵνα αἰώνιον αὐτὸν *ἀπέχῃς, οὐκέτι ὡς δοῦλον ἀλλ' ὑπὲρ δοῦλον, ἀδελφὸν ἀγαπητόν, μάλιστα ἐμοί, *πόσῳ δὲ μᾶλλον σοὶ καὶ ἐν σαρκὶ καὶ ἐν κυρίῳ. Εἰ οὖν με ἔχεις *κοινωνόν, *προσλαβοῦ αὐτὸν ὡς ἐμέ. εἰ δέ τι *ἠδίκησέν σε ἢ ὀφείλει, τοῦτο ἐμοὶ *ἐλλόγα· ἐγὼ Παῦλος ἔγραψα τῇ ἐμῇ χειρί, ἐγὼ *ἀποτίσω· ἵνα μὴ λέγω σοι ὅτι καὶ σεαυτόν μοι *προσοφείλεις.*ναί, ἀδελφέ, ἐγώ σου *ὀναίμην ἐν κυρίῳ· *ἀνάπαυσόν μου τὰ σπλάγχνα ἐν Χριστῷ.

(Philemon 4–20)

Appendix One: Extra Vocabulary

All of the words that occur fifty or more times in the New Testament, together with a number of other words, are featured in this textbook. The majority of vocabulary words are presented in lessons I–XXIX. This appendix features other common New Testament words.

Adjective

διάβολος, -ον   slanderous (used substantively, "the devil, the Slanderer")

Nouns

ἀγρός, ὁ   field

ἄρχων, -οντος, ὁ   ruler

θύρα, ἡ   door

μαρτυρία, ἡ   testimony

μάρτυς, -υρος, ὁ   witness

Verbs

ἅπτομαι   I touch

ἀσθενέω   I am weak, I am ill

βλασφημέω   I blaspheme

διακονέω   I serve, I minister to

διέρχομαι   I pass through

ἐκπορεύομαι   I go out

ἐπιστρέφω   I return, I turn toward

ἐπιτίθημι   I lay upon

κλαίω   I weep, I cry

μετανοέω   I repent

παραγίνομαι   I come, I arrive

παρίστημι   I am present

πάσχω   I suffer

περισσεύω   I abound

πράσσω   I do, I practice

Adverb

ἄρτι   now

Preposition

ὀπίσω   behind, after (with genitive; also used adverbially)

Interjection

οὐαί   woe!

Appendix Two: Common Proper Nouns

Most proper nouns in the Greek New Testament can be readily recognized. Many proper nouns are declined according to familiar patterns, as the first declension noun Γαλιλαία. Others, however, are declined in unexpected ways. For instance, the name Ἰησοῦς, which is the Greek form of both "Jesus" and "Joshua," is declined Ἰησοῦς, Ἰησοῦ, Ἰησοῦ, Ἰησοῦν (note the unpredictable dative form). Still others, like Ἀβραάμ, are *indeclinable* — that is, they take the same form in all cases.

Ἀβραάμ   Abraham (indeclinable)

Γαλιλαία, -ας, ἡ   Galilee

Δαυίδ   David (indeclinable)

Ἡρῴδης, -ου   Herod

Ἰάκωβος, -ου   Jacob (James)

Ἱεροσόλυμα, τά, ἡ   Jerusalem (neuter plural and feminine singular)

Ἱερουσαλήμ, ἡ   Jerusalem (feminine, indeclinable)

Ἰησοῦς, -ου   Jesus, Joshua

Ἰουδαία, -ας, ἡ   Judea

Ἰούδας, -α   Jude

Ἰσραήλ, ὁ   Israel (indeclinable)

Ἰωάννης, -ου   John

Μαρία, -ας   Mary

Μαριάμ   Mary, (indeclinable)

Μωϋσῆς, -έως   Moses

Παῦλος, -ου   Paul

Πέτρος, -ου   Peter

Πιλᾶτος, -ου   Pilate

Σίμων, -ωνος   Simon

Φαρισαῖος, -ου   Pharisee

Appendix Three: Textual Criticism

Textual criticism seeks to construct the best text from among the thousands of manuscript copies of the New Testament. Since every manuscript of the New Testament differs from all the others in some particulars, textual critics compare the various versions of a given passage in the New Testament to determine which of the variant readings most likely recaptures the wording of the first, original manuscript.

Textual critics judge readings by applying a variety of criteria. Some criteria are independent of the specific textual variant in question and depend instead upon the character of the manuscript itself. These are called *extrinsic criteria*. The geographic provenance of the manuscript (where is it from?) is important because textual variations that are represented in a wide variety of locales are more likely to be authentic than are variations restricted to a particular locale. The genealogy of the manuscript (do we know which other manuscript it was probably copied from?) reflects on the general quality of the text because some textual manuscript are very reliable, other families are quite unreliable. The date of the manuscript (how early or late is it?) makes a difference, though a recent copy of a trustworthy ancient manuscript is more reliable than is a much older copy of a corrupt manuscript. Other criteria depend on the specific variant. These are called *intrinsic criteria*. Is one text significantly longer than others? Would a familiar copying error explain the variant? Is the grammar smoother here than in other versions? Which variant best fits the style of the author in question? Which variant makes the least sense? Which variant makes it easiest to explain how the others arose? Some simple rules of text criticism are:

> *A more difficult reading is usually preferable since copyists rarely made the* text harder *to understand.*
> *Quality outweighs quantity. It is easy to make many copies of a bad manuscript, and a good manuscript may have looked "wrong" to scribes who were accustomed to bad manuscripts.*
> *A shorter reading is often to be preferred because scribes were somewhat more likely to add material than to delete material.*
> *Which of the readings would, if it were original, make it easiest to explain why scribes produced the variant readings?*

But these rules must be qualified since there are important exceptions in particular circumstances.

Morphology

First Declension

	Singular	Plural	Singular	Plural	Singular	Plural
N	ὥρα	ὧραι	γραφή	γραφαί	ἀσθένεια	ἀσθένειαι
G	ὥρας	ὡρῶν	γραφῆς	γραφῶν	ἀσθενείας	ἀσθενειῶν
D	ὥρᾳ	ὥραις	γραφῇ	γραφαῖς	ἀσθενείᾳ	ἀσθενείαις
A	ὥραν	ὥρας	γραφήν	γραφάς	ἀσθένειαν	ἀσθενείας
N	γλῶσσα	γλῶσσαι	μαθήτης	μαθῆται		
G	γλώσσης	γλωσσῶν	μαθήτου	μαθητῶν		
D	γλώσσῃ	γλώσσαις	μαθήτῃ	μαθήταις		
A	γλῶσσαν	γλώσσας	μαθήτην	μαθήτας		

Second Declension

	Singular	Plural	Singular	Plural	Singular	Plural
N	νόμος	νόμοι	δῶρον	δῶρα	ἄνθρωπος	ἄνθρωποι
G	νόμου	νόμων	δώρου	δώρων	ἀνθρώπου	ἀνθρώπων
D	νόμῳ	νόμοις	δώρῳ	δώροις	ἀνθρώπῳ	ἀνθρώποις
A	νόμον	νόμους	δῶρον	δῶρα	ἄνθρωπον	ἀνθρώπους

Third Declension

	Singular	Plural	Singular	Plural	Singular	Plural
N	πόλις	πόλεις	σάρξ	σάρκες	γυνή	γυναῖκες
G	πόλεως	πόλεων	σαρκός	σαρκῶν	γυναικός	γυναικῶν
D	πόλει	πόλεσι	σαρκί	σαρξί	γυναικί	γυναιξί
A	πόλιν	πόλεις	σάρκα	σάρκας	γυναῖκα	γυναῖκας
N	γένος	γένη	ἀνήρ	ἄνδρες	σῶμα	σώματα
G	γένους	γενῶν	ἀνδρός	ἀνδρῶν	σώματος	σωμάτων
D	γένει	γένεσι	ἀνδρί	ἀνδράσι	σώματι	σώμασι
A	γένος	γένη	ἄνδρα	ἄνδρας	σῶμα	σώματα
N	ὕδωρ	ὕδατα	σωτήρ	σωτῆρες	βασιλεύς	βασιλεῖς
G	ὕδατος	ὑδάτων	σωτῆρος	σωτήρων	βασιλέως	βασιλέων
D	ὕδατι	ὕδασι	σωτῆρι	σωτῆρσι	βασιλεῖ	βασιλεῦσι
A	ὕδωρ	ὕδατα	σωτῆρα	σωτῆρας	βασιλέα	βασιλεῖς
N	χείρ	χεῖρες	μήτηρ	μητέρες	ἄρχων	ἄρχοντες
G	χειρός	χειρῶν	μητρός	μητέρων	ἄρχοντος	ἀρχόντων
D	χειρί	χερσίν	μητρί	μητράσι	ἄρχοντι	ἄρχουσιν
A	χεῖρα	χεῖρας	μητέρα	μητέρας	ἄρχοντα	ἄρχοντας
N	χάρις	χάριτες	φῶς	φῶτα		
G	χάριτος	χαρίτων	φωτός	φώτων		
D	χάριτι	χάρισι	φωτί	φωσί		
A	χάριν	χάριτας	φῶς	φῶτα		

The Article

	Singular			Plural		
	M	*F*	*N*	*M*	*F*	*N*
N	ὁ	ἡ	τό	οἱ	αἱ	τά
G	τοῦ	τῆς	τοῦ	τῶν	τῶν	τῶν
D	τῷ	τῇ	τῷ	τοῖς	ταῖς	τοῖς
A	τόν	τήν	τό	τούς	τάς	τά

Adjectives

	Singular			Plural		
	M	*F*	*N*	*M*	*F*	*N*
N	καλός	καλή	καλόν	καλοί	καλαί	καλά
G	καλοῦ	καλῆς	καλοῦ	καλῶν	καλῶν	καλῶν
D	καλῷ	καλῇ	καλῷ	καλοῖς	καλαῖς	καλοῖς
A	καλόν	καλήν	καλόν	καλούς	καλάς	καλά
N	ἅγιος	ἁγία	ἅγιον	ἅγιοι	ἅγιαι	ἅγια
G	ἁγίου	ἁγίας	ἁγίου	ἁγίων	ἁγίων	ἁγίων
D	ἁγίῳ	ἁγίᾳ	ἁγίῳ	ἁγίοις	ἁγίαις	ἁγίοις
A	ἅγιον	ἁγίαν	ἅγιον	ἁγίους	ἁγίας	ἅγια
N	μείζων	μείζων	μεῖζον	μείζονες	μείζονες	μείζονα
G	μείζονος	μείζονος	μείζονος	μειζόνων	μειζόνων	μειζόνων
D	μείζονι	μείζονι	μείζονι	μείζοσι	μείζοσι	μείζοσι
A	μείζονα	μείζονα	μεῖζον	μείζονας	μείζονας	μείζονα
N	πλήρης	πλήρης	πλήρες	πλήρεις	πλήρεις	πλήρη
G	πλήρους	πλήρους	πλήρους	πλήρων	πλήρων	πλήρων
D	πλήρει	πλήρει	πλήρει	πλήρεσι	πλήρεσι	πλήρεσι
A	πλήρη	πλήρη	πλήρες	πλήρεις	πλήρεις	πλήρη
N	ταχύς	ταχεῖα	ταχύ	ταχεῖς	ταχεῖαι	ταχέα
G	ταχέως	ταχείας	ταχέως	ταχέων	ταχειῶν	ταχέων
D	ταχεῖ	ταχείᾳ	ταχεῖ	ταχέσι	ταχείαις	ταχέσι
A	ταχύν	ταχεῖαν	ταχύ	ταχεῖς	ταχείας	ταχέα

Irregular Adjectives

	Singular			Plural	
M	**F**	**N**	**M**	**F**	**N**
N	μέγας	μεγάλη	μέγα	μεγάλοι	μεγάλαι	μεγάλα
G	μεγάλου	μεγάλης	μεγάλου	μεγάλων	μεγάλων	μεγάλων
D	μεγάλῳ	μεγάλη	μεγάλῳ	μεγάλοις	μεγάλαις	μεγάλοις
A	μέγαν	μεγάλην	μέγα	μεγάλους	μεγάλας	μεγάλα
N	πολύς	πολλή	πολύ	πολλοί	πολλαί	πολλά
G	πολλοῦ	πολλῆς	πολλοῦ	πολλῶν	πολλῶν	πολλῶν
D	πολλῷ	πολλῇ	πολλῷ	πολλοῖς	πολλαῖς	πολλοῖς
A	πολύν	πολλήν	πολύ	πολλούς	πολλάς	πολλά
N	πᾶς	πᾶσα	πᾶν	πάντες	πᾶσαι	πάντα
G	παντός	πάσης	παντός	πάντων	πασῶν	πάντων
D	παντί	πάσῃ	παντί	πᾶσι	πάσαις	πᾶσι
A	πάντα	πᾶσαν	πᾶν	πάντας	πάσας	πάντα

Personal Pronouns

	First Person		Second Person	
	singular	*plural*	*singular*	*plural*
N	ἐγώ	ἡμεῖς	σύ	ὑμεῖς
G	ἐμοῦ, μου	ἡμῶν	σοῦ	ὑμῶν
D	ἐμοί, μοι	ἡμῖν	σοί	ὑμῖν
A	ἐμέ, με	ἡμᾶς	σέ	ὑμᾶς

Third Person

	Singular			Plural	
M	**F**	**N**	**M**	**F**	**N**
N	αὐτός	αὐτή	αὐτό	αὐτοί	αὐταί	αὐτά
G	αὐτοῦ	αὐτῆς	αὐτοῦ	αὐτῶν	αὐτῶν	αὐτῶν
D	αὐτῷ	αὐτῇ	αὐτῷ	αὐτοῖς	αὐταῖς	αὐτοῖς
A	αὐτόν	αὐτήν	αὐτό	αὐτούς	αὐτάς	αὐτά

Demonstrative Pronouns

	Singular			Plural		
	M	*F*	*N*	*M*	*F*	*N*
N	οὗτος	αὕτη	τοῦτο	οὗτοι	αὗται	ταῦτα
G	τούτου	ταύτης	τούτου	τούτων	τούτων	τούτων
D	τούτῳ	ταύτῃ	τούτῳ	τούτοις	ταύταις	τούτοις
A	τοῦτον	ταύτην	τοῦτο	τούτους	ταύτας	ταῦτα
N	ἐκεῖνος	ἐκείνη	ἐκεῖνο	ἐκεῖνοι	ἐκεῖναι	ἐκεῖνα
G	ἐκείνου	ἐκείνης	ἐκείνου	ἐκείνων	ἐκείνων	ἐκείνων
D	ἐκείνῳ	ἐκείνῃ	ἐκείνῳ	ἐκείνοις	ἐκείναις	ἐκείνοις
A	ἐκεῖνον	ἐκείνην	ἐκεῖνο	ἐκείνους	ἐκείνας	ἐκεῖνα

Relative Pronoun

	Singular			Plural		
	M	*F*	*N*	*M*	*F*	*N*
N	ὅς	ἥ	ὅ	οἵ	αἵ	ἅ
G	οὗ	ἧς	οὗ	ὧν	ὧν	ὧν
D	ᾧ	ᾗ	ᾧ	οἷς	αἷς	οἷς
A	ὅν	ἥν	ὅ	οὕς	ἅς	ἅ

Interrogative Pronoun
(*Without Accent = Indefinite Pronoun*)

	Singular			Plural		
	M	*F*	*N*	*M*	*F*	*N*
N	τίς	τίς	τί	τίνες	τίνες	τίνα
G	τίνος	τίνος	τίνος	τίνων	τίνων	τίνων
D	τίνι	τίνι	τίνι	τίσι	τίσι	τίσι
A	τίνα	τίνα	τί	τίνας	τίνας	τίνα

Reflexive Pronoun

	M	F	N	M	F	N
	First Person Singular			*Second Person Singular*		
G	ἐμαυτοῦ	ἐμαυτῆς	ἐμαυτοῦ	σεαυτοῦ	σεαυτῆς	σεαυτοῦ
D	ἐμαυτῷ	ἐμαυτῇ	ἐμαυτῷ	σεαυτῷ	σεαυτῇ	σεαυτῷ
A	ἐμαυτόν	ἐμαυτήν	ἐμαυτό	σεαυτόν	σεαυτήν	σεαυτό
	Third Person Singular			*All Persons Plural*		
G	ἑαυτοῦ	ἑαυτῆς	ἑαυτοῦ	ἑαυτῶν	ἑαυτῶν	ἑαυτῶν
D	ἑαυτῷ	ἑαυτῇ	ἑαυτῷ	ἑαυτοῖς	ἑαυταῖς	ἑαυτοῖς
A	ἑαυτόν	ἑαυτήν	ἑαυτό	ἑαυτούς	ἑαυτάς	ἑαυτά

Reciprocal Pronoun (Plural Only)

	M	F	N
G	ἀλλήλων	ἀλλήλων	ἀλλήλων
D	ἀλλήλοις	ἀλλήλαις	ἀλλήλοις
A	ἀλλήλους	ἀλλήλας	ἀλλήλα

Ω Verbs: Present Stem

	Singular	Plural	Singular	Plural
	Present Active Indicative		Present Middle/Passive Indicative	
1ST	λύω	λύομεν	λύομαι	λυόμεθα
2ND	λύεις	λύετε	λύῃ	λύεσθε
3RD	λύει	λύουσι	λύεται	λύονται
INF	λύειν		λύεσθαι	
	Imperfect Active Indicative		Imperfect Middle/Passive Indicative	
1ST	ἔλυον	ἐλύομεν	ἐλυόμην	ἐλυόμεθα
2ND	ἔλυες	ἐλύετε	ἐλύου	ἐλύεσθε
3RD	ἔλυεν	ἔλυον	ἐλύετο	ἐλύοντο
	Present Active Subjunctive		Present Middle/Passive Subjunctive	
1ST	λύω	λύωμεν	λύωμαι	λυώμεθα
2ND	λύῃς	λύητε	λύῃ	λύησθε
3RD	λύῃ	λύωσι	λύηται	λύωνται
	Present Active Imperative		Present Middle/Passive Imperative	
2ND	λῦε	λύετε	λύου	λύεσθε
3RD	λυέτω	λυέτωσαν	λυέσθω	λυέσθωσαν

Ω Verbs: Future Stem

	Singular	Plural	Singular	Plural
	Future Active Indicative		Future Middle/Passive Indicative	
1ST	λύσω	λύσομεν	λύσομαι	λυσόμεθα
2ND	λύσεις	λύσετε	λύσῃ	λύσεσθε
3RD	λύσει	λύσουσι	λύσεται	λύσονται
INF	λύσειν		λύσεσθαι	

Ω *Verbs: Aorist Stem*

	First Aorist		Second Aorist	
	singular	plural	singular	plural

Active Indicative

1ST	ἔλυσα	ἐλύσαμεν	ἔλιπον	ἐλίπομεν
2ND	ἔλυσας	ἐλύσατε	ἔλιπες	ἐλίπετε
3RD	ἔλυσεν	ἔλυσαν	ἔλιπεν	ἔλιπον
INF	λῦσαι		λιπεῖν	

Middle Indicative

1ST	ἐλυσάμην	ἐλυσάμεθα	ἐλιπόμην	ἐλιπόμεθα
2ND	ἐλύσω	ἐλύσασθε	ἐλίπου	ἐλίπεσθε
3RD	ἐλύσατο	ἐλύσαντο	ἐλίπετο	ἐλίποντο
INF	λύσασθαι		λιπέσθαι	

Active Subjunctive

1ST	λύσω	λύσωμεν	λίπω	λίπωμεν
2ND	λύσῃς	λύσητε	λίπῃς	λίπητε
3RD	λύσῃ	λύσωσι	λίπῃ	λίπωσιν

Middle Subjunctive

1ST	λύσωμαι	λυσώμεθα	λίπωμαι	λιπώμεθα
2ND	λύσῃ	λύσησθε	λίπῃ	λίπησθε
3RD	λύσηται	λύσωνται	λίπηται	λίπωνται

Active Imperative

2ND	λῦσον	λύσατε	λίπε	λίπετε
3RD	λυσάτω	λυσάτωσαν	λιπέτω	λιπέτωσαν

Middle Imperative

2ND	λῦσαι	λύσασθε	λιποῦ	λίπεσθε
3RD	λυσάσθω	λυσάσθωσαν	λιπέσθω	λιπέσθωσαν

Ω Verbs: Aorist Passive Stem

	Singular	Plural	Singular	Plural
	Aorist Passive Indicative		*Aorist Passive Indicative*	
1ST	ἐλύθην	ἐλύθημεν	ἐγράφην	ἐγράφημεν
2ND	ἐλύθης	ἐλύθητε	ἐγράφης	ἐγράφητε
3RD	ἐλύθη	ἐλύθησαν	ἐγράφη	ἐγράφησαν
INF	λυθῆναι		γραφῆναι	
	Aorist Passive Subjunctive		*Aorist Passive Imperative*	
1ST	λυθῶ	λυθῶμεν		
2ND	λυθῇς	λυθῆτε	λύθητι	λύθητε
3RD	λυθῇ	λυθῶσιν	λυθήτω	λυθήτωσαν
	Future Passive Indicative			
1ST	λυθήσομαι	λυθησόμεθα		
2ND	λυθήσῃ	λυθήσεσθε		
3RD	λυθήσεται	λυθήσονται		
INF	λυθήσεσθαι			

Ω Verbs: Perfect Stem

	Singular	Plural	Singular	Plural
	Perfect Active Indicative		*Pluperfect Active Indicative*	
1ST	λέλυκα	λελύκαμεν	ἐλελύκειν	ἐλελύκειμεν
2ND	λέλυκας	λελύκατε	ἐλελύκεις	ἐλελύκειτε
3RD	λέλυκεν	λελύκασι	ἐλελύκει	ἐλελύκεισαν
INF	λελυκέναι			

Ω Verbs: Perfect Passive Stem

	Singular	Plural		Singular	Plural
	Perfect Middle/Passive Indicative			*Pluperfect Middle/Passive Indicative*	
1ST	λέλυμαι	λελύμεθα		ἐλελύμην	ἐλελύμεθα
2ND	λέλυσαι	λέλυσθε		ἐλέλυσο	ἐλέλυσθε
3RD	λέλυται	λέλυνται		ἐλέλυτο	ἐλέλυντο
INF	λελύσθαι				

Contract Verbs: Present System

	Ἀγαπάω		Τηρέω		Πληρόω	
	singular	*plural*	*singular*	*plural*	*singular*	*plural*
			Present Active Indicative			
1ST	ἀγαπῶ	ἀγαπῶμεν	τηρῶ	τηροῦμεν	πληρῶ	πληροῦμεν
2ND	ἀγαπᾷς	ἀγαπᾶτε	τηρεῖς	τηρεῖτε	πληροῖς	πληροῦτε
3RD	ἀγαπᾷ	ἀγαπῶσιν	τηρεῖ	τηροῦσιν	πληροῖ	πληροῦσιν
INF	ἀγαπᾶν		τηρεῖν		πληροῦν	
			Present Middle/Passive Indicative			
1ST	ἀγαπῶμαι	ἀγαπώμεθα	τηροῦμαι	τηρούμεθα	πληροῦμαι	πληρούμεθα
2ND	ἀγαπᾷ	ἀγαπᾶσθε	τηρῇ	τηρεῖσθε	πληροῖ	πληροῦσθε
3RD	ἀγαπᾶται	ἀγαπῶνται	τηρεῖται	τηροῦνται	πληροῦται	πληροῦνται
INF	ἀγαπᾶσθαι		τηρεῖσθαι		πληροῦσθαι	
			Present Active Subjunctive			
1ST	ἀγαπῶ	ἀγαπῶμεν	τηρῶ	τηρῶμεν	πληρῶ	πληρῶμεν
2ND	ἀγαπᾷς	ἀγαπᾶτε	τηρῇς	τηρῆτε	πληροῖς	πληρῶτε
3RD	ἀγαπᾷ	ἀγαπῶσιν	τηρῇ	τηρῶσιν	πληροῖ	πληρῶσιν
			Present Middle/Passive Subjunctive			
1ST	ἀγαπῶμαι	ἀγαπώμεθα	τηρῶμαι	τηρώμεθα	πληρῶμαι	πληρώμεθα
2ND	ἀγαπᾷ	ἀγαπᾶσθε	τηρῇ	τηρῆσθε	πληροῖ	πληρῶσθε
3RD	ἀγαπᾶται	ἀγαπῶνται	τηρῆται	τηρῶνται	πληρῶται	πληρῶνται

	Ἀγαπάω		Τηρέω		Πληρόω	
	singular	*plural*	*singular*	*plural*	*singular*	*plural*

Imperfect Active Indicative

1ST	ἠγάπων	ἠγαπῶμεν	ἐτήρουν	ἐτηροῦμεν	ἐπλήρουν	ἐπληροῦμεν
2ND	ἠγάπας	ἠγαπᾶτε	ἐτήρεις	ἐτηρεῖτε	ἐπλήρους	ἐπληροῦτε
3RD	ἠγάπα	ἠγάπων	ἐτήρει	ἐτήρουν	ἐπλήρου	ἐπλήρουν

Imperfect Middle/Passive Indicative

1ST	ἠγαπώμην	ἠγαπώμεθα	ἐτηρούμην	ἐτηροῦμεν	ἐπληρούμην	ἐπληρούμεθα
2ND	ἠγαπῶ	ἠγαπᾶσθε	ἐτηροῦ	ἐτηρεῖσθε	ἐπληροῦ	ἐπληροῦσθε
3RD	ἠγαπᾶτο	ἠγαπῶντο	ἐτηρεῖτο	ἐτηροῦντο	ἐπληροῦτο	ἐπληροῦντο

Present Active Imperative

2ND	ἀγάπα	ἀγαπᾶτε	τήρει	τηρεῖτε	πλήρου	πληροῦτε
3RD	ἀγαπάτω	ἀγαπάτωσαν	τηρείτω	τηρείτωσαν	πληρούτω	πληρούτωσαν

Present Middle/Passive Imperative

2ND	ἀγαπῶ	ἀγαπᾶσθε	τηροῦ	τηρεῖσθε	πληροῦ	πληροῦσθε
3RD	ἀγαπάσθω	ἀγαπάσθωσαν	τηρείσθω	τηρείσθωσαν	πληρούσθω	πληρούσθωσαν

Present Active Participle

M	ἀγαπῶν	ἀγαπῶντες	τηρῶν	τηροῦντες	πληρῶν	πληροῦντες
F	ἀγαπῶσα	ἀγαπῶσαι	τηροῦσα	τηροῦσαι	πληροῦσα	πληροῦσαι
N	ἀγαπῶν	ἀγαπῶντα	τηρῶν	τηροῦντα	πληρῶν	πληροῦντα

Present Middle/Passive Participle

M	ἀγαπώμενος	ἀγαπώμενοι	τηρούμενος	τηρούμενοι	πληρούμενος	πληρούμενοι
F	ἀγαπωμένη	ἀγαπώμεναι	τηρουμένη	τηρούμεναι	πληρουμένη	πληρούμεναι
N	ἀγαπώμενον	ἀγαπώμενα	τηρούμενον	τηρούμενα	πληρούμενον	πληρούμενα

Mι Verbs: Present Stem

	Singular	Plural		Singular	Plural
	Present Active Indicative			*Present Middle/Passive Indicative*	
1ST	δίδωμι	δίδομεν		δίδομαι	διδόμεθα
2ND	δίδως	δίδοτε		δίδοσαι	δίδοσθε
3RD	δίδωσιν	διδόασιν		δίδοται	δίδονται
INF	διδόναι			δίδοσθαι	
	Imperfect Active Indicative			*Imperfect Middle/Passive Indicative*	
1ST	ἐδίδουν	ἐδίδομεν		ἐδιδόμην	ἐδιδόμεθα
2ND	ἐδίδους	ἐδίδοτε		ἐδίδοσο	ἐδίδοσθε
3RD	ἐδίδου	ἐδίδοσαν		ἐδίδοτο	ἐδίδοντο
	Present Active Subjunctive			*Present Middle/Passive Subjunctive*	
1ST	διδῶ	διδῶμεν		διδῶμαι	διδώμεθα
2ND	διδῷς	διδῶτε		διδῷ	διδῶσθε
3RD	διδῷ	διδῶσιν		διδῶται	διδῶνται
	Present Active Imperative			*Present Middle/Passive Imperative*	
2ND	δίδου	δίδοτε		δίδοσο	δίδοσθε
3RD	διδότω	διδότωσαν		διδόσθω	διδόσθωσαν

Mι Verbs: Aorist and Aorist Passive Stems

	Singular	Plural	Singular	Plural	Singular	Plural
	Active Indicative		*Middle Indicative*		*Passive Indicative*	
1ST	ἔδωκα	ἐδώκαμεν	ἐδόμην	ἐδόμεθα	ἐδόθην	ἐδόθημεν
2ND	ἔδωκας	ἐδώκατε	ἔδου	ἔδοσθε	ἐδόθης	ἐδόθητε
3RD	ἔδωκεν	ἔδωκαν	ἔδοτο	ἔδοντο	ἐδόθη	ἐδόθησαν
INF	δοῦναι		δόσθαι		δοθῆναι	
	Active Subjunctive		*Middle Subjunctive*		*Passive Subjunctive*	
1ST	δῶ	δῶμεν	δῶμαι	δώμεθα	δοθῶ	δοθῶμεν
2ND	δῷς	δῶτε	δῷ	δῶσθε	δοθῆς	δοθῆτε
3RD	δῷ	δῶσιν	δῶται	δῶνται	δοθῇ	δοθῶσιν
	Active Imperative		*Middle Imperative*		*Passive Imperative*	
2ND	δός	δότε	δοῦ	δόσθε	δόθητι	δόθητε
3RD	δότω	δότωσαν	δόσθε	δόσθωσαν	δοθήτω	δοθήτωσαν

Mι Verbs: Perfect and Perfect Middle/Passive Stems

	Singular	Plural	Singular	Plural
	Perfect Active Indicative		*Perfect Middle/Passive Indicative*	
1ST	δέδωκα	δεδώκαμεν	δέδομαι	δεδόμεθα
2ND	δέδωκας	δεδώκατε	δέδοσαι	δέδοσθε
3RD	δέδωκεν	δεδώκασιν	δέδοται	δέδονται
INF	δεδωκέναι			
	Pluperfect Active Indicative			
1ST	δεδώκειν	δεδώκειμεν		
2ND	δεδώκεις	δεδώκειτε		
3RD	δεδώκει	δεδώκεισαν		

Peculiar Μι Verbs

Ἀπόλλυμι				Δείκνυμι	
singular	plural			singular	plural

Present Active Indicative

			singular	plural
	1ST	δείκνυμι	*
ἀπολλύει	*	*3RD*	δείκνυσιν	*

Present Middle Indicative

ἀπόλλυμαι	ἀπολλύμεθα	*1ST*	*	*
*	*	*2ND*	*	*
ἀπόλλυται	ἀπόλλυνται	*3RD*	*	*

Present Active Imperative

ἀπόλλυε	*	*2ND*	*	*

Future Active Indicative

ἀπολῶ, ἀπολέσω	*	*1ST*	δείξω	*
*	ἀπόλητε	*2ND*		
ἀπολέσει	*	*3RD*	δείξει	*

Future Middle Indicative

*	ἀπολεῖσθε	*2ND*	*	*
ἀπολεῖται	ἀπολοῦνται	*3RD*	*	*

Aorist Active Indicative

*	*	*1ST*	ἔδειξα	*
*	*	*3RD*	ἔδειξεν	ἔδειξαν
ἀπολέσαι		*INF*	δεῖξαι	

Aorist Middle Indicative

ἀπολέσθαι		*INF*	*	

Aorist Active Subjunctive

ἀπολέσω	ἀπολέσωμεν	*1ST*	δείξω	*
*	ἀπολέσητε	*2ND*	*	*
ἀπολέση	ἀπολέσωσιν	*3RD*	*	*

Aorist Middle Subjunctive

*	ἀπόλησθε	*2ND*	*	*
ἀπόληται	ἀπόλωνται	*3RD*	*	*

Ἀπόλλυμι		Δείκνυμι	
singular	*plural*	*singular*	*plural*

Aorist Active Imperative

*	*	2ND	δεῖξον	δείξατε
*	*	3RD	δειξάτο	*

Participles

Ἀπόλλυμι	Δείκνυμι

Present Middle/Passive Masculine Nominative Plural

ἀπολλύμενοι　　　　　*

Present Middle/Passive Masculine/Neuter Genitive Singular

ἀπολλυμένου　　　　　*

Present Middle/Passive Masculine/Neuter Dative Plural

ἀπολλυμένοις　　　　　*

Present Middle/Passive Feminine Accusative Singular

ἀπολλυμένην　　　　　*

Aorist Active Masculine Nominative Singular

ἀπολέσας　　　　　*

Aorist Active Feminine Nominative Singular

ἀπολέσασα　　　　　*

Aorist Middle Masculine/Neuter Genitive Singular

ἀπολομένου　　　　　*

Aorist Passive Masculine Accusative Singular

　　　　　*　　　　　δειχθέντα

Perfect Active Masculine Nominative Singular

ἀπολωλώς　　　　　*

Perfect Active Neuter Accusative Singular

ἀπολωλός　　　　　*

Perfect Active Neuter Accusative Plural

ἀπολωλότα　　　　　*

Participles

	Singular			Plural	
M	*F*	*N*	*M*	*F*	*N*

Present Active

N	λύων	λύουσα	λῦον	λύοντες	λύουσαι	λύοντα
F	λύοντος	λυούσης	λύοντος	λυόντων	λυουσῶν	λυόντων
D	λύοντι	λυούσῃ	λύοντι	λύουσιν	λυούσαις	λύουσιν
A	λύοντα	λύουσαν	λῦον	λύοντας	λυούσας	λύοντα

Present Middle/Passive

N	λυόμενος	λυομένη	λυόμενον	λυόμενοι	λυόμεναι	λυόμενα
G	λυομένου	λυομένης	λυομένου	λυομένων	λυομένων	λυομένων
D	λυομένῳ	λυομένη	λυομένῳ	λυομένοις	λυομέναις	λυομένοις
A	λυόμενον	λυομένην	λυόμενον	λυομένους	λυομένας	λυόμενα

Aorist Active

N	λύσας	λύσασα	λῦσαν	λύσαντες	λύσασαι	λύσαντα
G	λύσαντος	λυσάσης	λύσαντος	λυσάντων	λυσασῶν	λυσάντων
D	λύσαντι	λυσάσῃ	λύσαντι	λύσασιν	λυσάσαις	λύσασιν
A	λύσαντα	λύσασαν	λῦσαν	λύσαντας	λυσάσας	λύσαντα

Aorist Middle

N	λυσάμενος	λυσαμένη	λυσάμενον	λυσάμενοι	λυσάμεναι	λυσάμενα
G	λυσαμένου	λυσαμένης	λυσαμένου	λυσαμένων	λυσαμένων	λυσαμένων
D	λυσαμένῳ	λυσαμένη	λυσαμένῳ	λυσαμένοις	λυσαμέναις	λυσαμένοις
A	λυσάμενον	λυσαμένην	λυσάμενον	λυσαμένους	λυσαμένας	λυσάμενα

Aorist Passive

N	λυθείς	λυθεῖσα	λυθέν	λυθέντες	λυθεῖσαι	λυθέντα
G	λυθέντος	λυθείσης	λυθέντος	λυθέντων	λυθεισῶν	λυθέντων
D	λυθέντι	λυθείσῃ	λυθέντι	λυθεῖσιν	λυθείσαις	λυθεῖσιν
A	λυθέντα	λυθεῖσαν	λυθέν	λυθέντας	λυθείσας	λυθέντα

Second Aorist Active

N	ἰδών	ἰδοῦσα	ἰδόν	ἰδόντες	ἰδοῦσαι	ἰδόντα
G	ἰδόντος	ἰδούσης	ἰδόντος	ἰδόντων	ἰδουσῶν	ἰδόντων
D	ἰδόντι	ἰδούσῃ	ἰδόντι	ἰδοῦσιν	ἰδούσαις	ἰδοῦσιν
A	ἰδόντα	ἰδοῦσαν	ἰδόν	ἰδόντας	ἰδούσας	ἰδόντα

	Singular			*Plural*	
M	F	N	M	F	N

Second Aorist Middle

N	ἰδόμενος	ἰδομένη	ἰδόμενον	ἰδόμενοι	ἰδόμεναι	ἰδόμενα
G	ἰδομένου	ἰδομένης	ἰδομένου	ἰδομένων	ἰδομένων	ἰδομένων
D	ἰδομένῳ	ἰδομένῃ	ἰδομένῳ	ἰδομένοις	ἰδομέναις	ἰδομένοις
A	ἰδόμενον	ἰδομένην	ἰδόμενον	ἰδομένους	ἰδομένας	ἰδόμενα

Perfect Active

N	λελυκώς	λελυκυῖα	λελυκός	λελυκότες	λελυκυῖαι	λελυκότα
G	λελυκότος	λελυκυίας	λελυκότος	λελυκότων	λελυκυιῶν	λελυκότων
D	λελυκότι	λελυκυίᾳ	λελυκότι	λελυκόσιν	λελυκυίαις	λελυκόσιν
A	λελυκότα	λελυκυῖαν	λελυκός	λελυκότας	λελυκυίας	λελυκότα

Perfect Middle/Passive

N	λελυμένος	λελυμένη	λελυμένον	λελυμένοι	λελυμέναι	λελυμένα
G	λελυμένου	λελυμένης	λελυμένου	λελυμένων	λελυμένων	λελυμένων
D	λελυμένῳ	λελυμένῃ	λελυμένῳ	λελυμένοις	λελυμέναις	λελυμένοις
A	λελυμένον	λελυμένην	λελυμένον	λελυμένους	λελυμένας	λελυμένα

Principal Parts of Verbs in the Vocabulary

ἀγαπάω	ἀγαπήσω	ἠγάπησα	ἠγάπηκα	ἠγάπημαι	ἠγαπήθην
ἁγιάζω	ἁγιάσω	ἡγίασα	—	ἡγίασμαι	ἡγιάσθην
ἀγοράζω	ἀγοράσω	ἠγόρησα	ἠγόρακα	ἠγόρασμαι	ἠγοράσθην
ἄγω	ἄξω	ἤγαγον	ἦχα	ἦγμαι	ἤχθην
αἴρω	ἀρῶ	ἦρα	ἦρκα	ἦρμαι	ἤρθην
αἰτέω	αἰτήσω	ᾔτησα	ᾔτηκα	ᾔτημαι	ᾐτήθην
ἀκολουθέω	ἀκολουθήσω	ἠκολούθησα	ἠκολούθηκα	ἠκολούθημαι	ἠκολουθήθην
ἀκούω	ἀκούσω	ἤκουσα	ἀκήκοα	ἤκουσμαι	ἠκούσθην
ἁμαρτάνω	ἁμαρτήσω	ἡμάρτησα ἥμαρτον	ἡμάρτηκα	ἡμάρτημαι	ἡμαρτήθην
ἀναβαίνω	ἀναβήσομαι	ἀνέβην	ἀναβέβημα	—	—
ἀναγινώσκω	ἀναγνώσομαι	ἀνέγνων	ἀνέγνωκα	ἀνέγνωσμαι	ἀνεγνώσθην
ἀνίστημι	ἀναστήσω	ἀνέστησα	ἀνέστηκα	ἀνέσταμαι	ἀνεστάθην
ἀνοίγω	ἀνοίξω	ἀνέῳξα ἠνέῳξα ἤνοιξα	ἀνέῳγα	ἀνέῳγμαι ἠνέῳγμαι	ἀνεῴχθην ἠνεῴχθην ἠνοίχθην
ἀπαγγέλλω	ἀπαγγελῶ	ἀπήγγειλα	—	—	ἀπηγγέλην
ἀπέρχομαι	ἀπελεύσομαι	ἀπῆλθον	ἀπελήλυθα	—	—
ἀποδίδωμι	ἀποδώσω	ἀπέδωκα ἀπεδόμην	—	—	ἀπεδόθην
ἀποθνῄσκω	ἀποθανοῦμαι	ἀπέθανον	—	—	—
ἀποκρίνομαι	—	ἀπεκρινάμην	—	—	ἀπεκρίθην
ἀποκτείνω	ἀποκτενῶ	ἀπέκτεινα	ἀπέκτονα	—	ἀπεκτάνθην

ἀπολύω	ἀπολύσω	ἀπέλυσα	—	ἀπολέλυμαι	ἀπελύθην
ἀποστέλλω	ἀποστελῶ	ἀπέστειλα	ἀπέσταλκα	ἀπέσταλμαι	ἀπεστάλην
ἄρχω	ἄρξω	ἦρξα	ἦρχα	ἦργμαι	ἤρχθην
ἄρχομαι	ἄρξομαι	[ἠρξάμην]	[ἦργμαι]	—	—
ἀσπάζομαι	ἀσπάσομαι	ἠσπασάμην	—	—	—
ἀφίημι	ἀφήσω	ἀφῆκα	ἀφεῖκα	ἀφεῖμαι	ἀφείθην
βάλλω	βαλῶ	ἔβαλον	βέβληκα	βέβλημαι	ἐβλήθην
βαπτίζω	βαπτίσω	ἐβάπτισα	—	βεβάπτισμαι	ἐβαπτίσθην
βασανίζω	βασανίσω	ἐβασάνισα	—	—	ἐβασανίσθην
βασιλεύω	βασιλεύσω	ἐβασίλευσα	—	—	—
βαστάζω	βαστάσω	ἐβάστασα	—	βεβάσταμμαι	ἐβαστάχθην
βλέπω	βλέψω	ἔβλεψα	βέβλεφα	βέβλεμμαι	ἐβλέφθην
βούλομαι	—	—	—	—	ἐβουλήθην
γεννάω 13ᵭ	γεννήσω	ἐγέννησα	γεγέννηκα	γεγέννημαι	ἐγεννήθην
γίνομαι	γενήσομαι	ἐγενόμην ἐγενήθην	γέγονα	γεγένημαι	ἐγενήθην
γινώσκω	γνώσομαι	ἔγνων	ἔγνωκα	ἔγνωσμαι	ἐγνώσθην
γνωρίζω	γνωρίσω	ἐγνώρισα	—	—	ἐγνωρίσθην
γράφω	γράψω	ἔγραψα	γέγραφα	γέγραμμαι	ἐγράφθην
δέχομαι	—	—	—	—	—
δέχομαι	δέξομαι	ἐδεξάμην	—	δέδεγμαι	ἐδέχθην
δηλόω	δηλώσω	ἐδήλωσα	δεδήλωκα	δεδήλωμαι	ἐδηλώθην
διδάσκω	διδάξω	ἐδίδαξα	δεδίδαχα	δεδίδαγμαι	ἐδιδάχθην
δίδωμι	δώσω	ἔδωκα	δέδωκα	δέδομαι	ἐδόθην

δικαιόω	δικαιώσω	ἐδικαίωσα	—	δεδικαίωμαι	ἐδικαιώθην
διψάω	διψήσω	ἐδίψησα	δεδίψηκα	—	—
διώκω	διώξω	ἐδίωξα	δεδίωχα	δεδίωγμαι	ἐδιώχθην
δοκέω	δόξω	ἔδοξα	—	—	—
δοξάζω	δοξάσω	ἐδόξασα	—	δεδόξασμαι	ἐδοξάσθην
δουλεύω	δουλεύσω	ἐδούλευσα	δεδούλευκα	—	—
δύναμαι	δυνήσομαι	—	—	—	ἐδυνήθην
ἐγγίζω	ἐγγιῶ	ἤγγισα	ἤγγικα	—	—
ἐγείρω	ἐγερῶ	ἤγειρα	ἐγήγερκα	ἐγήγερμαι	ἠγέρθην
εἰμί	ἔσομαι	—	—	—	—
εἰσάγω	—	εἰσῆγαγον	—	—	—
εἰσέρχομαι	εἰσελεύσομαι	εἰσῆλθον	εἰσελήλυθα	—	—
ἐκβάλλω	ἐκβαλῶ	ἐξέβαλον	ἐκβέβληκα	ἐκβέβλημαι	ἐξεβλήθην
ἐκτείνω	ἐκτενῶ	ἐξέτεινα	—	—	—
ἐλευθερόω	ἐλευθερώσω	ἠλευθέρωσα	—	—	ἠλευθερώθην
ἐλπίζω	ἐλπιῶ	ἤλπισα	ἤλπικα	—	—
ἐξέρχομαι	ἐξελεύσομαι	ἐξῆλθον	ἐξελήλυθα	—	—
ἔξεστιν	—	—	—	—	—
ἐπερωτάω	ἐπερωτήσω	ἐπηρώτησα	—	—	—
ἐπιγινώσκω	ἐπιγνώσομαι	ἐπέγνων	ἐπέγνωκα	—	ἐπεγνώσθην
ἐπιστρέφω	ἐπιστρέψω	ἐπέστρεψα	ἐπέστροφα	—	ἐπεστράφην
ἐπιτίθημι	ἐπιθήσω	ἐπέθηκα / ἐπέθην	—	ἐπιτέθειμαι	ἐπετέθην

ἐργάζομαι	—	ἐργασάμην / εἰργασάμην	—	εἴργασμαι	εἰργάσθην
ἔρχομαι	ἐλεύσομαι	ἦλθον	ἐλήλυθα	—	—
ἐρωτάω	ἐρωτήσω	ἠρώτησα	ἠρώτηκα	—	—
ἐσθίω	φάγομαι	ἔφαγον	—	—	—
ἑτοιμάζω	ἑτοιμάσω	ἡτοίμασα	ἡτοίμακα	ἡτοίμασμαι	ἡτοιμάσθην
εὐαγγελίζω	—	εὐηγγέλισα	—	εὐηγγέλισμαι	εὐηγγελίσθην
εὐλογέω	εὐλογήσω	εὐλόγησα	εὐλόγηκα	εὐλόγημαι	εὐλογήθην
εὑρίσκω	εὑρήσω	εὕρησα / εὗρον	εὕρηκα	εὕρημαι	εὑρέθην
εὐφραίνω	εὐφρανῶ	ηὔφρανα	—	—	ηὐφράνθην / εὐφράνθην
εὐχαριστέω	εὐχαριστήσω	εὐχαρίστησα	—	—	εὐχαριστήθην
ἔχω	ἕξω	ἔσχον	ἔσχηκα	ἔσχημαι	—
ζάω	ζήσω	ἔζησα	ἔζηκα	—	—
ζητέω	ζητήσω	ἐζήτησα	ἐζήτηκα	—	ἐζητήθην
θαυμάζω	θαυμάσομαι	ἐθαύμασα	τεθαύμακα	τεθαύμασμαι	ἐθαυμάσθην
θεάομαι	θεάσομαι	ἐθεασάμην	—	τεθέαμαι	ἐθεάθην
θέλω	θελήσω	ἠθέλησα	τεθέληκα	—	—
θεωρέω	θεωρήσω	ἐθεώρησα	τεθεώρηκα	—	—
θύω	θύσω	ἔθυσα	τέθυκα	τέθυμαι	ἐτύθην
θεραπεύω	θεραπεύσω	ἐθεράπευσα	—	τεθεράπευμαι	ἐθεραπεύθην
ἵστημι	στήσω	ἔστησα / ἔστην	ἕστηκα	ἕσταμαι	ἐστάθην

καθαρίζω	καθαριῶ	ἐκαθάρισα	—	κεκαθάρισμαι	ἐκαθαρίσθην
κάθημαι	καθήσομαι	—	—	—	—
καθίστημι	καταστήσω	κατέστησα	κατέστακα	κατέσταμαι	κατεστάθην
καλέω	καλέσω	ἐκάλεσα	κέκληκα	κέκλημαι	ἐκλήθην
καταβαίνω	καταβήσομαι	κατέβην	καταβέβηκα	—	—
καταλύω	καταλύσω	κατέλυσα	—	—	κατελύθην
κατοικέω	—	κατῴκησα	—	—	—
κηρύσσω	κηρύξω	ἐκήρυξα	κεκήρυχα	κεκήρυγμαι	ἐκηρύχθην
κράζω	κράξω	ἔκραξα	κέκραγα	—	—
κρατέω	κρατήσω	ἐκράτησα	κεκράτηκα	κεκράτημαι	—
κρίνω	κρινῶ	ἔκρινα	κέκρινα	κέκριμαι	ἐκρίθην
κωλύω	—	ἐκώλυσα	—	—	ἐκωλύθην
λαλέω	λαλήσω	ἐλάλησα	λελάληκα	λελάλημαι	ἐλαλήθην
λαμβάνω	λήμψομαι	ἔλαβον	εἴληφα	εἴλημμαι	ἐλήμφθην
λέγω	λέξω / ἐρῶ	εἶπον / ἔλεξα	εἴρηκα	εἴρημαι / λέλεγμαι	ἐρρέθην / ἐλέχθην
λείπω	λείψω	ἔλιπον	λέλοιπα / ἔλειψα	λέλειμμαι	ἐλείφθην
λογίζομαι	—	ἐλογισάμην	—	—	ἐλογίσθην
λυπέω	λυπήσω	ἐλύπησα	λελύπηκα	λελύπημαι	ἐλυπήθην
λύω	λύσω	ἔλυσα	λέλυκα	λέλυμαι	ἐλύθην
μαρτυρέω	μαρτυρήσω	ἐμαρτύρησα	μεμαρτύρηκα	μεμαρτύρημαι	ἐμαρτυρήθην

Present	Future	Aorist	Perfect Active	Perfect Mid/Pass	Aorist Passive
ἀγγέλλω	ἀγγελῶ	ἤγγειλα	—	—	—
αἰνέω	αἰνέσω	ᾔνεσα	—	—	—
μετανοέω	μετανοήσω	μετενόησα	—	—	—
μισέω	μισήσω	ἐμίσησα	μεμίσηκα	μεμίσημαι	—
μοιχεύω	μοιχεύσω	ἐμοίχευσα	—	—	ἐμοιχεύθην
νικάω	νικήσω	ἐνίκησα	νενίκηκα	νενίκημαι	ἐνικήθην
νομίζω	νομιῶ νομίσω	ἐνόμισα	νενόμικα	νενόμισμαι	ἐνομίσθην
ξηραίνω	ξηρανῶ	ἐξήρανα	—	ἐξήραμμαι	ἐξηράνθην
[οἶδα] *(perfect)*	εἰδήσω	[ᾔδειν] *(pluperf)*	οἶδα	—	—
οἰκοδομέω	οἰκοδομήσω	ᾠκοδόμησα	ᾠκοδόμηκα	οἰκοδόμημαι ᾠκοδόμημαι	οἰκοδομήθην ᾠκοδομήθην
ὁράω	ὄψομαι	εἶδον	ἑόρακα	—	ὤφθην
ὀφείλω	—	—	—	—	—
παραδίδωμι	παραδώσω	παρέδωκα	παραδέδωκα	παραδέδομαι	παρεδόθην
παρακαλέω	παρακαλέσω	παρεκάλεσα	παρακέκληκα	παρακέκλημαι	παρεκλήθην
παραλαμβάνω	παραλήμψομαι	παρέλαβον	—	—	παρελήμφθην
παρίστημι	παραστήσω	παρέστησα	παρέστηκα	—	παρεστάθην
παρατίθημι	παραθήσω	παρέθηκα	—	—	—
πάσχω	πείσομαι	ἔπαθον	πέπονθα	—	—
πείθω	πείσω	ἔπεισα	πέποιθα	πέπεισμαι	ἐπείσθην
πειράζω	πειράσω	ἐπείρασα	πεπείρακα	πεπείραμαι	ἐπειράσθην
πέμπω	πέμψω	ἔπεμψα	πέπομφα	πέπεμμαι	ἐπέμφθην

περιπατέω	περιπατήσω	περιεπάτησα	—	—	περιεπατήθην
πίνω	πίομαι	ἔπιον	πέπωκα	—	ἐπόθην
πίπτω	πεσοῦμαι	ἔπεσον	πέπτωκα	—	—
πιστεύω	πιστεύσω	ἐπίστευσα	πεπίστευκα	πεπίστευμαι	ἐπιστεύθην
πλανάω	πλανήσω	ἐπλάνησα	—	πεπλάνημαι	ἐπλανήθην
πληρόω	πληρώσω	ἐπλήρωσα	πεπλήρωκα	πεπλήρωμαι	ἐπληρώθην
ποιέω	ποιήσω	ἐποίησα	πεποίηκα	πεποίημαι	—
πορεύομαι	πορεύσομαι	—	—	πεπόρευμαι	ἐπορεύθην
προσέρχομαι	προσελεύσομαι	προσῆλθον	προσελήλυθα	—	—
προσεύχομαι	προσεύξομαι	προσηυξάμην	—	—	—
προσκυνέω	προσκυνήσω	προσεκύνησα	προσκεκύνηκα	—	—
προστίθημι	προσθήσω	προσέθηκα	—	προστέθειμαι	προσετέθην
προσφέρω	προσοίσω	προσήνεγκα / προσήνεγκον / προσένεγκα	προσενήνοχα	—	προσηνέχθην / προσηνείχθην
σαλεύω	σαλεύσω	ἐσάλευσα	—	σεσάλευμαι	ἐσαλεύθην
σκανδαλίζω	σκανδαλίσω	ἐσκανδάλισα	—	—	ἐσκανδαλίσθην
σπείρω	—	ἔσπειρα	—	ἔσπαρμαι	ἐσπάρην
σπλαγχνίζομαι	—	—	—	—	ἐσπλαγχνίσθην
σταυρόω	σταυρώσω	ἐσταύρωσα	ἐσταύρωκα	ἐσταύρωμαι	ἐσταυρώθην
στηρίζω	στηρίξω / στηρίσω	ἐστήριξα / ἐστήρισα	—	—	ἐστηρίχθην
συνάγω	συνάξω	συνήγαγον	—	συνῆγμαι	συνήχθην

Present	Future	Aorist	Perfect Active	Perfect Mid./Pass.	Aorist Passive
σύρω	συρῶ	ἔσυρα	σέσυρκα	σέσυρμαι	ἐσύρην
σώζω / σῴζω	σώσω	ἔσωσα	σέσωκα	σέσωσμαι	ἐσώθην
τελειόω	τελειώσω	ἐτελείωσα	τετελείωκα	τετελείωμαι	ἐτελειώθην
τηρέω	τηρήσω	ἐτήρησα	τετήρηκα	τετήρημαι	ἐτηρήθην
τίθημι	θήσω	ἔθηκα	τέθεικα	τέθειμαι	ἐτέθην
τιμάω	τιμήσω	ἐτίμησα	τετίμηκα	τετίμημαι	ἐτιμήθην
τυφλόω	τυφλώσω	ἐτύφλωσα	τετύφλωκα	τετύφλωμαι	ἐτυφλώθην
ὑπάγω	ὑπάξω	ὑπήγαγον	—	ὑπῆγμαι	ὑπήχθην
ὑπακούω	ὑπακούσομαι	ὑπήκουσα	—	—	—
ὑπάρχω	ὑπάρξομαι	ὑπηρξάμην	—	—	—
φανερόω	φανερώσω	ἐφανέρωσα	πεφανέρωκα	πεφανέρωμαι	ἐφανερώθην
φέρω	οἴσω	ἤνεγκα	ἐνήνοχα	ἐνήνεγμαι	ἠνέχθην

φημί (*3rd singular present active indicative* = φησίν, *3rd plural present active indicative* = φασίν, *imperfect active* = ἔφη)

Present	Future	Aorist	Perfect Active	Perfect Mid./Pass.	Aorist Passive
φιλέω	φιλήσω	ἐφίλησα	πεφίληκα	πεφίλημαι	ἐφιλήθην
φοβέομαι	—	—	—	—	ἐφοβήθην
φονεύω	φονεύσω	ἐφόνευσα	—	—	—
φωνέω	φωνήσω	ἐφώνησα	—	—	ἐφωνήθην
χαίρω	χαρήσομαι	ἐχάρην	κεχάρηκα	κεχάρημαι	ἐχάρην
χορτάζω	χορτάσω	ἐχόρτασα	—	—	ἐχορτάσθην
χρονίζω	χρονίσω / χρονιῶ	—	—	—	—

This book was designed and set into type by Kelby and Teresa Bowers,

and printed and bound by Versa Press in East Peoria, Illinois.

The text face is Kepler, designed by Robert Slimbach of Adobe Systems.